AN INTRODUCTION TO THE PHILOSOPHY
OF KNOWLEDGE

An Introduction to the Philosophy of Knowledge

Jennifer Trusted

Second Edition

palgrave

Published by PALGRAVE
Houndmills, Basingstoke, Hampshire RG21 6XS and
175 Fifth Avenue, New York, N. Y. 10010
Companies and representatives throughout the world

PALGRAVE is the new global academic imprint of
St. Martin's Press LLC Scholarly and Reference Division and
Palgrave Publishers Ltd (formerly Macmillan Press Ltd).

First edition 1981
Second edition 1997

Outside North America
ISBN 0–333–69185–7 hardcover
ISBN 0–333–69186–5 paperback

This book is printed on paper suitable for recycling and made from fully managed and sustained forest sources.

A catalogue record for this book is available from the British Library.

10   9   8   7   6   5   4   3
08   07   06   05   04   03   02   01

Printed and bound in Great Britain by
Antony Rowe Ltd, Eastbourne

Contents

Acknowledgements

I should like to thank Professor O'Connor and Professor Atkinson for their very great help and encouragement. I should also like to thank Professor Ayer for commenting on chapters 7, 8 and 9. Any mistakes in the text are, of course, my own.

J. T.

The author and publishers wish to thank the following who have kindly given permission for the use of copyright material: Professor Sir A. J. Ayer for extracts from *The Problem of Knowledge*; Basil Blackwell Publisher Limited for an abridged version of *Knowledge and Belief* by Norman Malcolm originally published in full in *Mind*, 51 (1952); Dr G. D. Chryssides for a winning entry in a competition published in *The Times Higher Education Supplement*; Faber & Faber Limited and Mrs Valerie Eliot for a letter to *The Times*, 10 February 1970; Manchester University Press for extracts from *Immanual Kant: Prolegomena* (Philosophical Classics Series) trans. by P. G. Lucas; The New American Library Inc. for extracts from *Great Dialogues of Plato*, trans. by W. H. D. Rouse and ed. by Philip G. Rouse and Eric H. Warmington, Copyright © 1956, 1961 by John Clive Graves Rouse; Thomas Nelson & Sons Limited for extracts from *Rene Descartes: Philosophical Writings*, trans. by E. Anscombe and P. T. Geach; Oxford University Press for selections from *Sense and Sensibilia* by J. L. Austin, ed. by G. J. Warnock, © 1962; from *The Oxford Translation of Aristotle*, ed. by W. D. Ross; from *The Problems of Philosophy* by Bertrand Russell (1912), and from *The Oxford Book of Literary Anecdotes* (pp. 242–3) ed. by James Sutherland (1975); Thames and Hudson Limited for extracts from *An Introduction to Western Philosophy*, by A. Flew; Weidenfeld & Nicolson Limited for extracts from *The Central Questions of Philosophy*, by A. J. Ayer.

Preface

The object of this book is to provide an introduction to philosophy for students; but it is also intended for the educated general reader who wishes to learn something of the nature of the subject.

Apart from Descartes and Kant, all the later philosophers discussed wrote in English but, even with this restriction, it is hoped that the general reader will find the book interesting, and will find it useful in bringing about an appreciation of essentially philosophical discussion and analysis.

For though a very large number of intelligent and alert people are attracted to philosophy, many of them have a very confused idea as to its nature. This is because philosophy is a subject which differs from all other subjects in that its aims and techniques *are* its content. Other subjects have their philosophies: philosophy of science, philosophy of history etc. and these philosophies may be appreciated with minimal knowledge of the content of the subjects. Certainly one can know something of the general aims and assumptions, and even something of the methods of the natural sciences, of history, of law, of the various arts without being a scientist, a historian, a lawyer, a musician or a painter. But the general aims, assumptions and methods of philosophy are themselves part of philosophy, and so one cannot know them without being a philosopher. That is why ignorance of the content of philosophy involves ignorance of the nature of philosophy – they are inseparable.

There are many books offering good elementary accounts of philosophy, of philosophers and of particular philosophical problems. These three topics cannot be distinguished as easily as can their analogues in other subjects. But, of course, there are degrees of emphasis. The author may give a simple account of certain philosophical problems as does Bertrand Russell in *The Problems of Philosophy*, or he or she may provide a historical picture of the work of many different philosophers, as Russell does in his *History of Western Philosophy*. A more detailed, though for that very reason a less comprehensive, historical account is given in *A Critical History of Western Philosophy* edited by D. J. O'Connor. This provides a more scholarly account than does Russell in his *History*, because different specialist writers can give a deeper and more critical assessment than can any one individual. At a more advanced level, A. J. Ayer presents a modern analysis of a wide range of philosophical problems in his *Central Questions of Philosophy*. This book is similar in some respects to Russell's *Problems of Philosophy*, and indeed comparison with Russell's book is invited, but it is more detailed and, as well as referring to works which had not appeared in Russell's day, it requires some philosophical background knowledge to be appreciated. Another approach to presenting elementary philosophy is shown by Antony Flew in *An Introduction to Western Philosophy*. Flew takes various philosophical themes and draws the attention of the reader to their treatment by different philosophers. There are long quotations from many different sources, and Flew provides comment and connection between the various writers and various themes.

Later works which appeared after my first edition went to press are *The History of Scepticism* by Richard H. Popkin, *Rationalism* by John Cottingham, *Modern Philosophy* by Roger Scruton and *Philosophy: the Basics* by Nigel Warburton. Popkin provides a historical background to the development of contemporary critical analysis but ends his account with Spinoza; his presentation does require some background knowledge to be fully appreciated. Cottingham's book is written for the general reader as well as for students and his account extends from Plato to Popper. His final chapter treats of falsifiability and current approaches in the philosophy of science. Scruton's book covers a wider range of topics. Those interested in philosophy of knowledge would find chapters 1 and 2 and chapters 22 and 23 particularly interesting.

Scruton implies that his text is accessible to the general reader but it is densely, though clearly, argued and those with no prior knowledge would probably find it difficult. By contrast Warburton's book is eminently readable and gives a lucid account of the nature of philosophy. A second, and slightly expanded, edition was published in 1995.

The approach here has something in common with all the books mentioned. Firstly, like all of them, it is an introduction to *Western* philosophy and, as already indicated, to Western philosophy as it is taught in many universities, that is with a marked bias towards an empiricist tradition. Secondly the treatment is historical as is the treatment in O'Connor, Flew, Russell, Popkin, Cottingham and (to a lesser extent) Russell, Scruton and Warburton. Thirdly, it is similar to Flew's book, though not to the others, in that there are very substantial quotations and a considerable portion of the text is devoted to quotation and comment. Where it differs from all these books, save for Warburton's, is that it is written as a basis for further study. The book is self-contained but it is meant to provide a foundation for students *as well as* being a text for the general reader.

It is for this reason that the theme is very much restricted, far more restricted than in the other books. The theme is epistemology and, in particular, the emergence of the distinction between the nature of the evidence required to justify a claim to empirical knowledge, as opposed to a claim to logical knowledge. I hope that the text allows the reader to appreciate how the notion of empirical knowledge as something having a different status from logical knowledge, gradually established itself; and how the quest for certainty about the nature of the empirical world had to be abandoned and replaced by a quest for understanding.

It seems to me that this theme is particularly well suited to historical treatment, for all philosophers have been concerned with knowledge, and the works of early writers are still influential and therefore still important today. In nine of the chapters of the book it is just nine philosophers whose works are discussed at any length. The selection is unlikely to surprise any teacher of philosophy, but it is inevitable that none of the philosophers considered can be fully discussed even when the subject is restricted to epistemology. It would be absurd to suggest that Plato's, Descartes' or Hume's view of knowledge could be comprehensively presented in twenty pages. The writings quoted and the interpretation are personal, but they are intended to make a coherent though elementary development of the theme. The aim is to show how philosophical ideas on this theme have evolved and how later philosophers responded to and made modifications of the work of their predecessors. The reader is encouraged to consider philosophy as an evolving whole, and to see the works of earlier philosophers as influencing those who came later.

In this way it is hoped that the book will lead to an appreciation of the flavour of philosophy and of the intellectual satisfaction that can come from philosophical analysis, philosophical criticism and philosophical speculation.

One of the problems of presenting philosophy is that a great deal of philosophical writing is very difficult to understand. This is not just because technical terms are used, though this does add to the difficulty, and not only because the writers are concerned with ideas rather than with people and with things. It is also because so much that must be read was written so long ago. It is difficult to follow eighteenth-century writing, because there are assumptions and references which are no longer obvious. It is even more difficult to understand works written 2000 years ago. These historical problems do not arise when we read contemporary philosophers but there is the difficulty of reference to the earlier philosophers, as well as the difficulty occasioned by much more frequent use of technical terms.

All the same, I am convinced that the only way to understand philosophy is to read the writings of philosophers – a gloss will not do – and that is why such a substantial part of this book is devoted to direct quotations. These have been selected to bear on the theme, and the accompanying explanation is intended to help understanding so that the book can be read without the *need* for further explanation of what is presented in its pages.

A selection of extracts, like the selection for any anthology, is always open to criticism. I have been guided by what I

judge is best related to the theme without being too difficult
to understand, and I have also been influenced by affection
for certain passages, such as Descartes's account of the wax,
and by the fame of certain accounts, such as Plato's cave.
There are also some philosophical ideas, such as the
Cartesian *cogito*, which trail their clouds of glory and which I
felt ought to be included.

The first chapter is by way of an introduction and is much
more general than subsequent chapters. Two passages, one
from Plato and one from J. L. Austin, are presented with the
purpose of showing the general nature of philosophical
analysis and philosophical problems. After reading this
chapter the reader should be in a position to decide whether
philosophy is of interest to him or her. Although the introduction is intended as a serious introduction to the nature of
philosophy, some lighter notes have been introduced (and
indeed there are lighter notes in later chapters), in the form
of secondary source extracts and anecdotes. This has been
done, not so much to 'sugar the pill', though it will have this
effect, but more to show that philosophical thought is not
different in kind from our everyday thinking and everyday
appreciation of sensible discussion. It is hoped that it will go
some way to dispelling a certain unhealthy mystique about
the nature of philosophy and the rather dubious belief that
philosophers are in some strange way removed from the
thinking of ordinary practical common sense.

The view taken here is that philosophical analysis is a
refinement of our daily common-sense analysis of the problems of daily life, just as scientific inquiry is a refinement of
our common-sense inquiry into the nature of the world
around us. In both cases skilled techniques are developed and
sophisticated safeguards against error are introduced, but
philosophy and natural science are both grounded in our
ordinary modes of thought and inquiry. Philosophy is *not*
opposed to common sense; it hopes to improve on common
sense – to make use of it. Because of this, readers of this
book may come to acknowledge that philosophy is a valuable
subject as well as being a source of intellectual pleasure.

To encourage further thought on the topics presented, I
have suggested some reading at the end of each chapter.

There are not many suggestions made, and often specific chapters or sections of chapters are given. In my experience short and specific lists of reading material are much more likely to be attended to than long lists. In addition, if the book is adopted as a text-book, different teachers will doubtless suggest different passages as well as supplementing the interpretations of the works offered here.

Technical terms used by me are defined as they are introduced, the more difficult of these, and other technical terms occurring in quotations, are explained in the glossary at the end of the book. The bibliography consists of a list of the books referred to in the text and in the 'Further Reading' lists at the end of the chapters. The full title, date and publisher are given there.

The conclusion reached in the book is that there can be empirical knowledge, as opposed to belief, and that it does not follow that there cannot be a claim to knowledge even though the knowledge is not logically indubitable. There is room for discussion here, and it is not intended that the reader be left with the impression that this particular problem, the problem of empirical knowledge, is one which has been resolved. I hope that what the reader will acquire is some idea as to the nature of the problem and about the way in which it has emerged and the ways in which it has been treated. In other words the text should leave readers with some understanding of the nature of philosophy and perhaps with a desire to understand more. This would be the best to be hoped because philosophy is not a subject to be learned merely by reading. As Plato said:

There is no written summary by me and never shall be. For it is not a thing that can be put into words, like other lessons for learning. But from a long communing over the thing itself and from living together, suddenly as though from a flame leaping a gap, a light kindles in the soul; and after that, it finds its own nourishment.

Trans A. R. Burn,
The Pelican History of Greece, p. 311

The Nature of Philosophy

Sir,
My husband, T. S. Eliot, loved to recount how late one evening he stopped a taxi. As he got in, the driver said: 'You're T. S. Eliot.' When asked how he knew, he replied: 'Ah. I've got an eye for a celebrity. Only the other evening I picked up Bertrand Russell, and I said to him: "Well, Lord Russell, what's it all about," and, do you know, he couldn't tell me.'

Yours faithfully,
VALERIE ELIOT

The Times, 10 February, 1970

The dictionary description of philosophy is given as 'the love, study, or pursuit of wisdom, or of knowledge of things and their causes, whether theoretical or practical' (O.E.D.). Therefore it does not seem unreasonable for the layman to suppose that philosophers should be concerned with what 'it' is all about.

From about 500 BC and up to the seventeenth century, Western philosophers (and only Western philosophy is considered here) aspired to embrace all knowledge: mathematics, logic, natural science, moral science, aesthetics, ethics, religion and metaphysics. All could be regarded as part of philosophy and the philosopher might attempt to study and debate about all of them. Thus philosophers would seek to answer questions relating to arithmetic and geometry, logical analysis, the nature of the heavens and earth, the structure of matter and material bodies, the knowledge given by perception, moral and aesthetic values, the nature of God and humanity. Philosophers were indeed trying to answer the indefinitely large number of questions implied in 'What's it all about?'

Though philosophy does not have such a vast field today, we can say that the disciplines now distinguished from philosophy — the branches of mathematics, the natural sciences, religion, aesthetics etc. — have emerged and have been distinguished as a result of the work of philosophers. One reason why philosophy has been valuable is that it has helped to establish these different fields with different assumptions, different purposes and different methods of inquiry. So philosophy itself might now seem to be left with very little: logic (a rather special branch), discussions of value judgements and metaphysical speculation. Even those who think that philosophy still has something to offer may feel that the subject needs to be justified in a way that the study of the natural sciences, of the law, of history, of the arts etc. does not.

It behoves philosophers to take note of this, to become aware of the extent of the criticisms, and to answer them.

It has to be admitted that philosophy is a subject which does appear to offer shelter to tendentious nonsense. The letter below won Dr Chryssides a prize from *The Times Higher Education Supplement* in a competition to devise the worst student essay of the year.

Philosophy essay: 'Universals'
Aristotle saw universals as existant *in re* and not *ante rem*, a piece of philosophical jargon which is certainly impressive although somewhat bewildering for the poor struggling student. Aristotle also said that the soul entered the body at the moment of contraception.

Locke's view was conceptualism which is best explained by contrasting it with Hobbes who was a nominalist. Leipzig held a different view. The former two views lack a basis in reality while Leipzig is not convincing to the modern mind.

Witgenstien had never read Aristotle, but yet equates with him to some extent, although he used the example of a game, this illustration occurred to him when he was passing a football field, just as the illustration of the car crash ocured to him in the West Trench. In his book on Witgenstein W. W. Bartley argues that he had disreputable sexual habits. However, by talking about language-*games*, Wetgenstien refused to see that language is a serious way of communicating, not a mere game to be played when we have nothing better to do.

Plato criticizes Witginstiens theories by claiming that the soul is reincarcerated, a doctrine that appeals to many people today, however it may be difficult to exept. The point is that philosophers still do not agree on this question and until they do it is impossible to decide.

In conclusion, the question is, can any of these theories of universals really be universal? If it cannot the theory is selfcontradictory, but if it can the problem is solved and theories are not needed. In fact philosophers do not seem to have noticed this and are attempting to solve problems which are irrelevant and not of universal interest.

G. D. Chryssides,
Senior lecturer in philosophy,
Plymouth Polytechnic.

Of course this nonsense is not philosophy, but it is a good satire because it shows what are not uncommonly held to be the failings of philosophy: its obscurity, its tendency to deal with totally ridiculous problems, and its involved arguments about technical terms. And the essay also indicates how it is that many people who respect philosophy respect it for the wrong reason: they think that philosophers possess some superior wisdom which endows them with a different way of thinking, such that ordinary mortals cannot comprehend their deep and wondrous wisdom. It is thought that the study of philosophy bestows the power to solve complex and mysterious problems.

A much more healthy attitude is the attitude of those who dismiss philosophy: who hold that the incomprehensible is not to be treated with awe but with suspicion. These critics say that obscurity implies muddle, that incomprehensible questions are unanswerable and not worth considering, and that those who devote their time to seeking answers to such questions lack sense – they are fools and only too often pretentious fools.

Both admirers and critics are misguided as to the nature of philosophy. Philosophers have not developed a *different* way of thinking and nor are they concerned with answering unanswerable (and therefore nonsensical) questions. They are concerned with using and developing our ordinary powers of thought to best advantage, and they are concerned with *criticising* questions. Their mode of understanding is the same as everyone else's, and they wish to understand by making problems clearer. For, in so doing, it becomes easier to find solutions. Philosophy today is concerned with developing our understanding through constructive and critical appraisal of questions as well as answers.

Another way in which philosophy develops our understanding and our critical powers is by analysing the nature of the assumptions underlying the various fields of knowledge and by analysing the nature of the problems in various fields. It involves consideration of what can count as an answer to questions and as a solution to problems – not so much specific answers and specific solutions but the *kind* of answer which is being sought and the *kind* of solution which would be acceptable. It also helps understanding by helping us to draw distinctions and to relate and inter-relate different subjects. For example: Are questions about the behaviour of an ideal gas to be considered as mathematical, scientific or metaphysical? Is the atomic theory a scientific theory or a metaphysical speculation? Are the problems of the ethics of abortion medical or moral or both? Is Marxism a scientific economic theory, a social theory, a moral theory or a religion? Is the beauty of a picture dependent on pure aesthetic judgement or on social conventions? Are the preceding questions fair questions?

Now these questions are ones which concern many people apart from philosophers; we need to show that they are clear, to improve them if they are not clear, and to seek answers. Philosophy helps us to understand the questions, by clarifying (and modifying them if necessary) and so helps in the task of seeking a satisfactory type of answer. An answer does not have to be accepted to be rated as a satisfactory type; to be satisfactory it has to be a *genuine* answer, one which is relevant to the question. Then, even if it is not accepted, it can be rated as a candidate for consideration, and therefore satisfactory in the sense that it was sensible, even though wrong.

This is why philosophers are concerned with language and it is the reason why it is sometimes thought that they are primarily concerned with language. That is a mistake; philosophers are primarily concerned with ideas and concepts, and their interest in language arises because it is largely in language that we think, and communicate with others. Language is the tool of thought and communication. Professor Ayer says:

> A philosopher who had no mastery of language would be as helpless as a mathematician who could not handle numerals;[1] but just as the mathematician was not concerned with numerals as such but rather with the numbers which they represented, so the philosopher's command of language was merely a necessary means to the investigation of the objective properties of concepts.
>
> (*The Concept of a Person*, p. 5)

It is misleading to regard words as simply representing concepts as numerals represent numbers. Ayer goes on to consider Wittgenstein's view that words muddle our thoughts if they are misused. Wittgenstein argued that philosophical problems arise through misuse of language because this misuse produces pseudo-concepts and pseudo-problems. Wittgenstein thought that:

> people made difficulties for themselves by failing to understand how their language worked. This led them to raise problems to which they could see no issue, to construct dilemmas which they could not resolve. In their efforts to escape from these they relapsed into talking nonsense. The remedy was to trace the muddle to its source by exposing the linguistic misconceptions from which it arose . . .
>
> (Ibid, p. 7)

This had been appreciated earlier of course. Lewis Carroll gives an excellent example:

> "And I haven't sent the two Messengers, either. They're both gone to the town. Just look along the road, and tell me if you can see either of them."
> "I see nobody on the road," said Alice.
>
> "I only wish *I* had such eyes," the King remarked in a fretful tone. "To be able to see Nobody! And at that distance too! Why, it's as much as *I* can do to see real people, by this light!"
>
> *(Alice Through the Looking Glass*, ch. VII)

To illustrate some of the points made in this chapter we shall consider two extracts, one from J. L. Austin and one from Plato. Both assume ordinary straight-forward ways of thinking and appeal to our ordinary common-sense way of reasoning. Both are concerned with the careful use of language, though this is more obvious in Austin's essay. Both are written with the prime purpose of increasing our understanding. Both have the same method of achieving that purpose, namely by critical analysis and discussion.

J. L. Austin (1910–1960) was an Oxford philosopher who was particularly concerned with showing how words and thoughts were related and how they interacted. In the extract below he is discussing the word 'real' and the significance of this word in regard to our ideas about reality and about what is real.

His chapter is presented first, as an example of first class modern philosophical writing. As well as being clear it is also entertaining. In addition, just like *Alice Through the Looking Glass*, it can be read at two levels. At first reading it can be enjoyed as a provocative and light-hearted lesson in lexicography. Its deeper philosophical meaning will be discussed afterwards.

But now, provoked largely by the frequent and unexamined occurrences of 'real', 'really', 'real shape', &c., in the arguments we have just been considering, I want to take a closer look at this little word 'real'. I propose, if you like, to discuss the Nature of Reality — a genuinely important topic, though in general I don't much like making this claim.

There are two things, first of all, which it is immensely important to understand here.

1. 'Real' is an absolutely *normal* word, with nothing new-fangled or technical or highly specialized about it. It is, that is to say, already firmly established in, and very frequently used in, the ordinary language we all use every day. Thus *in this sense* it is a word which has a fixed meaning, and so can't, any more than can any other word which is firmly established, be fooled around with *ad lib*. Philosophers often seem to think that they can just 'assign' any meaning whatever to any word; and so no doubt, in an absolutely trivial sense, they can (like Humpty-Dumpty[2]). There are some expressions, of course, 'material thing' for example, which only philosophers use, and in such cases they can, within reason, please themselves; but most words are *in fact* used in a particular way already, and this fact can't be just disregarded. (For example, some meanings that have been assigned to 'know' and 'certain' have made it seem outrageous that we should use these terms as we actually do; but what this shows is that the meanings assigned by some philosophers are *wrong*.) Certainly, when we have discovered how a word is in fact used, that may not be the end of the matter; there is certainly no reason why, in general, things should be left exactly as we find them; we may wish to tidy the situation up a bit, revise the map here and there, draw the boundaries and distinctions rather differently. But still, it is advisable always to bear in mind (a) that the distinctions embodied in our vast and, for the most part, relatively ancient stock of ordinary words are neither few nor always very obvious, and almost never just arbitrary; (b) that in any case, before indulging in any tampering on our own account, we need to find out what it is that we have to deal with; and (c) that tampering with words in what we take to be one little corner of the field is always *liable* to have unforeseen repercussions in the adjoining territory. Tampering, in fact, is not so easy

as is often supposed, is not justified or needed so often as is often supposed, and is often thought to be necessary just because what we've got already has been misrepresented. And we must always be particularly wary of the philosophical habit of dismissing some of (if not all) the ordinary uses of a word as 'unimportant', a habit which makes distortion practically unavoidable. For instance, if we are going to talk about 'real', we must not dismiss as beneath contempt such humble but familiar expressions as 'not real cream'; this may save us from saying, for example, or seeming to say that what is not real cream must be a fleeting product of our cerebral processes.

2. The other immensely important point to grasp is that 'real' is *not* a normal word at all, but highly exceptional; exceptional in this respect that, unlike 'yellow' or 'horse' or 'walk', it does not have one single, specifiable, always-the-same *meaning*. (Even Aristotle saw through this idea.) *Nor* does it have a large number of different meanings – it is not *ambiguous*, even 'systematically'. Now words of this sort have been responsible for a great deal of perplexity. Consider the expressions 'cricket ball', 'cricket bat', 'cricket pavilion', 'cricket weather'. If someone did not know about cricket and were obsessed with the use of such 'normal' words as 'yellow', he might gaze at the ball, the bat, the building, the weather, trying to detect the 'common quality' which (he assumes) is attributed to these things by the prefix 'cricket'. But no such quality meets his eye; and so perhaps he concludes that 'cricket' must designate a *non-natural* quality, a quality to be detected not in any ordinary way but by *intuition*. If this story strikes you as too absurd, remember what philosophers have said about the word 'good'; and reflect that many philosophers, failing to detect any ordinary quality common to real ducks, real cream, and real progress, have decided that Reality must be an *a priori* concept apprehended by reason alone.

Let us begin, then, with a preliminary, no doubt rather haphazard, survey of some of the complexities in the use of 'real'. Consider, for instance, a case which at first sight one might think was pretty straightforward – the case of 'real colour'. What is meant by the 'real' colour of a thing? Well, one may say with some confidence, that's easy enough: the *real* colour of the thing is the colour that it looks to a normal observer in conditions of normal or standard illumination; and to find out what a thing's real colour is, we just need to be normal and to observe it in those conditions.

But suppose (*a*) that I remark to you of a third party, 'That isn't the real colour of her hair.' Do I mean by this that, if you were to observe her in conditions of standard illumination, you would find that her hair did not look that colour? Plainly not — the conditions of illumination may be standard already. I mean, of course, that her hair has been *dyed*, and normal illumination just doesn't come into it at all. Or suppose that you are looking at a ball of wool in a shop, and I say, 'That's not its real colour.' Here I *may* mean that it won't look that colour in ordinary day-light; but I *may* mean that wool isn't that colour before it's dyed. As so often, you can't tell what I mean just from the words that I use; it makes a difference, for instance, whether the thing under discussion is or is not a type which is *customarily* dyed.

Suppose (*b*) that there is a species of fish which looks vividly multi-coloured, slightly glowing perhaps, at a depth of a thousand feet. I ask you what its real colour is. So you catch a specimen and lay it out on deck, making sure the condition of the light is just about normal, and you find that it looks a muddy sort of greyish white. Well, is *that* its real colour? It's clear enough at any rate that we don't have to say so. In fact, is there any right answer in such a case?

Compare: 'What is the real taste of saccharine?' We dissolve a tablet in a cup of tea and we find that it makes the tea taste sweet; we then take a tablet neat, and we find that it tastes bitter. Is it *really* bitter, or *really* sweet?

(*c*) What is the real colour of the sky? Of the sun? Of the moon? Of a chameleon? We say that the sun in the evening sometimes looks red — well, what colour is it *really*? (What are the 'conditions of standard illumination' for the sun?)

(*d*) Consider a *pointilliste* painting of a meadow, say; if the general effect is green, the painting may be composed of predominantly blue and yellow dots. What is the real colour of the painting?

(*e*) What is the real colour of an after-image? The trouble with this one is that we have no idea what an alternative to its 'real colour' might be. Its apparent colour, the colour that it looks, the colour that it appears to be? — but these phrases have no application here. (You might ask me, 'What colour is it really?' if you suspected that I had lied in telling you its colour. But 'What colour is it really?' is not quite the same as 'What is its real colour?')

Or consider 'real shape' for a moment. This notion cropped up, you may remember, seeming quite unproblematic, when we were considering the coin which was said to 'look elliptical' from some points of view; it had a real shape, we insisted, which remained unchanged. But coins in fact are rather special cases. For one thing their outlines are well defined and very highly stable, and for another they have a *known* and a *nameable* shape. But there are plenty of things of which this is not true. What is the real shape of a cloud? And if it be objected, as I dare say it could be, that a cloud is not a 'material thing' and so not the kind of thing which has to have a real shape, consider this case: what is the real shape of a cat? Does its real shape change whenever it moves? If not, in what posture *is* its real shape on display? Furthermore, is its real shape such as to be fairly smooth-outlined, or must it be finely enough serrated to take account of each hair? It is pretty obvious that there is *no* answer to these questions — no rules according to which, no procedure by which, answers are to be determined. Of course, there are plenty of shapes which the cat definitely is not — cylindrical, for instance. But only a desperate man would toy with the idea of ascertaining the cat's real shape 'by elimination'.

Contrast this with cases in which we *do* know how to proceed: 'Are those real diamonds?', 'Is that a real duck?' Items of jewellery that more or less closely resemble diamonds may not be real diamonds because they are paste or glass; that may not be a real duck because it is a decoy, or a toy duck, or a species of goose closely resembling a duck, or because I am having a hallucination. These are all of course quite different cases. And notice in particular (*a*) that, in most of them 'observation by a normal observer in standard conditions' is completely irrelevant; (*b*) that something which is not a real duck is not a *non-existent* duck, or indeed a non-existent anything; and (*c*) that something existent, e.g. a toy, may perfectly well not be real, e.g. not a real duck.

Perhaps by now we have said enough to establish that there is more in the use of 'real' than meets the cursory eye; it has many and diverse uses in many diverse contexts. We must next, then, try to tidy things up a little; and I shall now mention under four headings what might be called the salient features of the use of 'real' — though not *all* these features are equally conspicuous in all its uses.

1. First, 'real' is a word that we may call *substantive-hungry*. Consider:

'These diamonds are real';
'These are real diamonds'.

This pair of sentences looks like, in an obvious grammatical respect, this other pair:

'These diamonds are pink';
'These are pink diamonds'.

But whereas we can *just* say of something 'This is pink', we can't *just* say of something 'This is real'. And it is not very difficult to see why. We can perfectly well say of something that it is pink without knowing, without any reference to, what it *is*. But not so with 'real'. For one and the same object may be both a real *x* and not a real *y*; an object looking rather like a duck may be a real decoy duck (not just a toy) but not a real duck. When it isn't a real duck but a hallucination, it may still be a real hallucination — as opposed, for instance, to a passing quirk of a vivid imagination. That is, we must have an answer to the question 'A real *what*?', if the question 'Real or not?' is to have a definite sense, to get any foothold. And perhaps we should also mention here another point — that the question 'Real or not?' does not always come up, can't always be raised. We *do* raise this question only when, to speak rather roughly, suspicion assails us — in some way or other things may be not what they seem; and we *can* raise this question only if there *is* a way, or ways, in which things may be not what they seem. What alternative is there to being a 'real' after-image?

'Real' is not, of course, the only word we have that is substantive-hungry. Other examples, perhaps better known ones, are 'the same' and 'one'. The same *team* may not be the same *collection of players*; a body of troops may be one *company* and also three *platoons*. Then what about 'good'? We have here a variety of gaps crying out for substantives — 'A good *what*?', 'Good *at* what?' — a good book, perhaps, but not a good novel; good at pruning roses, but not good at mending cars.

2. Next, 'real' is what we may call a *trouser-word*. It is usually thought, and I dare say usually rightly thought, that what one might call the affirmative use of a term is basic — that, to understand '*x*', we need to know what it is to be *x*, or to be an *x*, and that knowing this apprises us of what it is *not* to be *x*, not to be an *x*. But with 'real' (as we briefly noted earlier) it is the *negative* use that wears the trousers. That is, a definite sense attaches to the assertion that something is real, a real such-and-such, only in the light of a specific way in which it might be, or might have been, *not* real. 'A real duck' differs from the simple 'a duck' only in that it is used to exclude various ways of being not a real duck — but a dummy, a toy, a picture, a decoy, &c.; and moreover I don't know *just* how to take the assertion that it's a real duck unless I know *just* what, on that particular occasion, the speaker has it in mind to exclude. This, of course, is why the attempt to find a characteristic common to all things that are or could be called 'real' is doomed to failure; the function of 'real' is not to contribute positively to the characterization of anything, but to exclude possible ways of being *not* real — and these ways are both numerous for particular kinds of things, and liable to be quite different for things of different kinds. It is this identity of general function combined with immense

diversity in specific applications which gives to the word 'real' the, at first sight, baffling feature of having neither one single 'meaning', nor yet ambiguity, a number of different meanings.

3. Thirdly, 'real' is (like 'good') a *dimension-word*. I mean by this that it is the most general and comprehensive term in a whole group of terms of the same kind, terms that fulfil the same function. Other members of this group, on the affirmative side, are, for example, 'proper', 'genuine', 'live', 'true', 'authentic', 'natural'; and on the negative side, 'artificial', 'fake', 'false', 'bogus', 'makeshift', 'dummy', 'synthetic', 'toy' — and such nouns as 'dream', 'illusion', 'mirage', 'hallucination' belong here as well. It is worth noticing here that, naturally enough, the *less* general terms on the affirmative side have the merit, in many cases, of suggesting more or less definitely what it is that is being excluded; they tend to pair off, that is, with particular terms on the negative side and thus, so to speak, to narrow the range of possibilities. If I say that I wish the university had a proper theatre, this suggests that it has at present a *makeshift* theatre; pictures are genuine as opposed to *fake*, silk is natural as opposed to *artificial*, ammunition is live as opposed to *dummy*, and so on. In practice, of course, we often get a clue to what it is that is in question from the substantive in the case, since we frequently have a well-founded antecedent idea in what respects the kind of thing mentioned could (and could not) be 'not real'. For instance, if you ask me 'Is this real silk?' I shall tend to supply 'as opposed to artificial', since I already know that silk is the kind of thing which can be very closely simulated by an artificial product. The notion of its being *toy* silk, for instance, will not occur to me.

A large number of questions arises here — which I shall not go into — concerning both the composition of these families of 'reality'-words and 'unreality'-words, and also the distinctions to be drawn between their individual members. Why, for instance, is being a *proper* carving-knife one way of being a real carving-knife, whereas being *pure* cream seems not to be one way of being *real* cream? Or to put it differently: how does the distinction between real cream and synthetic cream differ from the distinction between pure cream and adulterated cream? Is it just that adulterated cream still is, after all, *cream*? And why are false teeth called 'false' rather than, say, 'artificial'? Why are artificial limbs so-called, in *preference* to 'false'? Is it that false teeth, besides doing much the same job as real teeth, look, and are meant to look, *deceptively* like real teeth? Whereas an artificial limb, perhaps, is meant to do the same job, but is neither intended, nor likely, to be *passed off* as a real limb.

Another philosophically notorious dimension-word, which has already been mentioned in another connexion as closely comparable with 'real', is 'good'. 'Good' is the most general of a very large and diverse list of more specific words, which share with it the general function of expressing commendation, but differ among themselves in their aptness to, and implications in, particular contexts. It is a curious point, of which Idealist philosophers used to make much at one time, that 'real' itself, in certain uses, may belong to this family. 'Now this is a *real* carving-knife!' may be one way of saying that this is a good carving-knife. And it is sometimes said of a bad poem, for instance, that it isn't really a poem at all; a certain standard must be reached, as it were, even to *qualify*.

4. Lastly, 'real' also belongs to a large and important family of words that we may call *adjuster-words* — words, that is, by the use of which other words are adjusted to meet the innumerable and unforeseeable demands of the world upon language. The position, considerably oversimplified no doubt, is that at a given time our language contains words that enable us (more or less) to say what we want to say in most situations that (we think) are liable to turn up. But vocabularies are finite; and the variety of possible situations that may confront us is neither finite nor precisely foreseeable. So situations are practically bound to crop up sometimes with which our vocabulary is not already fitted to cope in any tidy, straightforward style. We have the word 'pig' for instance, and a pretty clear idea which animals, among those that we fairly commonly encounter, are and are not to be so called. But one

day we come across a new kind of animal, which looks and behaves very much as pigs do, but not *quite* as pigs do; it is somehow different. Well, we might just keep silent, not knowing what to say; we don't want to say positively that it *is* a pig, or that it is *not*. Or we might, if for instance we expected to want to refer to these new creatures pretty often, invent a quite new word for them. But what we could do, and probably would do first of all, is to say, 'It's *like* a pig.' ('Like' is *the* great adjuster-word, or, alternatively put, the main flexibility-device by whose aid, in spite of the limited scope of our vocabulary, we can always avoid being left completely speechless.) And then, having said of this animal that it's *like* a pig, we may proceed with the remark, 'But it isn't a *real* pig' — or more specifically, and using a term that naturalists favour, 'not a *true* pig'. If we think of words as being shot like arrows at the world, the function of these adjuster-words is to free us from the disability of being able to shoot only straight ahead; by their use on occasion, such words as 'pig' can be, so to speak, brought into connexion with targets lying slightly off the simple, straightforward line on which they are ordinarily aimed. And in this way we gain, besides flexibility, precision; for if I can say, 'Not a real pig, but like a pig', I don't have to tamper with the meaning of 'pig' itself.

But, one might ask, do we *have* to have 'like' to serve this purpose? We have, after all, other flexibility-devices. For instance, I might say that animals of this new species are 'piggish'; I might perhaps call them 'quasi-pigs', or describe them (in the style of vendors of peculiar wines) as 'pig-type' creatures. But these devices, excellent no doubt in their way, can't be regarded as substitutes for 'like', for this reason: they equip us simply with new expressions on the same level as, functioning in the same way as, the word 'pig' itself, and thus, though they may perhaps help us out of our immediate difficulty, they themselves may land us in exactly the same *kind* of difficulty at any time. We have this kind of wine, not real port, but a tolerably close approximation to port, and we call it 'port type'. But then someone produces a new kind of wine, not port exactly, but also not quite the same as what we now call 'port type'.

So what are we to say? Is it port-type type? It would be tedious to have to say so, and besides there would clearly be no future in it. But as it is we can say that it is *like* port-type wine (and for that matter rather like port, too); and in saying this we don't saddle ourselves with a *new word*, whose application may itself prove problematic if the vintners spring yet another surprise on us. The world ·'like' equips us *generally* to handle the unforeseen, in a way in which new words invented *ad hoc* don't, and can't.

(Why then do we need 'real' as an adjuster-word as well as 'like'?· Why exactly do we want to say, sometimes 'It is like a pig', sometimes 'It is not a real pig'? To answer these questions properly would be to go a long way towards making really clear the use, the 'meaning', of 'real'.)

It should be quite clear, then, that there are no criteria to be laid down *in general* for distinguishing the real from the not real. How this is to be done must depend on *what* it is with respect to which the problem arises in particular cases. Furthermore, even for particular kinds of things, there may be many different ways in which the distinction may be made (there is not just *one* way of being 'not a real pig') — this depends on the number and variety of the surprises and dilemmas nature and our fellow men may spring on us, and on the surprises and dilemmas we have been faced with hitherto. And of course, if there is *never* any dilemma or surprise, the question simply doesn't come up; if we had simply never had occasion to distinguish anything as being in any way like a pig but not a *real* pig, then the words 'real pig' themselves would have no application — as perhaps the words 'real after-image' have no application.

Again, the criteria we employ at a given time can't be taken as *final*, not liable to change. Suppose that one day a creature of the kind we now call a cat takes to talking. Well, we say to begin with, I suppose, 'This cat can talk.' But then other cats, not all, take to talking as well; we now have to say that some cats talk, we distinguish between talking and non-talking cats. But again we may, if talking becomes prevalent and the distinction between talking and not talking seems to us to be really important, come to insist that a *real* cat be a creature that can talk. And this will give us a new case of being 'not a real cat', i.e. being a creature just like a cat except for not talking.

Of course — this may seem perhaps hardly worth saying, but in philosophy it seems it does need to be said — we make a distinction between 'a real *x*' and 'not a real *x*' only if there is a way of telling the difference between what is a real *x* and what is not. A distinction which we are not in fact able to draw is — to put it politely — not worth making.

(J. L. Austin, *Sense and Sensibilia*, ch. VII)

Now this chapter is much more than a firework display of amusing examples. Austin's humour has sharpened our critical faculties much as Lewis Carroll's did; they both highlight the way that misuse of a word can lead to confused thought.

Thus the purpose is not merely to entertain, not merely to show that misuse of 'real' can lead to ridiculous statements analogous to those we get if we misuse 'nobody'. Austin aims to show the various different ways in which the word sets snares for the unwary, and he wants to stress that 'real' is not unique in this respect. He uses 'real' as an example, but he makes many general points about the meanings of words:

(1)   Words may be *substantive-hungry* in that they require attachment to a noun, or substantive, in order to be understood. If I ask 'Is it real?', my question cannot be properly understood unless the nature of 'it' is known. By contrast, if I ask 'Is it blue?' or 'Is it square?' or 'Is it holy?' it is not necessary to know what 'it' is in order to understand the question.[3]

(2)   Words may be *trouser-words* in that it is the negative (e.g. 'unreal' or 'not real') which makes the affirmative significant and therefore 'wears the trousers'. (Even as late as the 1950s it was relatively uncommon to see women habitually in trousers; it was also generally assumed that, in domestic affairs, the man (who wore the trousers) made the decisions. A wife who in fact managed might be said in a metaphorical sense to 'wear the trousers').

(3)   It is a *dimension-word* in that it comprehends more

specific words such as 'proper' and 'authentic'. Austin takes 'good' as another example of a dimension-word. 'Good' is also substantive-hungry but not a trouser-word.

(4) It is an *adjuster-word* in that it helps us to have a more flexible language and to introduce nuances of meaning which are actually more helpful if they are not too specific. Austin cites 'like' as another example of an adjuster-word.

By showing that the meaning and significance of what is a well-known, much-used and absolutely ordinary word like 'real' depend on the context to such a marked extent, Austin leads us to appreciate that there is no one meaning of 'real', and, by implication no one meaning of 'reality'. Thus questions such as 'Is the world real?' or 'What is reality?' leave us floundering. In the first case we are puzzled because we cannot say what an *unreal* world would be like, and it is the unreal which would give meaning to the real. In the second case we are puzzled because we are concerned with the problem of the nature of the substantive to which 'reality' must, by implication, be attached.

Austin's conclusion 'that there are no criteria to be laid down *in general* for distinguishing the real from the not real' is of very great importance because it applies not only to 'real' but to many other words. In respect of 'real' we can appreciate that questions about reality in general have to be treated with great circumspection, for, unless there is some further explanation, the question lacks significance. We shall be considering questions of reality in chapter 9 and we shall see that Austin's analysis helps us to avoid confusion, and so helps to clarify discussion of perception and knowledge. Austin's analysis is helpful because, like Wittgenstein, ultimately he is concerned, not with words but with concepts. He shows us how to take care of the tools with which we think.

In the next extract Plato is concerned with moral worth, which has here been translated as 'holiness'. The extract is very much shorter than the chapter from Austin, but considerably more difficult at first reading. This is partly because it is a translation, and moreover a translation of writings from nearly 2500 years ago, and partly because the mode of discussion is unfamiliar. The problem considered is:

'Is the holy loved by the Gods because it is holy, or is it holy because the Gods love it?'

In modern and secular terms it can be posed as:

'Is moral worth admired for its own sake, or is it held to be admirable because people in general (Society) admire it?'

This question raises the issue as to whether there is such a thing as absolute moral worth, objectively independent of what society (or a certain section of society) finds admirable. It is not difficult to find present-day examples of this problem.

Plato discusses the problem in the form of what is called the Socratic dialogue. Socrates (Plato's teacher, to whom Plato looked for philosophic guidance) poses the questions and Euthyphro is led to modify his original view. For Euthyphro begins by asserting that a thing is holy because the Gods love it, but he is so questioned that he comes to acknowledge that this is not the case, the holy is loved because it is holy; it is not holy because it is loved.

It would be as well to read the text carefully, and then to re-read it after looking at the commentary which follows it.

EUTHYPHRO: Well, I would say that the holy is this, what all the gods love, and the opposite, what all the gods hate, is unholy.

SOCRATES: We shall soon know better, my dear fellow. Just consider this argument. *Is the holy loved by the gods because it is holy, or is it holy because it is loved?*

EUTHYPHRO: I do not understand what you are saying, Socrates.

SOCRATES: Then I will try to say it more clearly. We speak of being carried and of carrying, of being led and leading, of being seen and seeing; and you understand in all such cases that and how the one thing differs from the other?

EUTHYPHRO: I think I do.

SOCRATES: Then there is being loved, and loving is something different from this?

EUTHYPHRO: Of course.

SOCRATES: Then tell me, is what is being carried what is being carried because someone is carrying it, or for some other reason?

EUTHYPHRO: No, for that reason.

SOCRATES: And what is being led is what is being led because someone is leading it, and what is seen is what is seen because someone is seeing it?

EUTHYPHRO: Certainly.

SOCRATES: Then someone does not see it because it is being seen but, on the contrary, because someone sees it it becomes something which is being seen. Again someone does not lead something because it is being led but it becomes something led in virtue of the fact that someone is leading it. So is it quite clear, Euthyphro, what I want to say?

EUTHYPHRO: Certainly.

SOCRATES: Now then, what shall we say about the holy, Euthyphro? It is, according to your account, what is loved by all the gods?

EUTHYPHRO: Yes.

SOCRATES: For this reason, because it is holy, or for some other reason?

EUTHYPHRO: No, for this reason.

SOCRATES: It is loved *because it* is holy, not holy because it is loved?

EUTHYPHRO: So it seems.

SOCRATES: But surely, that which is loved and that which is god-beloved is loved and god-beloved in virtue of the gods loving it?

EUTHYPHRO: Of course.

SOCRATES: Then the god-beloved is not the holy, Euthyphro, nor is the holy the god-beloved, as you were saying, but the one is different from the other.

EUTHYPHRO: How is that, Socrates?

SOCRATES: Because we agree, do we not, that the holy is loved because it is holy, rather than that it is holy because it is loved?

EUTHYPHRO: Yes.

SOCRATES: Also that what is god-beloved is god-beloved

because it is loved by gods, that is, by reason of this love, rather than that they love it because it is god-beloved?
EUTHYPHRO: You are right.
SOCRATES: So if the god-beloved and the holy were the same thing, my dear Euthyphro, and if the holy were loved in virtue of being holy then the god-beloved would be loved in virtue of being god-beloved; and if the god-beloved were god-beloved in virtue of being loved by gods, then the holy would be holy because it is loved. But you now see that the opposite is the case, in that both are entirely different from each other. For the one is beloved in virtue of being loved, whereas the other is loved because it is worthy to be loved. And it looks as if you, Euthyphro, when you were asked what the holy is were unwilling to reveal its essence to me, but instead mentioned an accident of this the holy — being loved by all gods. You have not yet said what it really is. If you please, then, do not hide it from me but begin over again from the beginning and tell me what the holy is. Forget about whether it is loved by gods or any other accident, for that is not the point at issue. Now, tell me frankly, what is the holy and what the unholy?

(Flew, p. 26—28)

Euthyphro maintains that the Gods love that which is holy, and he starts off by taking this as the essential nature of holiness: holiness *is* what the Gods love.

Socrates uses various analogies to show that if something is loved, it is loved because someone loves it. He grants that the holy is loved by all the Gods (or at least he accepts that this is what Euthyphro thinks!) but he asks if it is holy *because* they love it.

Euthyphro then says that this is not the case — the Gods love the holy because it is holy. So:

The holy is loved by the Gods because it is holy.

Socrates then gets Euthyphro to admit that:

The god-beloved is god-beloved because it is loved by all the Gods.

Hence the two things, the holy and the god-beloved, are what they are for different reasons and therefore they cannot be the same.

In our terms, Euthyphro begins by asserting that the morally good *is* that which Society admires, and comes to accept that this is not the essence of moral goodness. It may be that Society always does admire moral worth but this admiration does not in itself make the moral worth. If something is morally good, it will be so whether Society admires or whether it does not. Therefore, to be loved by the Gods, or to be approved by Society, is an incidental (or accidental) property of holiness, or of moral goodness; it does not give us the essential nature of holiness or of moral worth.

Socrates ends by asking what this essential nature is. He and Plato assume that there is a characteristic or feature of holiness which is essential and that this can be discovered. The philosophical discussion between Socrates and Euthyphro shows that one suggestion as to the essential nature, a suggestion which is still entertained today, is not acceptable. The discussion helps to clarify our concept (of holiness or of moral worth) even though it does not provide an answer to the question of what the essential nature might be.

In this chapter there has been an attempt to clear away some of the misconceptions about philosophy and to present an account of its general aims. Two philosophical works have been sampled in order to give examples of what philosophy is, i.e. the kinds of questions which philosophers ask and how they try to answer them. But there is more to philosophy than this: by encouraging critical thought it can free us from dogmatism, from assuming that our own ideas and/or the received ideas of our society are the only ones worth considering, and that our customary beliefs are beyond question. Russell says that by studying philosophy we become free of the tyranny of custom, we are liberated from our private world of self-interest and our horizons are extended:

> The man who has no tincture of philosophy goes through life imprisoned in the prejudices derived from common sense, from the habitual beliefs of his age or his nation, and from convictions which have grown up in his mind without the co-operation or consent of his deliberate reason.

To such a man the world tends to become definite, finite, obvious; common objects rouse no questions, and unfamiliar possibilities are contemptuously rejected.

(Problems of Philosophy, p. 91)

He adds that philosophy helps to release a person from the confines of Self:

Philosophy is to be studied, not for the sake of any definite answers to its questions, since no definite answers can, as a rule, be known to be true, but rather for the sake of the questions themselves; because these questions enlarge our conceptions of what is possible, enrich our intellectual imagination, and diminish the dogmatic assurance which closes the mind against speculation; but above all because, through the greatness of the universe which philosophy contemplates, the mind also is rendered great, and becomes capable of that union with the universe which constitutes its highest good. (Ibid, p. 93)

It is hoped that the account given in this chapter shows something of the nature of philosophy, at least sufficient to enable the reader to decide whether he or she thinks it interesting enough to devote time to the study of philosophy.

Subsequent chapters of this book are primarily concerned with one branch of philosophy, epistemology. Epistemology is the theory or science of the methods or grounds of knowledge. An historical account is given here, showing how epistemology emerged and showing the development of various ideas as to what we can know and how we justify claims to know.

Although epistemology is but one branch of philosophy, it is a particularly important branch because, as well as being a topic in its own right, it plays a part in other branches of philosophy such as metaphysics, ethics and aesthetics. It is an important aspect, also, of philosophy as applied to other subjects, the philosophy of science and the philosophy of history for example. Thus the study of epistemology can serve as an introduction to philosophy in general.

FURTHER READING

A. J. Ayer, *The Central Questions of Philosophy*, ch. 1, sec. A.
Bertrand Russell, *The Problems of Philosophy*, ch. 15.

NOTES

1. A numeral is simply a figure or symbol, for instance the written sign '2'. A number is what the numeral represents, e.g. the numeral '2' represents the number two, the concept of 'twoness' to us — so does the Roman numeral II, so does the English *word* 'two', the French word 'deux' etc.

2. Humpty Dumpty played his part in making a philosophical point:

> 'When *I* use a word,' Humpty Dumpty said, in rather a scornful tone, 'it means just what I choose it to mean — neither more nor less.'
> 'The question is, 'said Alice, 'whether you *can* make words mean so many different things.'
> 'The question is,' said Humpty Dumpty, 'which is to be master — that's all'
>
> (*Alice Through the Looking Glass*, ch. VI)

3. I am not concerned with the metaphorical uses of these words.

2

Plato's View of Knowledge

Plato (427—347 BC) lived in Athens. He was the son of a well-to-do citizen and he had no need to work in order to live comfortably; but he believed that it was a man's duty to contribute to the welfare of his fellow citizens. He founded the Academy at Athens, which was to provide a liberal education for young men who would be future leaders in the city state.

It is Plato's early ideas on knowledge which are the theme of this chapter, and it is not possible to distinguish these from those of his teacher, Socrates (470—399 BC). Most of the quotations come from Plato's earlier writings — the *Meno* is especially likely to reflect Socrates' views, and Socrates is one of the participants in the dialogue.

Plato took the main purpose of philosophy to be to encourage right conduct, and this was to be achieved by convincing people that they should be good, and also by showing them the way to be good. He did not regard knowledge as separate from ethics, for, like Socrates, he held that everyone wanted to be good and that any failure in virtue must, fundamentally, be due to ignorance. The truly wise would understand that their best interest was served by acting virtuously.

'Virtue' did not have the same meaning for Plato as it does for us. The Greek word *arete*, which we translate as 'virtue' had different connotations. Our concept of virtue is based, to a very large extent, on ideas which come from our Christian heritage: from the Bible, from Roman Catholic and from

Protestant (including Puritan, Quaker, Methodist etc.) interpretations. Their various views of virtue (in our sense of the
word) have influenced us, whether or no we be Christian
believers.

But, of course, none of these interpretations were part of
Plato's background. For the Greeks, *arete* could not stand on
its own as 'virtue' can for us. For them, to be virtuous or to
be good[1] was to be virtuous *in respect of* something or to be
good *at* something. So one would talk of a governing *arete*
(good at governing), or of a military *arete* (good at military
affairs). Plato speaks of the *arete* of dogs and horses, that is,
their ability to perform their special function (*ergon*) as dogs
or horses. Plato (and Socrates) reasoned that there must also
be a human *arete*, shown by a man who was good at being a
man, i.e. at performing specifically human functions, and
that was how the word was connected with virtue in our
sense of the word 'virtue'. The virtuous man was good at con-
ducting his life as a human being.

We can now see why Plato and Socrates thought that virtue
depended on knowledge. One had either to know how to be
good at being a man, or at least to have a true belief as to
how to be good. Plato would only bestow the accolade of
knowledge on what was indubitably and *necessarily* true.
What was true but might have been otherwise, i.e. what was a
contingent rather than a necessary truth, could only be an
object of opinion and, at best, it was held as a true belief,
never as knowledge. But, *as a practical guide to conduct*, true
belief was as good as knowledge. As we shall see in chapter 3,
this was also Aristotle's view and, indeed, Aristotle held that
ethics and human conduct generally could only be the objects
of true beliefs.

In the extract below Plato implies that knowledge is possible, though true belief will also guide to virtue:

SOCRATES: Then, in short, all the stirrings and endurings
of the soul, when wisdom leads, come to happiness in
the end, but when senselessness leads, to the opposite?'
MENON: So it seems.
SOCRATES: Then if virtue is one of the things in the soul,
and if it must necessarily be helpful, it must be wisdom:

since quite by themselves all the things about the soul are neither helpful nor harmful, but they become helpful or harmful by the addition of wisdom or senselessnes. According to this argument, virtue, since it is helpful, must be some kind of wisdom.

(Meno from Rouse, p. 54–5)

But *knowledge* was not necessary:

SOCRATES: And so long as he has right opinion about that which the other has knowledge, he will be quite as good a guide as the one who knows, although he does not know, but only thinks what is true.

MENON: Quite as good

SOCRATES: Then true opinion is no worse guide than wisdom, for rightness of action; and this is what we failed to see just now while we were enquiring what sort of a thing virtue is. We said then that wisdom alone guides to right action; but, really, true opinion does the same.

(Ibid, p. 64)

Grades of Apprehension: Knowledge and Opinion

Plato argued that since knowledge had to be indubitable the objects of knowledge had to be permanent and unchanging. For example: '2 + 2 = 4' is true, has always been true and always will be true. Likewise 'The angles of a (Euclidean) triangle sum to 180°' and 'All unicorns have one horn.'[2] These propositions are examples of necessary truths, they cannot be otherwise; hence such truths can be objects of knowledge. Moreover the knowledge of their truth is not arrived at by observation but by thought. Thus the objects of knowledge had to be necessary truths and they had to be apprehended by the mind, not by the senses. They were known by direct mental intuition or by ratiocination.

By contrast the objects which we perceived with our senses, were they shadows, rainbows, horses, mountains or people, did not have permanent properties or permanent existence. Hence any proposition about their properties could not be indubitable for, even if true they were not necessarily true, they might have been false. We could only claim to have opinions about them and, at best, these opinions would be but true beliefs.

Thus Plato distinguished two main grades of apprehension, according to the nature of the objects apprehended and the mode of apprehension. These were:

> Opinion — the objects of opinion were objects which could be apprehended by sense perception;
> Knowledge — the objects of knowledge were objects accessible only to the mind.

Plato invites us to conceive of two types of things — those that are perceived and those that can be thought about (but not perceived by any of the senses). He suggests that we can compare the clarity of apprehension of these two types of things with lines: the longer the line, the greater the clarity. Thus if we take a line AE and divide it at C, so that AC is less than CE, then the length AC represents the clarity of apprehension of things perceived and the length CE the clarity of apprehension of things thought about. These two lines AC and CE can be each divided again in the same ratio: AC is divided at B so that AB is less than BC; and CE is divided at D so that CD is less than DE. Since AB/BC = CD/DE = AC/CE then BC = CD. This is shown on the diagram below.

The World of Sight, and of things seen		The World of Mind, and of things thought	
A B	C	D	E
Images such as Shadows and Reflections	Objects such as Animals, Trees and Manufactured things	Thought-images, Ideas, such as Ideal Squares & Cubes	Ideas or Universals, such as Perfect Beauty, Justice & Goodness
(The changing world of the Senses)		Mathematical Thought	Dialectical Thought
CONJECTURE	BELIEF	UNDERSTANDING	EXERCISE OF REASON
◄---------- OPINION ----------►		◄----------- KNOWLEDGE -----------►	

SOURCE: *Republic*, Rouse, p. 369

We may note that the clarity of apprehension of objects perceived (measured by BC) is equal to the clarity of apprehension of mathematical ideas (measured by CD). Thus the higher grade of belief is as clear as the lower grade of understanding. But the higher grade of understanding, understanding of the Forms or Ideas is most clear.

The Forms or Ideas are like mathematical entities in not being accessible to sense perception: it is as difficult to find a perfectly just act, good man or beautiful statue in the experienced world as it is to find a perfectly straight line or pair of parallel lines. In addition to beauty, justice and goodness Plato recognised Forms for the horse, the mountain etc. Roughly speaking there is a Form or Idea corresponding to every kind of thing there is — but see p. 44 below for Platonic hesitations about this.

Forms or Ideas must not be taken to be concepts or ideas in the sense that we use the word 'idea' today. The latter are dependent on our minds and are produced by our mental activity. But the Forms are supposed to exist quite independently of us and our thoughts. For Plato they were *the* permanent objective reality to which, if we applied our mental powers, our concepts might correspond. Hence the term 'Idea' is misleading, and even the term 'Form' is misleading since it implies that non-material entities have a physical shape. A better word, which will be used henceforward, is 'Universal'.

The Nature of Universals

For Plato Universals were immaterial and completely independent entities which existed in an immaterial world of Universals. This world, and the Universals which made it, were the ultimate and objective reality. Plato is said to take a *realist* view of the nature of Universals. He held that whatever reality was ascribed to the world which we are aware of through sense perception, that is the world of entities which we see, hear, touch etc., was due to the fact that the objects of sense perception shared, though to a limited and imperfect extent, in the nature of the Universals.

The particulars which we perceived: particular acts of justice, particular beautiful things, existed as just acts and beautiful things in virtue of their participation in the Universals justice and beauty. Likewise particular mountains and horses existed as mountains and horses in virtue of their resemblance to the Universal mountain and horse. Though it was not possible to have knowledge of any particular which was observed, we could aspire to knowledge of the Universal. For example, we could not have knowledge of any particular horse because of its ever-changing attributes, but we could aspire to knowledge of the Universal horse because it would have the permanent and unchanging attributes which are essential to the nature of all horses. Likewise, though we could at best only aspire to true belief as to the nature of any particular just act, we could aspire to knowledge of the Universal justice because it would have the permanent attributes which constitute the essential nature of justice.

We can now appreciate the philosophical interest of the dialogue as to the essential nature of holiness which was presented in chapter 1. If we can find the essence of holiness (not just an accidental attribute) we can apprehend the Universal, and so acquire knowledge of holiness. It will be remembered that the Socratic dialogue did not guide us to the essential nature of holiness. We shall be returning to the problem of the discovery of essential natures in the next chapter, when we discuss Aristotle's approach to Universals.

But, apart from the difficulty of discovering essential nature, Plato's account of the relation between particulars and Universals, i.e. the nature of the participation and/or the basis of the resemblance, is vague and indeed he was aware that his explanations were unsatisfactory.

There have been other suggestions as to the nature of Universals and the way they relate to particulars. One proposal has been that a Universal is simply a name for the group of particulars which it subsumes. This is the *nominalist* view.

FIRST MUR.: We are men, my liege.
MACBETH: Ay, in the catalogue ye go for men;
As hounds and greyhounds, mongrels, spaniels, curs,
Shoughs, water-rugs and demi-wolves, are clept
All by the name of dogs: the valued file
Distinguishes the swift, the slow, the subtle,
The housekeeper, the hunter, every one
According to the gift which bounteous nature
Hath in him closed, whereby he does receive
Particular addition, from the bill
That writes them all alike:
(*Macbeth*, III, i)

So the Universal man stands for all men just as the Universal Dog stands for all dogs — they are catalogues or lists. There are of course subsidiary lists, corresponding to subsidiary Universals. But the problem which puzzled Aristotle (and Plato) is by-passed, for *what* determined the placing of any particular in any list? We have to know the Universal before we can make the list or complete the catalogue.

An alternative view was put forward by the seventeenth-century empiricist philosophers such as Locke and Berkeley (see chapter 6). Locke held that Universals were abstract ideas, what we might now call concepts. Berkeley suggested that when we want to think of men in a general way we have to imagine a particular man but, in reasoning about men in general, we take care not to deduce anything which could only be deduced from our imagined example. Now it may well be that this is the way we do reason about any kind of particulars, but again we have by-passed the question as to how we know that any particular man is a man. It is the 'something' which makes any particular man a man which is the Universal.

It seems that, as human beings, we have an innate capacity to 'pick out' the same features in different particulars. In chapter 3 we shall see how Aristotle accounted for our apprehension of Universals in this way.

In this chapter we shall accept the Platonic view of Universals, the view that they have an independent existence and that, because they are permanent and unchanging, they are proper objects of knowledge. Plato knew that he could not demonstrate the existence of Universals by rational deductive argument and that, at bottom, his account had to be accepted on the basis of an intuitive belief that ultimate reality was immaterial and not accessible to sense perception. But we should not, on that account, dismiss the Platonic conception of Universals and of knowledge. For *any* account that we give as to the nature of the world must ultimately rest on intuitive beliefs which cannot be rationally justified.

As we shall see in his allegory of the cave, Plato was well aware that our primitive and unreflecting instinctive belief is that the external world which we know through sense perception is the real world. Through metaphor he hoped to convince others that this belief was mistaken. Let us look first at his account of the conflict between the Gods and the Giants. The Giants hold the primitive instinctive belief, the Gods have a different belief, acquired by reflection.

> STRANGER: Look then, for there seems to be a sort of Battle of the Gods and the Giants going on among them because of their dispute about existence.
>
> THEAETETUS: How so?
>
> STRANGER: One side drags down everything from heaven and the unseen to earth, rudely grasping rocks and trees in their hands. For they get their grip on all such things and they maintain that that alone exists which can be handled and touched. They define body and existence as the same thing, and if anyone says that one of the other things which does not have body exists they completely despise him and are unwilling to listen to another word.
>
> THEAETETUS: Terrible men they are of whom you speak. I myself have met with a lot of them in my time.
>
> STRANGER: For that reason those who battle against them defend themselves very carefully from somewhere above in the unseen, contending that true existence consists in certain incorporeal Forms which are objects of the mind. But they pound the bodies of their opponents and what these call truth into small pieces in their arguments, denouncing it as a sort of motion and becoming. There is always, Theaetetus, an interminable battle going on between the two camps about these issues.
>
> THEAETETUS: True
>
> (secs 245E—246C in Flew, pp. 43—4)

The Giants are those who believe that sense perception gives knowledge of what *is*, i.e. knowledge of existence. For 'they define body and existence as the same thing' and 'that alone exists which can be handled and touched'. By contrast the Gods hold that true existence, true reality, is in the 'incorporeal Forms which are objects of the mind'. Here I must again stress that just because, if we are lucky, a Universal may become an object of our mind, something we think about, its existence does not depend on that.

But now we come to the famous metaphor of the cave. This tells us much more than the short account of Gods and Giants for it shows us not only why Plato held that sense perception could not be a basis for knowledge but it also shows how, in spite of this, we could aspire to knowledge, and it also shows that Plato fully appreciated that those who aspire to understand may be ridiculed.

'Next, then,' I said, 'take the following parable of education and ignorance as a picture of the condition of our nature. Imagine mankind as dwelling in an underground cave with a long entrance open to the light across the whole width of the cave; in this they have been from childhood, with necks and legs fettered, so they have to stay where they are. They cannot move their heads round because of the fetters, and they can only look forward, but light comes to them from fire burning behind them higher up at a distance. Between the fire and the prisoners is a road above their level, and along it imagine a low wall has been built, as puppet showmen have screens in front of their people over which they work their puppets.'

'I see,' he said.

'See, then, bearers carrying along this wall all sorts of articles which they hold projecting above the wall, statues of men and other living things, made of stone or wood and all kinds of stuff, some of the bearers speaking and some silent, as you might expect.'

'What a remarkable image,' he said, 'and what remarkable prisoners!'

'Just like ourselves,' I said. 'For, first of all, tell me this: What do you think such people would have seen of themselves and each other except their shadows, which the fire cast on the opposite wall of the cave?'

'I don't see how they could see anything else,' said he, 'if they were compelled to keep their heads unmoving all their lives!'

'Very well, what of the things being carried along? Would not this be the same?

'Of course it would.'

'Suppose the prisoners were able to talk together, don't you think that when they named the shadows which they saw passing they would believe they were naming things?'

'Necessarily.'

'Then if their prison had an echo from the opposite wall, whenever one of the passing bearers uttered a sound, would they not suppose that the passing shadow must be making the sound? Don't you think so?'

'Indeed I do,' he said.

'If so,' said I, 'such persons would certainly believe that there were no realities except those shadows of handmade things.'

'So it must be,' said he.

'Now consider,' said I, 'what their release would be like, and their cure from these fetters and their folly; let us imagine whether it might naturally be something like this. One might be released, and compelled suddenly to stand up and turn his neck round, and to walk and look towards the firelight; all this would hurt him, and he would be too much dazzled to see distinctly those things whose shadows he had seen before. What do you think he would say, if someone told him that what he saw before was foolery, but now he saw more rightly, being a bit nearer reality and turned towards what was a little more real? What if he were shown each of the passing things, and compelled by questions to answer what each one was? Don't you think he would be puzzled, and believe what he saw before was more true than what was shown to him now?'

'Far more,' he said.

'Then suppose he were compelled to look towards the real light, it would hurt his eyes, and he would escape by turning them away to the things which he was able to look at, and these he would believe to be clearer than what was being shown to him.'

'Just so,' said he.

'Suppose, now,' said I, 'that someone should drag him thence by force, up the rough ascent, the steep way up, and never stop until he could drag him out into the light of the sun, would he not be distressed and furious at being dragged; and when he came into the light, the brilliance

would fill his eyes and he would not be able to see even
one of the things now called real?'

'That he would not,' said he, 'all of a sudden.'

'He would have to get used to it, surely, I think, if he is
to see the things above. First he would most easily look at
shadows, after that images of mankind and the rest in water,
lastly the things themselves. After this he would find it
easier to survey by night the heavens themselves and all
that is in them, gazing at the light of the stars and moon,
rather than by day the sun and the sun's light.'

'Of course.'

'Last of all, I suppose, the sun; he could look on the sun
itself by itself in its own place, and see what it is like, not
reflections of it in water or as it appears in some alien setting.'

'Necessarily,' said he.

'And only after all this he might reason about it, how
this is he who provides seasons and years, and is set over all
there is in the visible region, and he is in a manner the cause
of all things which they saw.'

'Yes, it is clear,' said he, 'that after all that, he would
come to this last.'

'Very good. Let him be reminded of his first habitation,
and what was wisdom in that place, and of his fellow-pris-
oners there; don't you think he would bless himself for the
change, and pity them?'

'Yes, indeed.'

'And if there were honours and praises among them and prizes for the one who saw the passing things most sharply and remembered best which of them used to come before and which after and which together, and from these was best able to prophesy accordingly what was going to come — do you believe he would set his desire on that, and envy those who were honoured men or potentates among them? Would he not feel as Homer says, and heartily desire rather to be serf of some landless man on earth and to endure anything in the world, rather than to opine as they did and to live in that way?'

'Yes indeed,' said he, 'he would rather accept anything than live like that.'

'Then again,' I said, 'just consider; if such a one should go down again and sit on his old seat, would he not get his eyes full of darkness coming in suddenly out of the sun?'

'Very much so,' said he.

'And if he should have to compete with those who had been always prisoners, by laying down the law about those shadows while he was blinking before his eyes were settled down — and it would take a good long time to get used to things — wouldn't they all laugh at him and say he had spoiled his eyesight by going up there, and it was not worth-while so much as to try to go up? And would they not kill anyone who tried to release them and take them up, if they could somehow lay hands on him and kill him?'

'That they would!' said he.

'Then we must apply this image, my dear Glaucon,' said I, 'to all we have been saying. The world of our sight is like the habitation in prison, the firelight there to the sunlight here, the ascent and the view of the upper world is the rising of the soul into the world of mind; put it so and you will not be far from my own surmise, since that is what you want to hear; but God knows if it is really true. At least, what appears to me is, that in the world of the known, last of all, is the idea of the good, and with what toil to be seen! And seen, this must be inferred to be the cause of all right and beautiful things for all, which gives birth to light and the king of light in the world of sight,

and, in the world of mind, herself the queen produces truth
and reason; and she must be seen by one who is to act with
reason publicly or privately.'

(*Republic*, Book VII, Rouse, pp. 371—6)

If we rely on sense perception, we remain like the prisoners
in the cave and are aware only of shadows; we take these to
be reality. But if we use our understanding and aspire to the
light (i.e. try to become enlightened) then the fetters of
sense perception may be broken. At first we shall feel puzzled
and afraid, but once we have become used to the light we
shall appreciate that we have knowledge which was not available in the cave. However, if we go back to the cave we may
find ourselves ridiculed and perhaps in danger, for, having
been enlightened, it will be difficult for us to see things as we
used to see and in the way that those in the cave still see
them. We aspire to knowledge and we acquire knowledge by
using our understanding, *not* by means of perception with
our senses — sight, hearing, touch, taste and smell. But, since
this is so, Plato has to say, more explicitly than by metaphor,
how it is that we have even the beginning of the notion of
Universals. He has to explain how we come to apprehend
Universals so that they can illuminate us, and so that we
thereby begin to apprehend true reality. His explanation was
that, by thought, we were able to *remember* that world of
Universals which the soul inhabited before its earthly life
began. It was Socrates who expounded this view of the soul
and Plato developed his ideas. For Plato's doctrine of Universals depends on acknowledging that the soul is immortal, or,
at the very least, existed before it came to the material world.

Plato held that the immaterial soul was independent of and
also superior to the material body. This view of body and soul
as two independent and *different* substances is a form of
dualism. As we shall see later, Plato's dualism is in many
respects similar to that of Descartes. Both regarded the soul
as immaterial, as providing rational and understanding capacities, and also as probably being immortal. By contrast the
body was a material, changing and impermanent substance.

Plato said that the soul belonged to the changeless and
external world of Universals, not to the changing, imperman-

ent and shadowy world of sense perception. After death it
might go back to the world of Universals, though it might
return from thence to this material world again. But each
time it returned within a body it was as though it had been
once more imprisoned. It longed for release in order to return
to the world of Universals. Yet, whilst in a material body it
became polluted, sometimes very much polluted, and for this
reason it would at least partially forget the world of Universals.
Sense perception might serve to *remind* it of that world, but
it could only begin to apprehend Universals because it had
once known them fully. 'For now I see as in a glass darkly,
but then face to face.'

'Now come,' said he, 'in ourselves one part is body and
one part soul?'

'Just so,' he said.

'Then which kind do we say the body would be more
like and akin to?'

'The visible,' he said, 'that is clear to anyone.'

'And the soul — is it visible, or unseen?'

'Not visible to mankind at least, Socrates,' he said.

'But when we say visible and not visible, we mean to
human senses, don't we?'

'Yes, we do.'

'Then what of the soul — do we say that is visible or
invisible?'

'Not visible.'

'Unseen, then?'

'Yes.'

'Then soul is more like to the unseen, and body to the
visible.'

'It surely must be.'

'Now you remember that we were saying some time ago
that the soul, when it has the body to help in examining
things, either through sight or hearing or any other sense —
for to examine something through the body means through
the senses — then it is dragged by the body towards what is
always changing, and the soul goes astray and is confused
and staggers about like one drunken because she is taking
hold of such things.'

'Certainly.'

'But when she examines by herself, she goes away yonder to the pure and everlasting and immortal and unchanging; and being akin to that, she abides ever with it, whenever it becomes possible for her to abide by herself. And there she rests from her wanderings, and while she is amongst those things she is herself unchanging because what she takes hold of is unchanging: and this state of the soul has the name of wisdom?'

'Most excellent and true, Socrates.'

'Then which of the two kinds is she more like and more akin to, judging from what we said before and what we are saying now?'

'Everyone, even the most ignorant, would admit, I think, Socrates,' he said, 'from that way of reasoning, that soul is wholly and altogether more like the unchanging than the changing.'

'And the body?'

'More like the changing.'

'Look at it in this way also: When soul and body are together, our nature assigns the body to be slave and to be ruled, and the soul to be ruler and master; now, then, further, which of the two seems to be like the divine, and which like the mortal? Don't you think the divine is naturally such as to rule and to guide, and the mortal such as to be ruled and to be a slave?'

'I do.'

'Then which is the soul like?'

'It is clear, Socrates, that the soul is like the divine, and the body like the mortal.'

'Consider now, Cebes, whether it follows from all that we have said, that the soul is most like the divine and immortal and intellectual and simple and indissoluble and selfunchangeable, but on the contrary, the body is most like the human and mortal and manifold and unintellectual and dissoluble and ever-changing. Can we say anything to contradict that, my dear Cebes, or is that correct?'

'We cannot contradict it.'

'Very well. This being so, is it not proper to the body to be quickly dissolved, but on the contrary to the soul to be wholly indissoluble or very nearly so?'

'Of course.'

'You understand, then,' he said, 'that when the man dies, the visible part of him, the body — that which lies in the visible world, and which we call the corpse, for which it is proper to dissolve and disappear — does not suffer any of this at once but instead remains a good long time, and if a man dies with his body in a nice condition and age, a very long time. For if the body is shrivelled up and mummified like the mummies in Egypt it lasts almost whole, for an incredibly long time. And some portions of the body, even when it decays, bones and sinews and so forth, may almost be called immortal.'

'Yes.'

'But the soul, the "unseen" part of us, which goes to another place noble and pure and unseen like itself, a true unseen Hades, to the presence of the good and wise God, where, if God will, my own soul must go very soon — shall our soul, then, being such and of such nature, when released from the body be straightway scattered by the winds and perish, as most men say? Far from it, my dear Simmias! This is much more likely: If it is pure when it gets free, and drags nothing of the body with it, since it has no communion with the body in life if it can help it, but avoids the body and gathers itself into itself, since it is always practising this — here we have nothing else but a soul loving wisdom rightly, and in reality practising death — don't you think this would be a practice of death?'

'By all means.'

'Then, being thus, it goes away into the unseen, which is like itself, the divine and immortal and wise, where on arrival it has the opportunity to be happy, freed from wandering and folly and fears and wild loves and all other human evils, and, as they say of the initiated, really and truly passing the rest of time with the gods. Is that what we are to say, Cebes?'

'Yes indeed,' said Cebes.

'But if contrariwise, I think, if it leaves the body polluted and unpurified, as having been always with it and attending it and in love with it and bewitched by it through desires

and pleasures, so that it thinks nothing to be true but the
bodily — what one could touch and see and drink and eat
and use for carnal passion: if what is darksome to the eyes
and "unseen" but intellectual and to be caught by philosophy, if this, I say, it is accustomed to hate and fear and
flee; do you think a soul in that state will get away pure
and incorrupt in itself?'

'By no possible means whatever,' he said.

'No, I think it is interpenetrated by the bodily, which
the association and union with it of the body has by constant practice made ingrained.'

'Exactly.'

'A heavy load, my friend, we must believe that to be,
heavy and earthy and visible; and such a soul with this on
board is weighed down and dragged back into the visible
world, by fear of the unseen, Hades so-called, and cruises
about restless among tombs and graves, where you know
shadowy apparitions of souls have often been seen, phan-
toms such as are produced by souls like this, which have
not been released purely, but keep something of the visible,
and so they are seen.

'That is likely, Socrates.'

'Indeed it is likely; and likely that these are not the souls
of the good, but souls of the mean, which are compelled to
wander about such places as a penalty for their former way
of life, which was evil; and wander they must until by desire
for the bodily which is always in their company they are
imprisoned once more in the body.

(*Phaedo*, Rouse, pp. 556—8)

But if the soul has not been too much polluted it will return
to the world of Universals. Here it will again have knowledge.
But, when it returns to the material world it must drink at
least a little of the water of forgetfulness.

Everyone was compelled to drink a measure of this water;
but those who were not saved by prudence drank more
than the measure, and whoever drank forgot everything.
When they were laid to sleep and midnight came, there
was thunder and earthquake and then suddenly they were

carried upward this way and that to birth, like shooting
stars.   (*Republic*, Book X, Rouse, p. 490)

A rather picturesque account of the theory of knowledge
by recollection is given in this story of the young Shelley.

One Sunday we had been reading Plato together so dili-
gently, that the usual hour of exercise passed away unperceived: we sallied forth hastily to take the air for half an
hour before dinner. In the middle of Magdalen Bridge we
met a woman with a child in her arms. Shelley was more
attentive at that instant to our conduct in a life that was
past, or to come, than to a decorous regulation of the
present according to the established usages of society, in
that fleeting moment of eternal duration styled the nineteenth century. With abrupt dexterity he caught hold of
the child. The mother, who might well fear that it was
about to be thrown over the parapet of the bridge into the
sedgy waters below, held it fast by its long train.
    'Will your baby tell us anything about pre-existence,
Madam?' he asked, in a piercing voice, and with a wistful
look.
    The mother made no answer, but perceiving that Shelley's
object was not murderous, but altogether harmless, she dismissed her apprehension, and relaxed her hold.
    'Will your baby tell us anything about pre-existence,
Madam?' he repeated, with unabated earnestness.
    'He cannot speak, Sir,' said the mother seriously.
    'Worse and worse,' cried Shelley, with an air of deep
disappointment, shaking his long hair most pathetically
about his young face; 'but surely the babe can speak if he
will, for he is only a few weeks old. He may fancy perhaps
that he cannot, but it is only a silly whim; he cannot have
forgotten entirely the use of speech in so short a time; the
thing is absolutely impossible.'
    'It is not for me to dispute with you, Gentlemen,' the
woman meekly replied, her eye glancing at our academical
garb; 'but I can safely declare that I never heard him speak,
nor any child, indeed, of his age.'
    It was a fine placid boy; so far from being disturbed by

the interruption, he looked up and smiled. Shelley pressed his fat cheeks with his fingers, we commended his healthy appearance and his equanimity, and the mother was permitted to proceed, probably to her satisfaction, for she would doubtless prefer a less speculative nurse. Shelley sighed deeply as we walked on.

'How provokingly close are those new-born babes!' he ejaculated; 'but it is not the less certain, notwithstanding the cunning attempts to conceal the truth, that all knowledge is reminiscence: the doctrine is far more ancient than the times of Plato, and as old as the venerable allegory that the Muses are the daughters of Memory . . . '

(*The Oxford Book of Literary Anecdotes*, pp. 190—1)

Why was there such emphasis on recollection and why was knowledge possible only if there was recollection? Of course Plato had to suggest some basis or grounds for knowledge and, since he eschewed sense perception, the source of knowledge must be the mind. It might then be asked why it was that the mind (or soul) did not arrive at knowledge by interpreting the data of sense. As we have seen, Plato did grant that true belief (which was based on sense perception) might *prompt* the soul, but it was prompted to remembrance.

Plato asserted that the material objects and events which we could observe were never perfect embodiments of Universals. He also asserted that from sense perception of imperfect entities we would never be able to apprehend perfection. Therefore merely by perceiving imperfect particular things, we could not possibly comprehend the corresponding Universals — the best that perception could do was to *remind* us of the Universals. For example, no two lines are of exactly equal length, and no two objects are of exactly equal weight etc. and *yet* we do have an understanding of equality — of the Universal, Equality. Since we cannot possibly have got this apprehension by direct observation we must have remembered it. We must have been reminded by the nearly but not quite equal things which we observe in the material world, of the absolute equality which we knew in the world of Universals. Similarly there was no object in the material world which was completely and absolutely beautiful, but observation of objects which showed beauty in some degree would remind the soul of Beauty, the Universal, which it had known in the immaterial world of Universals. Plato was undecided on the status of such entities as dirt or hair. Originally he had proposed a world of Universals which excluded these but it seems that he finally concluded that all our general notions, whether elevated or sordid, must be derived from Universals in the real, immaterial world of Universals. We may summarise Plato's view of knowledge as follows:

(1)   Knowledge is permanent and certain, i.e. it is not subject to correction.
(2)   It is not possible to claim knowledge on the basis of sense perception and therefore it is not possible to claim knowledge of any object or event in the material world. The best we can aspire to is true belief (right opinion).
(3)   True belief can guide us and can prompt the soul to remember the world of Universals.
(4)   Universals are eternal and changeless and therefore they *can* be objects of knowledge.
(5)   Universals cannot be perceived by the senses; it is only the intellect which makes us aware of them.
(6)   Thus we can *know* only by virtue of our intellect, and by its capacity for recollection.

This view of the nature of the soul, an immaterial intellectual entity from the immaterial world of Universals permeates Plato's writing. The philosopher must cultivate his soul; he must strive to recollect and to come out of the cave into the sunlight. When he has apprehended reality he must return to the cave in order to persuade others to see. He may well be ridiculed and perhaps may be persecuted but it is his duty to help others to the light. From knowledge there will be goodness and this is the end for which the philosopher, and, in the ideal Platonic state the philosopher king, should strive.

But there is another personal aspiration for each philosopher. The study of philosophy educates the soul of the philosopher and prepares it for the true life which could follow death. After release from the prison of the body, the soul could stay permanently in the world of Univerals and never more be polluted by a material body.

'The lovers of learning understand', said he, 'that philosophy found their soul simply imprisoned in the body and welded to it, and compelled to survey through this as if through prison bars the things that are, not by itself through itself, but wallowing in all ignorance; and she saw that the danger of this prison came through desire, so that the prisoner himself would be a chief helper in his own imprisonment.

. . .

So the soul of the true philosopher believes that it must not oppose this deliverance, and therefore abstains from pleasures and desires and griefs and fears as much as possible, counting that when a man feels great pleasure or fear or pain or desire, he suffers not only the evil that one might think (for example, being ill or squandering money through his desires), but the greatest and worst of all evils, which he suffers and never counts.

. . .

Because each pleasure and pain seems to have a nail, and nails the soul to the body and pins it on and makes it bodily, and so it thinks the same things are true which the body says are true. For by having the same opinion as the body, and liking the same things, it is compelled, I believe, to adopt the same ways and the same nourishment and to become such as never could come pure to the house of Hades, but would always go forth infected by the body; so it would fall quickly into another body and there be sown and grown, and therefore would have neither part nor lot in communion with the divine and pure and simple.

. . .

. . . it is for these reasons . . . that those who rightly love learning are decent and brave.

. . .

Such would be the reasons of the philosopher. His soul would not think it right that philosophy should set her free, and that while being set free she herself should surrender herself back again in bondage to pleasure and pains . . . she thinks she must calm these passions; and, following reason and keeping always in it, beholding the true and the

divine and the certain, and nourishing herself on this, his
soul believes that she ought to live thus, as long as she does
live, and when she dies she will join what is akin and like
herself, and be rid of human evils.'

(*Phaedo*, Rouse, pp. 560—1)

We can now appreciate more fully how knowledge and
virtue were so intimately connected in Plato's philosophy.
With true knowledge, apprehension of Universals, the futility
and also the snares of the world of sense perception is realised
and the virtuous soul will avoid the pleasures (and pains) of
the senses. We may regard this as a rather arid, perhaps puri-
tanical view of the nature of virtue and it is arguable that the
plea to disregard the material world can rather too easily be
held to encourage disregard of the material wants of others as
well as our own wants. Plato's view of virtue is indeed open
to criticism.

There have also been criticisms of Plato's contention that
knowledge comes from recollection and that only Universals
can be objects of knowledge. There has been criticism of
Plato's view that Universals are more real than the particulars
which we sense. One of the critics was Plato's pupil Aristotle;
his view of knowledge will be discussed in the next chapter.
Today there would be criticisms arising from our view that
there can be no knowledge without a mind and no mind
without a brain. So that there can be knowledge without at
least part of a corporeal body. How, therefore, could an immaterial entity acquire knowledge, a knowledge which could
be later recollected in a material brain? Even if the possibility
of the existence of an immaterial soul is admitted, Plato's
account of knowledge by recollection seems far-fetched to us.

Yet it remains true that Plato did bring out problems of
knowledge, and the problem of the relationship between
sense perception and reasoning, which are still with us today.
We may not agree with Plato's conclusions, but we should
study them sympathetically, for, unless we make a real effort
to understand and to appreciate his thoughts we are in no
position to criticise, still less to undermine, his position.

FURTHER READING

W. K. C. Guthrie, *The Greek Philosophers.*
P. M. Huby, 'Socrates and Plato' from D. J. O'Connor (ed.),
A Critical History of Western Philosophy.
W. H. D. Rouse (ed. & trans), *The Complete Texts of Great Dialogues of Plato.*

NOTES

1. The English word 'good' is similar to *arete* in that it needs a context to be significant. It is an example of one of Austin's substantive-hungry words, like 'real'. However, here we have the context, for we are concerned with the moral good of human beings.

2. The unicorn is a mythical animal *defined* as having one horn; we can claim knowledge by definition. Euclidean triangles are also mythical, and knowledge of them is knowledge by definition (see glossary).

3

Aristotle's View of Knowledge

Aristotle, 384–322 BC, was born 43 years after Plato but, since Plato lived till he was 80, their lives overlapped enough for Plato to have had considerable direct influence on Aristotle. Aristotle came to Plato's Academy in Athens when he was 18 years old and stayed there until Plato died; he was the most distinguished of all Plato's disciples and also one of the most critical. We need to take these criticisms very seriously because, despite accusations that Aristotle misinterpreted Plato, his criticisms are the criticisms of someone who had been able to talk and discuss philosophy with Plato. Moreover it is likely that Aristotle had at least as good and very possibly much better understanding of Plato's ideas than we have. As O'Connor says:

> It has sometimes been suggested that many of Aristotle's criticisms of Plato are unfair and that the theory he attacked is only a caricature of Plato's real views. This may be so. But Aristotle was a pupil of Plato for many years and we may reasonably suppose him to have been better acquainted with Plato's meaning than any scholar today.
>
> (*Crit. Hist. West. Phil.*, p. 47)

After Plato's death, 347 BC, Aristotle left the Academy and went to Assos in Asia Minor. Here he established a school of philosophy. At that time, and indeed until the nineteenth century, philosophy embraced natural philosophy, which we now call natural science. Aristotle made many observations of the flora and fauna, and these observations are still of interest today. He also married the daughter[1] of the king Hermias. This is worth noting, for it shows that in his own lifetime Aristotle was an eminent and highly respected figure. It is not surprising that Philip of Macedon invited him to be tutor to his son, Alexander, the future Alexander the Great. Aristotle went to the Macedonian court in 343 BC. Many people have speculated as to the influence Aristotle had on Alexander. I am rather inclined to agree with Bertrand Russell:

> . . . we are left free to conjecture whatever seems to us most plausible. For my part, I should suppose it *nil*. Alexander was an ambitious and passionate boy, on bad terms with his father, and presumably impatient of schooling. . . . I cannot imagine his pupil regarding him as anything but a prosy old pedant, set over him by his father to keep him out of mischief.   (*Hist. West. Phil.*, p. 174)

Later, 335 BC, Aristotle returned to Athens and set up his own school of philosophy, known as the Lyceum. The teachers walked about as they discussed with their students, and hence they were called peripatetic philosophers and the school was also called Peripatos. The Macedonians were not popular in Athens and, after Alexander died in 323 BC, Aristotle was, or at least thought he was, in some danger. It is said that he moved from the city so that the citizens should not again sin as they had sinned when they killed Socrates. At all events he left for Chalcis, and died there the next year; he was 62 years old.

Aristotle's work is staggering both in its range and in its depth. His texts were rediscovered piece-meal, and they do not have the elegance and 'flow' of Plato's writings. Also, and this is a difficulty in common with Plato, they are written against a very different intellectual background from our own. It was a pre-Christian and relatively primitive society and this difference in background makes it necessary to be wary in interpreting the text. Nevertheless, Aristotle's works can only fill us with respect and admiration. He is one of the great philosophers who have had an influence on all subsequent thought and who have affected far more people than those who have read him. But he speaks even more powerfully to these, and even in translation the impact of his ideas comes through with great force.

Perhaps the least regarded parts now are his writing on cosmology and physics. Indeed it is still sometimes said that Aristotle held back the progress of scientific knowledge for centuries. I doubt if this is true for his writings epitomise the two fundamental characteristics of scientific inquiry: curiosity about the natural world and the belief that through observation and reason we can acquire knowledge of its nature.

Aristotle held that the cosmos was closed and finite. The spherical earth was at the centre and around it the moon, sun and the known planets (Mercury, Venus, Mars, Saturn and Jupiter) revolved — each embedded in a transparent crystalline sphere. Beyond these spheres was the sphere containing the fixed stars — unlike the other heavenly bodies they remained in the same positions relative to each other. The revolutions of all these spheres was controlled by another outer sphere — the sphere of the unmoved mover, but, since circular motion was natural to the heavens, no force was necessary to keep the spheres revolving. The observed irregularities of the planets were accounted for by proposing a series of subsidiary circular motions.

The moon was in the sphere nearest to the earth and, within this sphere (the sub-lunar region), natural motion was upwards or downwards. Here all other motion, such as circular motion or horizontal motion, required a force. Everything in the sub-lunar region was composed of the four elements: earth, air, fire and water. Fire and air moved upwards naturally, earth and water downwards (i.e. towards the centre of the earth and the centre of the cosmos). Hence there was perpetual change and corruption since the elements were striving to attain their natural places.

By 'earth', 'air' etc., Aristotle did not refer to lumps of earth or to the air around us but to the underlying essence of earthiness, airiness etc which made solid or gaseous material. The many different substances were compounded of more than one element and their observed qualities were held to be due to an inner essence or *form* which was imposed on the crude matter. We shall not pursue this aspect of Aristotle's philosophy further, but, as we shall see in chapter 4, Aristotle's view of matter and indeed of the earth itself and of the heavenly bodies, implied a latent animism. He drew no clear distinction between the animate and inanimate. In this respect his view of all matter was not unlike our present-day view of DNA and of viruses.

However, for Aristotle, all was different beyond the sphere of the moon. Here everything was composed of a fifth element, the quintessence, and was not subject to change and decay. The heavenly bodies and their spheres were perfect and incorruptible.

Aristotle's cosmological scheme was developed and elaborated by others and in particular by Ptolemy (90–168 AD) but his basic picture of the universe remained virtually unchallenged until the publication of Copernicus' *On the Revolutions of the Celestial Orbs* in 1543. It was therefore the basis of astronomy and cosmology for centuries. It was a basis for scientific thought, for philosophical speculation and for poetic imagination. The heavenly music, the music of the spheres as they revolved, was an inspiration to poets up to the time of Shakespeare and the cosmological scheme inspired Dante's Divine Comedy.

Yet it was unfortunate for scientific inquiry that the Aristotelian theories were incorporated with Christian doctrines for they became 'elevated' to the rank of dogmatic and divinely inspired truths which it would be heretical to question. This rigidity was further encouraged by the Renaissance tradition which was that the wisdom of the Ancients, and of Aristotle in particular, was beyond criticism. Therefore medieval and Renaissance philosophers directed their inquiries to the study and analysis of Greek and Roman texts and, with a few exceptions,[2] made no experiments and few observations of the world around them.

But we can hardly blame Aristotle for this. He himself did not proceed in this way. He developed older ideas and he also suggested new theories, prompted and stimulated by what he observed. Most of his scientific theories have been superseded, but this is the fate of empirical theories, and we cannot reasonably discount Aristotle's contribution to natural science for that reason. However, though he did make observations, and though he did not rely on appeal to earlier authority, his mode of scientific inquiry is open to *modern* criticism in two respects: firstly because his view of causal explanation and the role of measurement in empirical inquiry was unhelpful; this will be discussed in chapter 4. Secondly because his belief that certain properties of materials were necessarily associated led him to the view that indubitable knowledge could be found by discovering these necessary and essential properties. This will be discussed and criticised below.

A third criticism, which cannot be so severe is that he relied too much on the direct evidence provided by observation. His account of the cosmos and of events in the world is *more* in accord with what we actually observe than are the accounts given by Copernicus, Galileo and those who followed. After all, we only have to look up to see that the sun and other heavenly bodies move round the earth, we can observe that the earth is at rest, that if objects are to keep moving they must be pushed or pulled and that heavy objects fall to the ground more quickly than light objects. And we must remember that Aristotle's interpretations did not invariably mislead: he appreciated that the moon was not a source of light, but reflected light from the sun, he understood the reason for eclipses, he realised that because the planets were much nearer than the stars they did not twinkle. As indicated at the beginning of this chapter, many of his observations of living creatures were relevant to what interests us today. Therefore, in spite of what we now consider to be mistaken assumptions as to the nature of physical explanations, we can at least discuss the possibility that Aristotle contributed to the laying of the foundations of scientific inquiry. In any case, whatever the verdict on the value of his contribution to science, there can be no doubt that his contribution to logic was of the very greatest value. Although he analysed only one type of argument, those arguments based on syllogisms, and although he did not explicitly lay down formal rules of inference, he established a scheme of deductive reasoning which is the basis of mathematical as well as logical argument and which also plays an essential role in natural science.

Aristotle showed that the validity of an argument depends not on its content, i.e. not on the particular classes of propositions with which it deals, but on its structure, that is on the way the contents are related. His introduction of symbols, A, B, C, etc. to stand for the items making up the content was a highly original and important innovation. For, by using symbols, the structure of the argument is made plain, and arguments of totally different content can be structurally compared and criticised. For over 2000 years Aristotle's analysis remained undisputed and was held to be definitive. Not until the nineteenth century was deductive logic modified and developed further by Frege, Russell and others.

Aristotle did not regard logic as part of philosophy — it was an adjunct, a tool to be used to help philosophical analysis. He distinguished two main branches of philosophy: practical and speculative. Practical philosophy was concerned with conduct, with ethics and politics, with *arete*, with knowing how to be good at being a man and a citizen. Aristotle, like Plato regarded this knowledge as the ultimate aim of philosophy. He opens his book on Ethics with:

> Every art and every investigation, and similarly every action and pursuit, is considered to aim at some good. Hence the Good has been rightly defined as 'that at which all things aim'.   (*Ethics*, p. 63)

Practical philosophy was concerned with establishing general rules of conduct which would apply in most cases; but, because conduct depended on men's desires, the rules were liable to modification. Therefore they could not be absolute and therefore they could not be logically necessary and logically demonstrable. They were to be contrasted with physical laws which Aristotle thought did hold with logical necessity.[3] It followed that practical philosophy could not be a source of knowledge in the strict sense; for Aristotle agreed with Plato that true knowledge (scientific knowledge) had to be indubitable and therefore logically necessary.

The other branch of philosophy, speculative philosophy, was concerned with abstract principles which could be logically derived from self-evident first premises. Thus speculative philosophy could lead to scientific knowledge. For Aristotle 'scientific knowledge' included not only knowledge of the natural world (the province of what we now call science) but also mathematics and metaphysics.

Now in the previous chapter, we saw that Plato had argued that it was only possible to have knowledge of mathematical entities and Universals, and that this knowledge had to be acquired by mental activity. The senses could not give knowledge for they could only inform as to particulars, and, for Plato, the ever-changing and impermanent particulars could not be objects of knowledge. Aristotle agreed that they could not be objects of knowledge *qua* particulars, but he did think that sense perception could and indeed had to play a part in the acquisition of knowledge. This was because he had a different view of the nature of the particulars and of the relation of Universals to particulars. He also had a different view of how we came to apprehend Universals.

Aristotle did not think that Universals could exist independently of particulars; the relation between them was not analogous to the relation between an object and its shadow. He thought that Universals and particulars were *inter*-dependent, so that neither could exist without the other. For example, a particular horse could only be a horse because there was a Universal horse[4] (i.e. the complex of characteristics the possession of which by a creature made it a horse), but the existence of the Universal horse depended on there being at least one particular horse.

In addition Aristotle did not believe that our knowledge of Universals was innate, depending on recollection from an existence in the world of Universals. Plato had said that sense perception might *help* to remind us of our innate memory, but Aristotle believed that sense perception was *required* for the development of our ability to apprehend Universals; it was not just a help, it played an essential role. In the extract below he considers the problem as to how we come to apprehend Universals:

> . . . it is strange if we possess them from birth; for it means that we possess apprehensions more accurate than demonstration and fail to notice them. If on the other hand we

acquire them and do not previously possess them, how could we learn without a basis of pre-existent knowledge?

(Ross, 99b 26)

we conclude these states of knowledge are neither innate in a determinate form, nor developed from other higher states of knowledge, but from sense perception. It is like a rout in a battle stopped by first one man making a stand and then another, until the original formation has been restored. The soul is so constituted as to be capable of this process.   (Ibid, 100a)

The rout is analogous to the hurly burly of sensations which pervade us at birth. When we begin to appreciate similarity an early[5] Universal has 'made a stand', and we start to classify. We *respond* to sensations in this way for 'the soul is so constituted as to be capable of this process'. Modern suggestions that we have an innate expectation of order are not so very different from the Aristotelian explanation. Aristotle continues:

When one of a number of logically indiscriminable particulars has made a stand, the earliest Universal is present in the soul; for though the act of sense perception is of the particular, its content is Universal — is Man, for example, not the man Callias. A fresh stand is made among these rudimentary Universals, and the process does not cease until the indivisible concepts, the true Universals, are established: e.g. such and such a species of animal is a step towards the genus animal, which by the same process is a step towards a further generalisation.

(Ibid, 13)

'The act of sense perception is of the particular but its *content* is Universal' — we can, after all, only recognise the man Callias *as* a man if we already understand what it is to be a man. In other words we must apprehend the Universal in order to interpret the particular; but we have to have sense experience of particulars to apprehend the Universal.

An established hierarchy of Universals gives us a classifying scheme and any universal can be defined by its place in the scheme. The lowest Universal is a species, which is contained within a higher Universal, its genus. A species is distinguished from other species in the genus by its unique and essential characteristics. For example the species man is in the genus animal, and it is differentiated from other animals by its unique and essential characteristic of rationality; hence man is the species of rational animal. (In fact Aristotle classed man as *political animal*, 'political' meaning 'living in a social group' and derived from the Greek *polis* (city). The specification 'rational' comes from medieval philosophers. But there is little doubt that Aristotle would have accepted this, and so 'rational' will be used as the species characteristic here.)

We must bear in mind that an important feature of Aristotle's scheme of classification and of knowledge was that it was only possible to have knowledge of Universals, not of the particulars which make up the species; this is because particulars cannot be defined. To appreciate this we must understand the distinction between a definition and a description. A particular can be described and identified but it cannot be defined, i.e. there are no attributes which are essential to it *as a particular*, no attributes which are required to make it the particular entity which it is. For example, take a particular woman, Margaret Thatcher; she can of course be described, she is prime minister in 1980, she is a Conservative politician, she has a husband, she has two children, she is a certain weight and height and so on. This description identifies her but are any of these properties essential to her being Margaret Thatcher? Would she be regarded as Margaret Thatcher if she lacked any or all of these?[6] If these properties alter will she still be Margaret Thatcher? *As an individual* she has no essential properties and therefore she cannot be defined; the essential properties she does possess she possesses as a member of the human species.

But to return to our Universals; the defining and therefore the essential properties are such that they apply to all the particulars subsumed by the Universal and to no others. Thus the defining property for the Universal man is 'rational animal'. All men are rational animals and all rational animals are men (in this context 'man' embraces 'woman'). The attribute 'rational animal' is one which Aristotle would say was *commensurately universal*:

> I term 'commensurately universal' an attribute which belongs to every instance of its subject, and to every instance essentially as such; from which it follows clearly that all commensurately universals inhere necessarily in their subjects ... triangle as such has two right angles, for it is essentially equal to two right angles.   (Ross, 73b 27)

Aristotle took the geometrical figure, the triangle, as his example and it is indeed to geometrical figures that his classificatory scheme of knowledge can be most successfully applied. For, with geometrical figures, defining attributes are essential attributes and further properties can be logically deduced from these essential attributes. For example, the defining and essential attribute of circles is that all points on the circumference are equidistant from the centre, and all figures with all points on their circumference equidistant from their centre are circles. Taking this definition along with the Euclidean axioms (which effectively define the higher Universals in the classifying scheme) we can deduce other attributes of circles and thus obtain scientific knowledge – knowledge which cannot be otherwise.

But the situation is different when we come to consider objects in the world. For, even if we assume that species, say man or horse, have essential attributes (and we shall question this assumption later) we cannot *postulate* these in the same way as we can postulate the attributes of a geometric figure. However, Aristotle did not think that it was impossible to *discover* them. He appreciated that we could not *start* by defining an existent species in the way that we could define a mythical creature like a unicorn, but he thought that there was a defining attribute (or set of defining attributes), and, by observing the particular individuals, this could be discovered. The process of generalising, making a general assertion about properties by appealing to evidence from observation of particulars, is known as *induction*. It is important to note that Aristotle did not think that induction would give knowledge of essential attributes but that it was a method of guiding to possible essential attributes. It did not give us certain knowledge for, even if an attribute were observed to be common to *all* individuals of a species and unique to those individuals, it might not be an essential attribute.

For example, observation shows that all humans are featherless bipeds and that only featherless bipeds are humans, so it might be assumed that this is an essential attribute, one which is commensurately universal. But Aristotle would have denied this; he would have said that observation could show that it was a universal attribute,[7] but could not show that it was an essential attribute. In other words, although as a matter of contingent fact all humans are featherless bipeds, that attribute is not necessarily part of the essential nature of humans. It *might* be, but this must be established by means other than observation. To show it is essential we must show *why* humans possess the attribute; otherwise it can only be rated as an accidental or contingent property, just as the attribute of being god-beloved is an accidental or contingent property of holiness. Aristotle said that such contingent or accidental properties could not give knowledge.

> . . . since accidents are not necessary one does not necessarily have reasoned knowledge of a conclusion drawn from them. (This is so even if the accidental properties are invariable . . . for though the conclusion be actually essential, one will not know it is essential nor know its reason); but to have reasoned knowledge of a conclusion is to know it through its cause. (Ross, 75a)

It was only if causal connection could be established that it was justifiable to assert that a property was essential and therefore necessary. Having shown a causal connection a plain fact became a *reasoned fact*. For example, take the plain fact that the planets do not twinkle − non-twinkling is an attribute of all planets. It is made into a reasoned fact by the causal explanation that the planets are near.

'What is near does not twinkle
The planets are near
Therefore the planets do not twinkle.'

Aristotle stressed that we have to observe, i.e. we have to

be aware of the plain fact in order to be able to show that it is a reasoned fact, though the fact and its reason may be apprehended simultaneously:

> When we are aware of a fact we seek its reason, and though sometimes the fact and the reason dawn on us simultaneously, yet we cannot apprehend the reason a moment sooner than the fact; and clearly in just the same way we cannot apprehend a thing's definable form[8] without apprehending that it exists, since, while we are ignorant whether it exists we cannot know its essential nature. Moreover we are aware whether a thing exists or not sometimes through apprehending an element in its character, and sometimes accidentally, as, for example, when we are aware of thunder as a noise in the clouds, of eclipse as privation of light . . . . As often we have accidental knowledge that the thing exists, we must be in a wholly negative state as regards awareness of its essential nature; for we have not got genuine knowledge even of its existence, . . . the degree of our knowledge of a thing's essential nature is determined by the sense in which we are aware that it exists.   (Ross, 93a 16)

> Now to know its essential nature is, as we have said, to know the cause of a thing's existence, and the proof of this depends on the fact that a thing must have a cause.
>
> (Ibid, 93a 3)

But how did we know that we had indeed found a true definition and a true cause? How did we know that we had a reasoned fact? Aristotle said that we knew this by intuition or *nous*. *Nous* was a superior kind of apprehension. It was more reliable than deduced scientific knowledge since it was known directly. We shall see later (chapter 4) that Descartes had precisely the same opinion as to the superiority of intuitively apprehended truths over those which were arrived at by demonstration, i.e. by logical deduction.

The important features of Aristotle's analysis of knowledge are as follows:

(1)   Like Plato, Aristotle was a realist; the Univerals had an

objective existence. Moreover Aristotle did not think that it was necessary to convince others of their existence by appeals to metaphor. He took their existence for granted just as he took the existence of physical objects for granted.

(2)   Unlike Plato Aristotle believed that Universals could not exist without particulars; particulars and Universals were interdependent.

(3)   Plato held that knowledge could only come by recollecting the permanent and changeless Universals which the soul had known in its pre-bodily existence. Aristotle held that knowledge was arrived at with the help of sense-perception of particulars.

(4)   All Universals had necessary attributes which defined them and from which, along with their relation to other Universals, their properties could be logically deduced.

(5)   Observation guided to discovery of essential properties by showing the plain facts of association of properties.

(6)   Intuition or *nous* showed causes of associations and therefore showed reasoned facts.

(7)   Reasoned facts were the basis of scientific knowledge and further scientific knowledge was arrived at by deduction. This knowledge was indubitable; it could not be otherwise.

(8)   Thus empirical inquiry (inquiry into the world we perceived) could yield knowledge which was as certain as mathematical knowledge.

Here we must begin to assess and criticise: these points cannot be accepted *in toto*, though there is much that is acceptable. We can accept, in a general sense, the reliance on *nous*, for, at the last, we *must* rely on our intuition (see also chapter 5, p. 99—100) — we must trust our powers of thought and reason. But we can object to the assumption that reason is an infallible guide to causes of events in the world, and that it can show us that attributes are necessarily associated. We must also object to the assumption that there *are* some properties which are necessarily associated and so we must object to the inference, from that assumption, that a system of classification based on purportedly necessary associations of properties will reflect a necessary order in nature.

The view that knowledge about the world could be found by logical deduction from associations of essential properties, and that it would be certain and indubitable, persisted right into the seventeenth century. As we shall see in chapter 4, it permeates the philosophy of Descartes, and, as we shall see in chapter 6, it was also fundamental to Locke's view of empirical knowledge. Both the rationalist Descartes and the empiricist Locke[9] regarded mathematical knowledge as the paradigm of all knowledge, and thereby show their debt to Plato and to Aristotle. It was the paradigm, because mathematical knowledge could be arrived at by deduction from the defining (and therefore the essential) properties of mathematical entities.

As we shall see in chapter 6, Locke believed that it was impossible to know what the essential attributes of materials were, so that he accepted that it was impossible, *in practice*, to deduce their properties and have indubitable knowledge. But he believed that there *were* essential properties of the tiny corpuscles which made up all matter and that if these could have been observed then indubitable knowledge would be possible; hence, for Locke such knowledge was possible in principle.

Today we do not accept that there are any properties which are necessarily associated, and therefore our attitude to classification and to knowledge is quite different. For us classifying schemes are simply schemes that are devised for making convenient groupings of entities in virtue of some property (or more usually a set of properties) which they *happen* to have in common. The association of these properties is a contingent association, not a necessary association.[10]

We learn by experience that certain properties are regularly associated and therefore that certain schemes of classification are useful. We may indeed *feel* that there is some logical inevitability about familiar associations: we have an expectation that the transparent odourless liquid coming from the tap must quench our thirst if we drink it, must boil if we heat it, must eventually solidify if we cool it etc., etc. We shall see in chapter 7 that there is no logical justification for these expectations. Familiarity masks the fact that the associations are contingent and not logically inevitable.

In regard to living organisms (plants and animals) we find associations of characteristics which are made the basis of a comprehensive classifying scheme. We believe that the similarities and differences between the species are the result of evolution. But this evolution is itself a contingent fact and hence the relations which our classification exhibits so clearly are contingent relations. But our classification, though not reflecting a logical order in nature, can guide us to empirical knowledge. It can indicate possible properties of the ancestors of present species, the precursors of man, horse and other animals and plants. These surmises have sometimes been confirmed by the discovery of fossils and of bones. The scheme can also suggest the structure and appearance of extinct species on the basis of very sparse evidence. The great French paleontologist, Cuvier (1769–1832), who lived before the Darwinian theory gave a rationale for the classification, was able to reconstruct the appearance of extinct animals from one or two bones, by comparing them with bones of animals which the scheme indicated as having similar attributes. These structures may be said to have been deduced in just the manner that Aristotle would have advocated. So classifying does not have to be mere cataloguing, it can help in discovery.[11]

It is not only classification of living organisms which can give knowledge. Observation of the properties of elements led to a scheme of classification, the periodic table, proposed by Mendeleeff (1834–1907) in 1869. When first proposed it was, like the classification of living organisms, just a convenient grouping based on observed associations of properties — it was a classification based on facts, not on reasoned facts. Nevertheless it enabled Mendeleeff to predict that certain new elements would be discovered and that they would possess certain properties. These predictions were spectacularly successful. That very success prompted search for an explanation and played a part in the development of a theory of atomic structure which effectively turned the simple facts into reasoned facts.

Thus Aristotle's belief that empirical knowledge (scientific knowledge in our sense of 'scientific') can be obtained by observing relations between materials is not to be dismissed; it is indeed the basis of discovery through analogy. Classification, by revealing analogies, prompts the imagination to conjecture an explanation, it may stimulate predictions, and it may prompt us to check observations which do not 'fit' the classifying scheme.

But, unlike Aristotle, we do *not* conclude that even the most successful and helpful of classifications shows a necessary hierarchy and reveals necessary associations of properties. After the acceptance of the electronic theory of atomic structure it could be said that the Mendeleeff periodic table represented a necessary classification[12] but it was necessary *in relation to the theory*, not necessary in an absolute sense. Thus, though it is true that many of our scientific laws are deduced, deduced from an explanatory theory, we differ from Aristotle in that we do not therefore regard them as embodying logically necessary truths. We may have found a reason for the fact, but that does not guarantee indubitable knowledge. Whether our theories are speculative conjectures, or well-established and themselves explained by higher theories, they are *always* subject to correction and even to rejection.

Neither Aristotle nor Plato considered the possibility that different kinds of knowledge, that is knowledge about different kinds of objects (mathematical entities as opposed to empirical facts) might be justified in different ways. For them all knowledge had to be logically necessary and indubitable. For Plato the objects of knowledge were Universals, intuitively apprehended by mental contemplation. For Aristotle there could be knowledge of existent entities *in so far as* their species attributes, i.e. their Universal attributes, were concerned. Knowledge depended on mental intuition (which gave the cause) and deduction, but it also required sense experience.

As already indicated the view that all knowledge had to be logically necessary and analogous to mathematical knowledge persisted for centuries, but there were different opinions as to how it could be obtained and whether it could be obtained. In the next two chapters we shall discuss the Cartesian quest.

FURTHER READING

D. J. O'Connor, Article 3 'Aristotle', from *A Critical History of Western Philosophy*.

W. D. Ross (ed.), *The Works of Aristotle translated into English*, vol. I.

A. E. Taylor, *Aristotle*, chs 2 and 3.

NOTES

1. Bertrand Russell says that Aristotle's wife must have been Hermias' sister or niece, because Hermias was a eunuch (Russell, *Hist. West. Phil.*, p. 173); but O'Connor refers to a daughter. It is unlikely that we shall ever be sure of the relationship now! But the fact that it was close is enough to tell us that Aristotle was highly esteemed in his day.

2. Such men as Roger Bacon (1214–94), Jean Buridan (1297–1358), Nicolas Oresme (1320–82) and Nicolas of Cusa (1401–64) were exceptional.

3. The view that scientific laws were logically necessary remained virtually unchallenged until the eighteenth century (see chapter 7).

4. It is important to remember that the Platonic (and Aristotelian) Universals are *not* our ideas or concepts; for they were held to exist quite independently of human thoughts. Aristotle's Universals depended on the existence of particulars, but not on the existence of any person's thoughts.

5. Aristotle's scheme of classification entailed a hierarchy of Universals, for example man, animal, living creature. The early and rudimentary Universals were the lowest in the hierarchy. The baby will first apprehend these: man, cat, dog etc. and then learn to apprehend the higher Universals, animal etc.

6. We have no definite ruling as to what and/or how many changes of attributes would bring about such a change that we should say that a given particular was no longer the same particular. We shall not discuss this problem here. The point at issue in this context is that no one attribute is essential for the preservation of the identity of a particular (or individual) *qua* particular.

7. In chapter 7 we shall discuss whether observation can

ever show that an attribute is universal, but Aristotle's position is accepted here.

8. The Universal which subsumes it, e.g. the definable form of an individual person would be the Universal Man.

9. Descartes did not rely entirely on reason, as did Plato, but, since his ideal was to acquire knowledge by deduction, he can be regarded as a rationalist. As we shall see, Locke did not rely entirely on sense experience, but he rated it as fundamental, and therefore he is regarded as an empiricist.

10. Of course the association of many properties can be deduced by reference to a theory; but the theory is itself contingent so that, ultimately, the association of all properties is contingent.

11. Present-day biologists wish to abandon species classifications because they find the concept of species unhelpful, but we will ignore this modern view here.

12. In fact the original Mendeleeff table has been much modified, but that is irrelevant to the argument.

4

Descartes – the Quest for Certainty

Descartes (1596–1650) was born at La Haye, a small town near to Tours in France. His father was prosperous, a magistrate and one of the lesser nobility. Descartes had private means throughout his life. His mother died a year after he was born and at the age of eight or ten (authorities differ) he was sent to the new Jesuit College of La Flèche at Anjou. He remained there until he was eighteen years old. The intellectual atmosphere at the school was relatively liberal, and even though he later said that all that he learned there was some mathematics, Descartes remained sympathetic to the Jesuits throughout his life. He was a Roman Catholic throughout his life and he remained a believer in a personal and benevolent God. His philosophy of knowledge *depended* on a belief in God and, though it is clear that he secretly rejected certain literal interpretations of the Scriptures – secretly because it would have been dangerous to reject them openly – there is little doubt that he truly believed that intuitive knowledge, given by God, was the most certain knowledge. It was his absolute confidence that God was perfect, and therefore no deceiver, which led him to trust those ideas which, he perceived, clearly and distinctly to be true. This criterion, clear and distinct perception, was the test for truth and those ideas which survived that test could be bases for knowledge.

In 1614 Descartes went to Poitiers and took a degree in law in 1616. Two years later he joined a Dutch army commanded by Maurice of Nassau which was based in Holland. He joined not in order to fight but in order to travel. Whilst he was in the army, and in Germany (1619), he had a very vivid series of dreams on one night which affected him so powerfully that he resolved to devote himself to mathematics and philosophy. He was indeed to become an outstanding mathematician; his success here illustrates how successful is the rationalist approach when used by a great thinker in the appropriate field: a purely abstract subject which is essentially a development of implications contained in the axioms, or premises, which define the field.

Descartes's rationalist approach was not to be so successful in natural philosophy, what today we call natural science. Even so he had a profound effect on the subsequent course of science. He expounded an entirely new way of explaining events in the world which is now taken for granted and is basic to our view of what a scientific explanation is. The new attitude to explanation also affected scientific method, in a way not completely anticipated by Descartes.

Descartes differed from the early Christian and medieval philosophers in *not* appealing to authorities of various sorts (the Ancient Greeks and the Bible) as giving the foundations of truth and as being the source of truth. He has been called the father of modern philosophy because he did *not* take the views of older writers, or even the accounts in the Scriptures as axiomatically true. (Of course he did not explicitly say he doubted the latter, but he would have argued strongly that the critical mind would *find them* to be true; they did not have to be accepted unquestioningly.) In this respect one can say that Descartes was like Plato and Aristotle in that he evolved his own philosophy. He was of course influenced by the Greeks, just as they had been influenced by earlier thinkers, but he developed his own views.

He was undoubtedly affected by the sixteenth- and seventeenth-century discoveries and ideas in astronomy and physics. There was the Copernican cosmos of a sun-centred solar system (later to lead to the notion of an infinitely large universe with stars acting as other suns for other (invisible) planets) which replaced the Aristotelian closed and finite universe with the earth at its centre. Copernicus had published his work in 1543 and it had become a physically possible description (as opposed to a device for calculating the positions of the heavenly bodies) with the emergence of Galileo's new physics in the 1590s. Galileo broke away from the laws of Aristotelian physics when he postulated inertial motion (in a circle) and a speed of free fall which was independent of the weight of the falling object. In 1609 Galileo used the newly invented telescope to show that the heavenly bodies were not perfect spheres, as Aristotle had taught: the telescope revealed that the moon had mountains, the face of the sun had spots. In addition the milky way could be seen as a mass of stars so that the universe, even if not infinite, had to be much bigger than had been supposed. In 1610 he announced the discovery of the four Medicean stars, the satellites of Jupiter, and thereby showed that the earth was not unique in having its moon. All these astronomical discoveries were verified by Jesuit astronomers in Rome and Descartes heard of the Medicean stars in 1611 whilst he was still at La Flèche.

After his decision to devote his life to mathematics and philosophy, Descartes turned to the new astronomy, cosmology and physics. He held that, as a matter of logic,[1] the entire cosmos must be a plenum (there was no empty space) and that all motion was in swirling vortices. He expounded what he took to be logically necessary laws of motion, and argued that inertial motion would be motion in a straight line. He wrote on optics and, in particular, on the bending of light as it passed from one transparent medium to another. He correctly deduced Snell's law (when light passes from one medium to another of different density it is bent (refracted) so that the ratio of the sine of the angle of incidence to the sine of the angle of refraction is constant). But, in general, his contribution to the advance of natural philosophy, *as expressed by specific scientific laws* was slight. It happens that Snell's law is correct but Descartes's deduced laws of motion are not. Descartes himself regarded *all* his deduced laws as logically certain; he was the first to use the term 'laws of nature'. He coined this phrase to indicate that they were ordained by

God and were logically necessary laws as to the behaviour of phenomena in the natural world.

We can see the influence of Aristotle here; scientific knowledge *could not be otherwise*. Thus, although Descartes did carry out some experiments, especially in dissecting animals, and although he appealed to experimental results to support his deductions, he did not think that *knowledge* of the world could come from observation; experiment and observation could give the fact, but not the reasoned fact. *Knowledge* had to be logically deduced. For this reason he was contemptuous of Galileo's laws of falling bodies; they were mere generalisations from what was observed and could not be deduced from self-evident first premises. To be fair to Descartes we must bear in mind that observations could be nothing like as accurate in the seventeenth century as we can assume them to be today. Galileo had to measure time with his pulse or with a water clock; his 'dilution' of gravity by rolling a ball down an inclined plane meant that the fall observed was a rotary motion not a free glide, and his weighing methods could not be very accurate.

But, to return to Descartes, though his laws of motion were not correct, his concept of inertial motion in a straight line has been of great value. (By 'inertial motion' is meant motion of a body which will continue indefinitely unless it is altered by some external force.) But we should bear in mind that this is not so much a law of nature but a guiding principle. It is a principle which has proved useful in helping us to explain how bodies do in fact move. It has been found more helpful than the Aristotelian principle of a body *requiring* a force in order to maintain it in motion.

An even more fundamental contribution to natural science was Descartes's new view of cause, and the nature of causal explanations. Aristotle had argued that the final and ultimate cause of an object or event was a cause which expressed purpose, in terms of some desired end. Such explanations are called teleological explanations. We still use them when explaining human actions: 'Why are you going to London?' 'Because I want to see the new play at the Lyttleton.' But we don't now use them to explain physical events: 'Why did the car stop?', 'Because it ran out of petrol.' We should not regard the answer 'Because it was thirsty and wanted petrol' as anything more than funny. On the other hand if someone said they were walking along the road *because* there were certain nerve impulses going to their muscles which were then contracting we should regard that explanation as inappropriate except in very special circumstances, e.g. if the person had been paralysed. Generally such an 'explanation' would be considered, at best, as a starting point; the fundamental answer expected is an answer in terms of the person's purpose. Now, in Ancient Greek times and indeed in medieval times and up to the seventeenth century the *final* cause that is the fundamental answer would always have to be in terms of purpose: for physical events as well as for human actions. There was a latent animism, a view of 'things' having purposes. The fall of a stone to the ground was explained as the stone seeking its proper place near the centre of the earth. The heavenly bodies were also thought to be animate and indeed the question of their being alive was left open even by Galileo:

> among physical propositions there are some with regard to which all human science and reason cannot supply more than a plausible opinion and a probable conjecture in place of a sure and demonstrated knowledge; for example, whether the stars are animate.
>
> (G. Galilei, 'Letter to the Grand Duchess Christina')

It is also worth noting that even Galileo, who relied on observation far more than Descartes, still regarded knowledge as having to be demonstrated, i.e. it had to be established by logical argument.

Descartes completely rejected the teleological causal explanations. Final causes were known only to God and we humans could know nothing of His purposes. We must be content to seek explanations of physical events in terms of prior physical events. This type of causal explanation was based on a mechanistic view of the material world — all physical events were events in a vast machine. Such was the Cartesian mechanical universe. Descartes held that all physical objects, including animals, worked like machines; all physical movement could be explained in the same way as the movement of a machine was explained. Only human beings were different though even with them those parts of their bodies which worked without volition: e.g. digestion, heartbeat, were also to be explained mechanically. But human beings had an immaterial soul as well and this controlled their voluntary actions. Voluntary actions were, therefore, not to be explained in the same way as physical events. Teleological explanations *were* in order for these, but only for these, because the immaterial soul was not subject to the mechanical laws of nature which *must* hold for all material objects. This dualism: the material body along with an immaterial mind is clearly derived from Plato. It led to great difficulties; but we shall not be concerned with problems arising from that aspect of Descartes's view of knowledge. We need to consider what he thought could be known and how he thought it could come to be known.

Descartes rejected authority *per se* and he rejected the Aristotelian animistic view of causal explanation. He also rejected Aristotelian cosmology and physics yet he was profoundly influenced by Greek thought. In particular he was influenced by the Platonic and Aristotelian doctrine that knowledge could only *be* knowledge if it were indubitable and logically certain. We have seen that Galileo thought that knowledge must, at the last, be demonstrated; but Galileo would have argued that the demonstration might come by generalising from observations. We shall be examining this view, the view that certainty can be achieved by induction or ampliative inference, but whatever opinion we may come to, we must recognise that such a form of inference would not have been accepted by Descartes. He held that it was necessary to start from indubitable premises and, by logical deduction, to arrive at conclusions which would also be indubitable. This is Aristotelian rationalism and, like Aristotle, Descartes was a rationalist. Both philosophers allowed that observation (sense experience) could be of help – we have seen that Aristotle rated its value higher than did Plato – but still it could only corroborate or confirm knowledge. Sense perception could not be used as a basis for knowledge; it could not provide the solid basic premises from which other conclusions could be deduced. Descartes, again like Aristotle, thought that mathematical deduction supplied the pattern for all reasoning. To have true knowledge of the world, scientific knowledge, knowledge which could not be otherwise, it was necessary to follow the same method as in mathematical inquiry.

How then did Descartes differ from Aristotle? What was distinctive about his approach to the search for certain knowledge? Unlike Aristotle, he did not accept that intuitive conviction, *nous*, was a guarantee of truth. After his dream, when still a very young man, he arrived at his decision to study philosophy. Then he came to doubt whether most of the things which men had claimed to know, and which *he* had claimed to know, should be accepted so readily. He came to question the truth of all beliefs, even those of which he had been most certain: the evidence provided by the senses and the truths of arithmetic and geometry:

> Some years ago now I observed the multitude of errors that I had accepted as true in my earliest years, and the dubiousness of the whole super-structure I had since then reared on them; and the consequent need of making a clean sweep for once in my life, and beginning again from the very foundations, if I would establish some secure and lasting result in science . . . . Today is my chance; I have banished all care from my mind, I have secured myself peace, I have retired by myself; at length I shall be at leisure to make a clean sweep, in all seriousness and with full freedom, of all my opinion.
>
> . . .
>
> What I have so far accepted as true *par excellence*, I have got either from the senses or by means of the senses. Now I have sometimes caught the senses deceiving me; and a wise man never entirely trusts those who have once cheated him . . . .
>
> . . .
>
> . . . suppose I am dreaming and these particulars, that I open my eyes, shake my head, put out my hand, are incorrect, suppose even that I have no such hand, no such body; at any rate it has to be admitted that the things that appear in sleep are like painted representations, which cannot have

been formed except in the general likeness of real objects. So at least these general kinds of things, eyes, head, hands, body, must not be imaginary but real objects. ... even if these general kinds of things, eyes, head, hands and so on, could be imaginary, at least it must be admitted that some simple and more universal kinds of things are real, and are as it were the real colours out of which there are formed in our consciousness (*cogitatione*) all our pictures of real and unreal things. To this class there seem to belong: corporeal nature in general, and its extension; the shape of extended objects; quantity, or the size and number of these objects; place for them to exist in, and time for them to endure through; and so on.

At this rate we might be justified in concluding that whereas physics, astronomy, medicine, and all other sciences depending on the consideration of composite objects, are doubtful; yet arithmetic, geometry, and so on, which treat only of the simplest and most general subject-matter, and are indifferent whether it exists in nature or not, have an element of indubitable certainty. Whether I am awake or asleep, two and three add up to five, and a square has only four sides; and it seems impossible for such obvious truths to fall under suspicion of being false.

But there has been implanted in my mind the old opinion that there is a God who can do everything, and who has made me such as I am. How do I know he has not brought it about that, while in fact there is no earth, no sky, no extended objects, no shape, no size, no place, yet all these things should appear to exist as they do now? Moreover, I judge that other men sometimes go wrong over what they think they know perfectly well; may not God likewise make me go wrong, whenever I add two and three, or count the sides of a square, or do any simpler thing that might be imagined? ...

I am obliged in the end to admit that none of my former ideas are beyond legitimate doubt; and this, not from inconsideration or frivolity, but for strong and well-thought-out reasons. So I must carefully withold assent from them just as if they were plainly false, if I want to find any certainty.

(*First Meditation*, Anscombe and Geach, pp. 61–5)

It is important to appreciate that though Descartes *questioned* all accepted beliefs he was not a sceptic. Unlike a true sceptic such as Montaigne (1533–92), he did not think that knowledge was impossible to attain. His method of doubt was to be used to find the firm foundation of knowledge. His clerical friends advised him to say, not that he doubted, but that he was pretending to doubt. This might be advice dictated by prudence but it is perhaps a better description of what Descartes was doing. As we shall see, his belief in God enabled him to decide to accept many of the beliefs which he had professed to doubt.

Nevertheless, as his *First Meditation* shows, he began with a radical attack: we know the senses can deceive so how can we be sure *beyond doubt* of the evidence they provide; we know that we can make mistakes in calculation, so how can we be sure *beyond doubt* that a given calculation is correct.

He admits that it is hard to maintain these doubts:

> But it is not enough to have observed this; I must take care to bear it in mind. My ordinary opinions keep on coming back; and they take possession of my belief, on which they have a lien by long use and the right of custom, even against my will. I shall never get out of the habit of assenting to and trusting them, so long as I have a view of them answering to their real nature; namely, that they are doubtful in a way, as has been shown, but are yet highly probable, and far more reasonably believed than denied. So I think it will be well to turn my will in the opposite direction; deceive myself, and pretend they are wholly false and imaginary; until in the end the influence of prejudice on either side is counterbalanced, and no bad habit can any longer deflect my judgment from a true perception of facts. For I am sure no danger or mistake can happen in the process, and I cannot be indulging my scepticism more than I ought; because I am now engaged, not in action, but only in thought.
>
> I will suppose, then, not that there is a supremely good God, the source of truth; but that there is an evil spirit, who is supremely powerful and intelligent, and does his utmost to deceive me. I will suppose that sky, air, earth,

colours, shapes, sounds and all external objects are mere
delusive dreams, by means of which he lays snares for my
credulity. I will consider myself as having no hands, no
eyes, no flesh, no blood, no senses, but just having a false
belief that I have all these things. I will remain firmly fixed
in this meditation, and resolutely take care that, so far as
in me lies, even if it is not in my power to know some
truth, I may not assent to falsehood nor let myself be imposed upon by that deceiver, however powerful and intelligent he may be. But this plan is irksome, and sloth brings
me back to ordinary life. I am like a prisoner who happens
to enjoy an imaginary freedom during sleep, and then
begins to suspect he is asleep; he is afraid to wake up, and
connives at the agreeable illusion. So I willingly slip back
into my old opinions, and dread waking up, in case peace-
ful rest should be followed by the toil of waking life, and I
should henceforth have to live, not in the light, but amid
the inextricable darkness of the problems I raised just now.

(Ibid, p. 64)

Even so he resolved to persevere in his method of doubt:

But I will make an effort, and try once more the same path
as I entered upon yesterday; I will reject, that is, whatever
admits of the least doubt, just as if I had found it was
wholly false; and I will go on until I know something for
certain — if it is only this, that there is nothing certain.

(*Second Meditation*, Anscombe and Geach, p. 66)

Here is the influence of the sceptics and of Montaigne. Descartes allowed that it was possible that there was nothing
certain. But he was going to inspect every belief carefully and
so hope to separate the true from the false, just as he might
separate good and bad apples in a basket:

If you have a basket of apples, some of which (as you
know) are bad and will spoil and poison the rest, you have
no other means than to empty your basket completely and
then take and test the apples one by one, in order to put

the good ones back in your basket and throw away those
that are not.

(Letter to Father Bourdin, Anscombe and Geach, xxi)

It is *possible* that all the apples will be bad, but the method is
being used in order to put the good ones back; so the assumption is that some good apples will be found.

But what was the criterion for true belief? It is easier to
pick out good apples than true beliefs. Descartes, like Aristotle,
relied on understanding, but it had to be a much more critical
understanding than the Aristotelian intuitive *nous*. Moreover
it could be aided by sense (i.e. sense perception — this was
also accepted by Aristotle), by memory and by imagination:

> Only two things are relevant to knowledge: ourselves, the
> subjects of knowledge; and the objects to be known. In
> ourselves there are just four faculties that can be used for
> knowledge: understanding, imagination, sense, and memory.
> Only the understanding is capable of perceiving truth, but
> it must be aided by imagination, sense and memory, so
> that we may not leave anything undone that lies within
> our endeavour.
>
> (Rule XII, Anscombe and Geach, p. 165)

When Descartes referred to imagination, he was using the
term in a sense closer to imaging than to conjecturing. His
distinction between understanding and imagination was given
very clearly:

> , . . when I imagine a triangle, I do not just understand that
> it is a figure enclosed in three lines; I also at the same time
> see the three lines present before my mind's eye, and this
> is what I call imagining them. Now if I want to think of a
> chiliagon, I understand just as well that it is a figure of a
> thousand sides as I do that a triangle is a figure of three
> sides; but I do not in the same way imagine the thousand
> sides, or see them as presented to me. I am indeed accus-
> tomed always to imagine something when I am thinking of
> a corporeal object; so I may confusedly picture to myself
> some kind of figure; but obviously this picture is not a

chiliagon, since it is in no way different from the one I should form if I were thinking of a myriagon, or any other figure with very many sides;

. . .

In the act of understanding the mind turns as it were towards itself, and contemplates one of the ideas contained in itself; in the act of imagining, it turns to the body, and contemplates something in it resembling an idea understood by the mind itself or perceived by sense.
(*Sixth Meditation*, Anscombe and Geach, pp. 109—10)

To guide his understanding Descartes's basic rule was:

. . . never to accept anything as true if I had not evident knowledge of its being so; that is, carefully to avoid precipitancy and prejudice, and to embrace in my judgement only what presented itself to my mind so clearly and distinctly that I had no occasion to doubt it.
(*Discourse*, Part Two, Anscombe and Geach, p. 20)

In fact he devised a whole set of 'Rules for the *Direction of the Mind*', Some of them are rather banal, though all are obviously sensible *after* being stated. The point is that Descartes stated them!

Rule III   As regards any subject we propose to investigate, we must inquire not what other people have thought, or what we ourselves conjecture, but what we clearly and manifestly perceive by intuition or deduce with certainty. For there is no other way of acquiring knowledge. [Note the explicit rationalist view.]

By *intuition* I mean, not the wavering assurances of the senses, or the deceitful judgement of a misconstructing imagination, but a conception formed by unclouded mental attention, so easy and distinct as to leave no room for doubt in regard to the thing we are understanding.

Rule VIII   If in the series of subjects to be examined we come to a subject of which our intellect cannot gain a good enough intuition, we must stop there; and we must not examine other matters that follow, but must refrain from futile toil.

Rule XII   Finally we must make use of all the aids of understanding, imagination, sense and memory; and our aim in doing this must be, first to gain distinct intuitive knowledge of simple propositions; secondly to relate what we are looking for to what we already know, so that we may discern the former; thirdly to discover those truths which should be correlated with each other, so that nothing is left that lies within the scope of human endeavour.

(Ibid, p. 153 *et seq*)

The intuitive understanding, the apprehension, had to be clear and distinct. These two terms are constantly used by Descartes: clarity meant at an idea was fully before the mind, distinctness meant that it was not only fully before the mind but that it was precisely delineated and could not be confused with anything else. A clear and distinct idea was *completely* apprehended, and, if seen to be true, it would indeed *be* true.

XLV . . . I call a perception *clear* when, if the mind attends to it, it is present and manifest; just as we may say we see clearly what is present to the gaze of our eye and has a sufficiently strong and manifest effect upon it. I call a perception *distinct* if it is not only clear but also precisely distinguished from all others, so that it contains no element that is not clear.

XLVI. . . . when a man feels great pain, he has a very clear perception of pain, but not always a distinct one; for men commonly confuse this perception with an obscure judgement as to the nature of pain; they think there is something in the painful spot resembling the sensation of pain, but the sensation is all that they perceive clearly. So a percep-

tion may be clear without being distinct, though not distinct
without being clear.

(*Principles of Philosophy*, Part I,
Anscombe and Geach, p. 190)

Descartes held that if a belief was stated as a proposition
then, if that proposition was clearly and distinctly understood
we should *know* whether it was true or false. The understanding of a proposition was a necessary and a sufficient condition
for knowledge of its truth or falsity.

Now, in the field of mathematics and geometry this is so.
If we understand a proposition clearly and distinctly it is not
only fully before our mind as a meaningful proposition (it is
clear) but we also distinguish it from others by understanding
how it is deduced from the basic axioms (it is distinct). Then
we can know if it is validly deduced and we can know if it is
true or false. For example, if I understand the Pythagorean
theorem[2] clearly I can state it and state it meaningfully — not
like a parrot. If I also understand it distinctly I can distinguish
it from all others and therefore can deduce it from the
Euclidean axioms, and prior theorems. So knowing the theorem clearly and distinctly I *know* that it is true. By contrast
if I understand clearly the squaring of the circle, I know what
it means and can state it meaningfully. If I can follow Hobbes's[3] 'proof' I can give his argument *and* can show the error.
Therefore I know Hobbes's theorem of the squaring of the
circle clearly and distinctly and I *know* that it is false (see
also chapter 7, p. 155), I *know* that Hobbes's 'proof' is incorrect, and that the theorem has not been established as true.
Today mathematicians can produce arguments, which if
understood clearly and distinctly will give knowledge that the
theorem must be false.

But Descartes's criteria do not apply when we are making
claims to know facts about the world. I may understand the
proposition 'The earth travels round the sun' clearly. Also, in
so far as I can relate it to physical theories, such as the theory
of gravitational attraction, I may claim that I can understand
it distinctly. But understanding 'The earth travels round the
sun' clearly and distinctly, and understanding that the deductions from the theories are valid does not show that the state-

ment *must* be true. The physical theories are not like arithmetical and geometrical axioms which we accept as the indubitable bases of our arithmetic and our geometry. The physical theories are themselves supported by observations, in this case observations made with our eyes and with telescopes. Observation is an *essential* part of the support for the theory; and this is not a matter of rational understanding pure and simple but a matter of what *is*, and this can always be disputed. Take a much more simple example: 'Toadstools are poisonous'. We can perfectly well understand the proposition and relate it to our knowledge of poisonous chemicals, but whether it is true or false depends on observations on the toadstools themselves and/or on the chemicals. There is always a logical possibility that we have made a mistake.

It may seem strange that Descartes failed to appreciate so obvious a distinction between arithmetical and factual propositions, but here we must take care. It is no great help when studying the ideas and opinions of great men to dismiss them summarily in the light of what is suggested in our own time — indeed it may turn out that our present views are also misguided, and that posterity may rate the Cartesian approach more highly than our own. In any case, to appreciate Descartes's originality and genius we need to understand how he came to profess his views of knowledge.

First we should note that up till well on in the nineteenth century, the basis axioms of arithmetic and geometry were held not only to be the axioms forming the bases of mathematical systems but to apply in the world of things, of time and of space. Space, for instance, was held to be Euclidean space — the shortest distance between two points was a straight line, parallel lines would never meet etc. — so that the Euclidean theorems, which followed logically from the axioms, e.g. the angles of a triangle sum to 180, were logically and necessarily true *in the world*, not just within the Euclidean system. It seemed that our critical intuitive powers of reason *showed* that these axioms were true beyond doubt. (Descartes did profess to doubt them, but of course re-established them, as we shall see in the next chapter). Since it was possible to understand how the theorems were arrived at, by valid deduction from the axioms, we could *know* certain mathematical truths about the world. Thus there seemed no reason why we could not *know* non-mathematical truths about the world as well. Of course it was more difficult to find the fundamental premises but there seemed no reason why it should be impossible.

Another aspect of the claim to *know* facts was that, until the eighteenth century and the doubts expounded by Hume (see chapters 7 and 8), it was firmly believed that by observing events it was possible to establish relations between them such that one event, the cause, necessarily produced another event, the effect. Many natural philosophers held that observation of one event which was invariably followed by another event *proved* (logically) that the cause and effect were necessarily related. It was the view of Galileo (see above), of Newton (though he did qualify by 'little short of certainty') and of all the great natural philosophers of the time. In fact it was *not* Descartes's view. He would have been more sympathetic to Hume's ideas than were Hume's contemporaries. For Descartes did not think that certain truth (knowledge) could come from mere observation. Nevertheless he did regard physical causal relations to be established as necessarily true if they could be *deduced*. Therefore we may claim that he was influenced by the assumption of the necessary connection between cause and effect. In a sense, by emphasising rationalist methodology he avoided the problem of induction; the trouble was that, though induction from observation cannot lead to logically certain scientific laws, it has turned out, so far, to be of great help in giving us information about the world. But in the early seventeenth century this was by no means so clear as it is today.

Descartes eschewed this approach. He held that from first principles, clearly and distinctly perceived, he could deduce the general laws of nature and therefore the causal relations between events:

if the only principles we use are such as we see to be self-evident; if we infer nothing from them except by mathematical deductions and if all these inferences agree accurately with natural phenomena; then we should, I think be wronging God if we were to suspect this discovery of the causes of things to be delusive.

and

our aim is to deduce an account of the effects from the causes, not to deduce an account of the causes from the effect. (*Principles of Philosophy*, Pt. III, pp. 223—4)

The second quote specifically rejects induction (building up from observed effects); but the first quote shows that Descartes did not regard observation as valueless in *confirming* a deduction. (His methodology has something in common with Popper's hypothetico-deductive-method,[4] though Popper starts from conjecture rather than intuitive first principles and therefore does not claim that certain truth is attained.) Descartes made vast claims:

Then I showed how the great part of the matter of this chaos must, in consequence of these laws, dispose and arrange itself in such a way as to resemble the heavens in our world; and how accordingly some of its parts must form an earth; and others, planets and comets, a sun and fixed stars. Here I developed the subject of light; I explained at length the nature of the light that must be found in the sun and stars, and how it instantaneously travelled across the immense distances of the heavens, and how it was reflected from the planets and comets to the earth. I added several points about the substance, situation, movement, and all the various qualities of these heavens and stars; and I thought I had thus said enough to show that nothing is observed in the heavens and stars of the real world but must — or at least could — present a similar appearance in the world I was describing. From that I proceeded to a special discussion of the earth; how, although I had expressly supposed that God had given no gravity to the matter of which it was composed, yet none the less all its parts would tend exactly towards its centre; and how, there being water and air on its surface, the arrangement of the heavens and the heavenly bodies, in particular the moon, must cause

a flux and reflux similar in all regards to what is observed
in our seas . . . .   (*Discourse*, Part Five, p. 39)

But Descartes had to take care; it was not prudent to deny
the book of Genesis. He avoided the difficulty by saying that
these suppositions were made only in order to help us understand what the world was now like:

> . . . in order to explain natural objects the better, I shall
> pursue my inquiry into their causes further back than I
> believe the causes ever in fact existed. There is no doubt
> that the world was first created in its full perfection; there
> were in it a Sun, an Earth, a Moon, and the stars; and on
> the earth there were not only the seeds of plants, but also
> plants themselves; and Adam and Eve were not born as
> babies, but made as full-grown human beings. This is the
> teaching of the Christian faith; and natural reason convinces
> us that it was so;'
> (*Principles of Philosophy*, Pt. III, XLV, p. 224)

It is impossible to say how sincere Descartes was. In the
next chapter we shall see that his belief in the existence of
God can hardly be questioned, although his writings certainly
tend to undermine much of the Bible. He lived for most of
his adult life in Protestant Holland and the Church did not
persecute him. But his works were held to be subversive and
in 1664 they were put on the Index of the Roman Catholic
church.

Although his deductions in natural philosophy[5] are of little
interest to practising scientists today they are valuable in
helping us to understand the rationalist aspiration to knowledge. Also we need to remember that Descartes's appeal to
deductive reasoning was part of his view of explanation in
terms of prior physical events; part of his view of the inanimate world as a mechanical world to be explained by physical
processes. One of the features of Cartesian mechanism was
that all matter was composed of tiny particles, corpuscles.
These corpuscles were not atoms since they could be subdi-
vided indefinitely and, indeed, since Descartes believed that
it was logically impossible for there to be a vacuum (he

defined matter as extension and extension as matter so that empty space, empty extension, was impossible), some of the corpuscles had to be indefinitely small to fill up the spaces between the bigger ones. Any given material and any given object was held to be composed of characteristic corpuscles. We need not go into the details of the Cartesian scheme but the corpuscles of any object were responsible for the *primary* qualities of the body. For Descartes the primary qualities were extension (size) and motion (others who developed this idea introduced further primary qualities, see chapter 6). The primary qualities of the *corpuscles* also gave the *body* its primary qualities, i.e. *its* size and motion. But of course the bodies which we sense, which we see, touch, and taste etc. have other qualities. For example a lemon looks yellow, has a rough skin and an acid taste. These qualities were called *secondary* qualities; they were due to the corpuscles acting on our sense organs. They were secondary in that they depended as much on us, the perceivers, as on the object, e.g. the lemon. As we shall see, the notion of primary and secondary qualities was to be developed and also criticised. But it has remained with us and supports a certain philosophy of perception: this is the philosophy which suggests that the qualities which we sense (secondary qualities) are not the *real* (primary) qualities. Philosophers such as Bertrand Russell take the (primary) qualities to be those shown by science, especially physics:

> We think that grass is green, that stones are hard, and that snow is cold. But physics assures us that the greenness of grass, the hardness of stones, and the coldness of snow, are not the greenness, hardness, and coldness that we know in our own experience, but something very different. The observer, when he seems to himself to be observing a stone, is really, if physics is to be believed, observing the effects of the stone on himself.
>
> (B. Russell *An Inquiry into Meaning and Truth*, p. 15)

This view is open to severe criticism and is so criticised by A. J. Ayer (*The Central Questions of Philosophy*, pp. 82–8), but it has proved very helpful to science and credit should be given to Descartes as the originator.

We need also to acknowledge Descartes's contribution to our understanding of perception. Aristotle had appreciated that perception was not entirely a passive process in that the Universal had to be grasped, 'though the act of sense-perception is of the particular its content is Unversal'. Nevertheless, it was held that there was no interpretation involved in perceiving familiar objects. Descartes showed that even the most simple material was not apprehended merely by sense appreciation of its qualities, nor even by stimulation of the imaginative (imaging) capacity but by use of the intellectual or reasoning capacity in us.

Consider the objects commonly thought to be the most distinctly known, the bodies we touch and see. I will take, not body in general, for these generic concepts (*perceptiones*) are often the more confused, but one particular body; say, this wax. It has just been extracted from the honeycomb; it has not completely lost the taste of the honey; it retains some of the smell of the flowers from which it was gathered; its colour, shape, size are manifest; it is hard, cold, and easily handled, and gives out a sound if you rap it with your knuckle; in fact it has all the properties that seem to be needed for our knowing a body with the utmost distinctness. But while I say this, the wax is put by the fire. It loses the remains of its flavour, the fragrance evaporates, the colour changes, the shape is lost, the size increases; it becomes fluid and hot, it can hardly be handled, and it will no longer give out a sound if you rap it. Is the same wax, then, still there? 'Of course it is; nobody denies it, nobody thinks otherwise.' Well, what was in this wax that was so distinctly known? Nothing that I got through the senses; for whatever fell under taste, smell, sight, touch, or hearing has now changed; yet the wax is still there.

'Perhaps what I distinctly knew was what I am now thinking of: namely, that the wax was not the sweetness, nor the fragrance of the flowers, nor the whiteness, nor the shape, nor the sound, but body; manifested to me previously in those aspects, and now in others.' But what exactly am I thus imagining? Let us consider; let us remove what is not proper to the wax and see what is left: simply, something extended, flexible, and changeable. But what is its being 'flexible' and 'changeable'? Does it consist in my imagining the wax to be capable of changing from a round shape to a square one and from that again to a triangular one? By no means; for I comprehend its potentiality for an infinity of such changes, but I cannot run through an infinite number of them in imagination; so I do not comprehend them by my imaginative power. What again is its being 'extended'? Is this likewise unknown? For extension grows greater when the wax melts, greater still when it boils, and greater still again with increase of heat; and I should mistake the nature of wax if I did not think this piece capable also of more changes, as regards extension, than my imagination has ever grasped. It remains then for me to admit that I know the nature even of this piece of wax not by imagination, but by purely mental perception. (I say this as regards a particular piece of wax; it is even clearer as regards wax in general.) What then is this wax, perceived only by the mind? It is the very same wax as I see, touch, and imagine — that whose existence I believed in originally. But it must be observed that perception of the wax is not sight, not touch, not imagination; nor was it ever so, though it formerly seemed to be; it is a purely mental contemplation (*inspectio*); which may be either imperfect or confused, as it originally was, or clear and distinct, as it now is, according to my degree of attention to what it consists in.

But it is surprising how prone my mind is to errors. Although I am considering these points within myself silently and without speaking, yet I stumble over words and am almost deceived by ordinary language. We say we see the wax itself, if it is there; not that we judge from its colour or shape that it is there. I might at once infer: I see the wax by ocular vision, not by merely mental contemplation. I chanced, however, to look out of the window, and see men walking in the street; now I say in ordinary language that I 'see' them, just as I 'see' the wax; but what can I 'see' besides hats and coats, which may cover automata? I judge that they are men; and similarly, the objects that I thought I saw with my eyes, I really comprehend only by my mental power of judgment.

It is disgraceful that a man seeking to know more than the mass of mankind should have sought occasions for doubt in popular modes of speech! Let us go on, and consider when I perceived the wax more perfectly and manifestly; was it when I first looked at it, and thought I was aware of it by external senses, or at least by the so-called 'common' sense, i.e. the imaginative faculty? or is it rather now, after careful investigation of its nature and of the way that I am aware of it? It would be silly to doubt as to the matter; for what was there distinct in my original perception? Surely any animal could have one just as good. But when I distinguish the wax from its outward form, and as it were unclothe it and consider it in its naked self, I get something which, mistaken as my judgment may still be, I need a human mind to perceive.

. . .

These observations about the wax apply to all external objects. Further, if the perception of the wax is more distinct when it has become known to me not merely by sight or by touch, but from a plurality of sources; how much more distinct than this must I admit my knowledge of myself to be! No considerations can help towards my perception of the wax or any other body, without at the same time all going towards establishing the nature of my mind. And the mind has such further resources within itself from which its selfknowledge may be made more distinct, that the information thus derived from the body appears negligible.

I have thus got back to where I wanted; I now know that even bodies are not really perceived by the senses or the imaginative faculty, but only by intellect; that they are perceived, not by being touched or seen, but by being understood; . . .
(*Second Meditation*, Anscombe and Geach, pp. 72–4)

Cartesian rationalism did take Descartes too far for the sucessful pursuit of scientific inquiry and for discovery. His relative failure in this field shows very sharply by contrast to his brilliant successes in mathematics. But the failure *was* relative; he did after all have some success in optics. Moreover, in a fundamental sense Cartesian philosophy contributed greatly to science. The mechanistic view of matter and motion, involving a new approach to explanation and a new way of accounting for the properties of materials and objects, was originated by Descartes. Along with this went the development of a new philosophy (and psychology) of perception which affected philosophers, including natural philosophers.

Descartes is the father of modern philosophy in that he reintroduced the questioning attitude of the Ancient Greeks and also developed a critical rational approach to the study of knowledge (epistemology). He can also be regarded as at least one of the progenitors of our present natural philosophy or natural science.

FURTHER READING

Descartes, *Philosophical Writings*, ed. and trans. G. E. M. Anscombe and P. T. Geach.

J. L. Watling, 'Descartes', from O'Connor (ed.), *A Critical History of Western Philosophy*.

B. Williams, *Descartes*.

NOTES

1. Descartes held that matter was equivalent to extension so that it was logically inevitable that space (extension) was full of matter, i.e. that it was a plenum. The logical necessity depended on the definition and concept of matter; just as the logical necessity that a bachelor is unmarried depends on the definition and concept of bachelors.

2. The Pythagorean theorem states that for a rightangle-triangle the square on the hypotenuse is equal to the sum of the squares on the other two sides.

3. Thomas Hobbes 1588—1679, an English materialist philosopher who thought, mistakenly, that the area of a circle

could be exactly calculated if the radius were known — this is
called 'squaring the circle'.

4. Sir Karl Popper, 1902 — holds that science progresses by
imaginative conjecture followed by testing, not by generalising
from experience, i.e. not be induction.

5. The term 'natural philosophy' applied to what we
should, today, call 'science'. Natural philosophers were, in
our terms, scientists. But the words 'science' and 'scientists'
were not used in their modern sense until the nineteenth
century.

Descartes – the 'Cogito'

Descartes had decided that in order to gain knowledge it was necessary to start from first premises which could not be doubted. *All* beliefs had to be tested, and if they could be doubted they must be rejected (like bad apples) — at least until such time as they could be established by some other independent test. They could not be used, in the first instance, as a foundation of knowledge.

As we have seen, Descartes argued that the evidence of the senses could be doubted, and also the axioms and calculations of arithmetic and geometry could be doubted. Therefore these could not be used as a foundation for knowledge. After much thought he came to the conclusion that the *only* thing which it was impossible for him to doubt was that he existed *as a thinking thing.*

I do not know whether I need tell you of my first meditations; for they are perhaps too metaphysical and uncommon for the general taste. At the same time I am in a way obliged to speak of them so as to make it possible to judge whether the foundation I have chosen is secure enough. I had noticed long before, as I said just now, that in conduct one sometimes has to follow opinions that one knows to be most uncertain just as if they were indubitable; but since my present aim was to give myself up to the pursuit of truth alone, I thought I must do the very opposite, and reject as if absolutely false anything as to which I could imagine the least doubt, in order to see if I should not be left at the end believing something that was absolutely indubitable. So, because our senses sometimes deceive us, I chose to suppose that nothing was such as they lead us to imagine. Because there are men who make mistakes in reasoning even as regards the simplest points of geometry and perpetrate fallacies, and seeing that I was as liable to error as anyone else, I rejected as false all the arguments I had so far taken for demonstrations. Finally, considering that the very same experiences (*pensées*) as we have in waking life may occur also while we sleep, without there being at that time any truth in them, I decided to feign that everything that had entered my mind hitherto was no more true than the illusions of dreams. But immediately upon this I noticed that while I was trying to think everything false, it must needs be that I, who was thinking this (*qui le pensais*), was something. And observing that this truth 'I am thinking (*je pense*), therefore I exist' was so solid and secure that the most extravagant suppositions of the sceptics could not overthrow it, I judged that I need not scruple to accept it as the first principle of philosophy that I was seeking.

I then considered attentively what I was; and I saw that while I could feign that I had no body, that there was no world, and no place existed for me to be in, I could not feign that I was not; on the contrary, from the mere fact that I thought of doubting (*je pensais à douter*) about other truths it evidently and certainly followed that I existed. On the other hand, if I had merely ceased to be conscious (*de penser*), even if everything else that I had ever imagined had been true, I had no reason to believe that I should still have existed. From this I recognised that I was a substance whose whole essence or nature is to be conscious (*de penser*) and whose being requires no place and depends on no material thing. Thus this self (*moi*), that is to say the soul, by which I am what I am, is entirely distinct from the body, and is even more easily known; and even if the body were not there at all, the soul would be just what it is.　　　　(*Discourse*, Part Four, pp. 31–2)

This was to be his foundation. But he did not use 'I am thinking, therefore I am' as a premise from which he could *deduce* other propositions which would then be equally certain. We need at least two statements in order to make further deductive inferences and Descartes's reflections had provided him with but one. No, he used this certain truth to guide him to the *criteria* by which he could test his beliefs. Reflecting on the certainty of 'I think therefore I am' he decided that the test of a true belief was that it could be clearly and distinctly apprehended as true.

> After this I considered in general what is requisite to the truth and certainty of a propositon; for since I had just found one that I knew to have this nature, I thought I must also know what this certainty consists in. Observing that there is nothing at all in the statement 'I am thinking, therefore I exist' which assures me that I speak the truth, except that I see very clearly that in order to think I must exist, I judged that I could take it as a general rule that whatever we conceive very clearly and very distinctly is true; only there is some difficulty in discerning what conceptions really are distinct. (*Discourse*, Part Four, p. 32)

It was *clear* because doubting and therefore thinking were before the mind; it was *distinct* in that the argument from thinking to existence, (or the connection between thinking and existence) could be understood and seen to be valid. Hence Descartes argued that he *knew* that he existed as a thinking thing (or conscious being) because he had a clear and distinct conception of the truth of the proposition 'I think (therefore) I am'. From this he went on to infer that *anything* which was clearly and distinctly conceived as true must *be* true. There was some difficulty in establishing whether a conception was distinct but this was a practical matter — if the test could be made it was a sure one. *Anything* which stood up to the test could be held to be true and therefore could provide knowledge.

Later we shall return to the question of whether Descartes's view 'I think (therefore) I am' *is* a basis for a test for knowledge. In the first instance it does not seem too difficult to grant him *that*. What does seem puzzling is to accept his conclusion that because *this* belief ('I think (therefore) I am') is clear and distinct then *anything* clearly and distinctly conceived as true is true. We are back to the problem discussed in the previous chapter. There I argued that, in the seventeenth century mathematical propositions were not so clearly separated from factual propositions so that the rationalist view did not seem so misguided then as it seems to us today. However we need to see how Descartes used his criteria before dismissing them as insufficient.

Descartes had a sincere and unquestioning belief in God. He had only pretended to doubt the existence of God when he had come to the conclusion that the only thing which he could hold as truly indubitable was his own existence. But, following his avowed method he used the criteria established by the *cogito* to prove (logically as he thought) that God existed.

He, Descartes, had a clear and distinct idea of something more perfect than himself. Indeed he had a clear and distinct idea of a fully perfect being, namely God. Now Descartes followed the current philosophical view that it was logically impossible for a cause to contain or to be less than any effect that it produced. (This was simply accepted as a rule of deductive inference; one might say that it was part of the contemporary concept of cause and the cause/effect relation.) Imperfection was less than perfection; therefore, since Descartes could clearly and distinctly conceive of a supremely perfect being and, since he knew that he was not himself supremely perfect, it must follow that a supremely perfect being had caused Descartes to have the conception.

> Next, I reflected on the fact that I was doubting, and that consequently my being was not wholly perfect (for I saw clearly that knowledge was a greater perfection than doubt). I decided to enquire whence I had learnt to think of something more perfect than myself, and I recognised it as evident that this idea must come from some nature that was really more perfect. As regards my ideas of many other external things — the sky, the earth, light, heat, and innumerable other objects — I was not so much concerned to

know their source; for I discovered nothing in them that appeared to make them higher than myself. If they were true, they might depend on my own nature, in so far as it had some degree of perfection; if not, I might have got them from nothingness — they might be in me because I had some defect. But this could not hold good for the idea of an existence more perfect than my own; it was manifestly impossible to have got this from nothingness; and since it is no less contradictory that the more perfect should follow from and depend on the less perfect, than that something should proceed from nothing, likewise I could not have got it from myself. So the only possibility left was to hold that the idea had been put in me by a nature really more perfect than myself, and in fact possessing all the perfections of which I could have any idea; that is to say, to explain myself in one word, by God. And to this I added that since I knew of some perfections that I did not possess, I was not the only being in existence (here, by your leave, I will freely use scholastic terms), but that there must needs be some other more perfect being on whom I depended, and from whom I received all that I had. For if I had been alone and independent of everything else, so that my slight participation in perfect being were from myself, I could by parity of reasoning have had from myself all the remainder of perfection that I knew I lacked; I could myself have been infinite, eternal, immutable, omniscient, almighty — in short, have had all the perfections I discovered in God. For, according to the arguments I have just used, all that I had to do in order to know God's nature, as far as my own allowed, was to consider, as regards every property of which I found any idea in myself, whether the possession of it was a perfection or not; and I was certain that no property that indicated any imperfection was in God, but that all others were. Thus, I saw that doubt, inconstancy, sorrow, and so on could not be in God; for I myself should have liked to be rid of them. Further, I had ideas of a plurality of sensible and corporeal things; for even if I were to suppose that I was dreaming and that all I saw or imagined was a sham, I yet could not deny that these ideas were really in my consciousness. But I had already recognised quite clearly in my own case that the intelligent and the corporeal nature are distinct; so, considering that all composition is a sign of dependence and dependence is manifestly a defect, I concluded that it could not be a perfection in God to be composed of these two natures, and consequently that he was not; but that if there were any bodies in the world, or again any intelligences or other natures that were not entirely perfect, then their being must depend on his power, so that without him they could not subsist for a single moment.   (*Discourse*, Part Four, pp. 32–4)

Descartes argued, and here we would agree with him, that the certainty of geometrical proofs depends on their being distinctly conceived. But, said he, though we can say that a triangle *must* have internal angles summing to 180° (two right angles), this does not prove that a perfect triangle has ever been drawn. On the other hand, if we, the less perfect, can distinctly conceive of God, the supremely perfect, then God must exist. This is called the ontological argument for the existence of God and it had been used by earlier philosophers. (It was originally stated by St Anselm and Descartes's version is much the same as St Anselm's.)

After this I wished to seek for other truths; I took the subject-matter of geometry, which I conceived to be a continuous body or a space indefinitely extended in length, breadth, and height or depth, divisible into distinct parts, which may have distinct shapes and sizes and may be moved or transposed in all sorts of ways; for the geometers assume all this in their subject-matter. I went through some of the simpler proofs, and observed that their high degree of certainty is founded merely on our conceiving them distinctly (according to the principle mentioned above). I also observed that there was nothing in them to assure me of the existence of the subject-matter. For instance, I saw quite well that, assuming a triangle, its three angles must be equal to two right angles; but for all that I saw nothing that assured me that there was any triangle in the real world. On the other hand, going back to an examination of my

idea of a perfect Being, I found that this included the existence of such a Being; in the same way as the idea of a
triangle includes the equality of its three angles to two right
angles, or the idea of a sphere includes the equidistance of
all parts (of its surface) from the centre; or indeed, in an
even more evident way. Consequently it is at least as certain
that God, the perfect Being in question, is or exists, as any
proof in geometry can be.

(*Discourse*, Part Four, pp. 34–5)

Descartes argued forcefully that the existence of God was
more certain than the existence of objects in the material
world, the objects we perceived with our senses. However,
having established that God *must* exist, he could then begin
to build up knowledge. If he clearly and distinctly conceived
(i.e. by reason, not by sense or imagination) a judgement as
being true, then it would be true. For God, being supremely
perfect, would not deceive him.

The reason why many people are convinced that there is
difficulty in knowing God, and even in knowing what their
soul is, is that they never raise their mind above sensible
objects, and are so used to think of things only by way of
imagining them (a mode of thought specially adapted to
material things) that whatever is unimaginable appears to
them unintelligible. This is clear from the maxim held even
by scholastic philosophers, 'there is nothing in the intellect
but has previously been in sense'; and yet the ideas of God
and the soul have certainly never been in sense. And it
seems to me that those who try to use their imagination to
understand them are acting just as though they tried to use
their eyes to hear sounds or smell odours. There is, however,
also this difference: the sense of sight gives us no less assurance of the reality of its objects than the senses of smell or
hearing; whereas neither our imagination nor our senses
can ever assure us of anything at all, except with the aid of
our understanding.

Finally, if there are still men not sufficiently convinced
of the existence of God and of their soul by the reasons I
have brought forward, I would have them know that every-

thing else that seems to them more sure — that they have a body, that there are stars and an earth, and so on — is really less certain. For while we are morally certain of these things, so that it seems we cannot doubt them without being extravagant; at the same time, if it is a question of metaphysical certainty, one cannot reasonably deny that there is good reason for not being entirely certain of them. One need only consider that in sleep one may imagine in just the same way that one has a different body, and that one sees different stars and a different earth, while none of this is so. How do we know that the experiences (*pensées*) occurring in our dreams are any more illusory than the others? They are often no less lively and distinct. And if the best minds study the question as much as they like, I think they will find no adequate grounds for removing this doubt, if they do not presuppose the existence of God. For in the first place, what I took just now as a principle, viz. that whatever we conceive very clearly and distinctly is true, is assured only because God is or exists, and is a perfect being, and everything in us comes from him. It follows that, since our ideas or notions have positive reality and proceed from God, in so far as they are clear and distinct, they must to this extent be true. If we often have ideas with some error in them, these must be among those that contain some confusion or obscurity; for in this regard they participate in nothingness; that is, they occur in us in this confused form only because we are not wholly perfect. And clearly there is no less contradiction in God's originating error or imperfection as such, than in the origin of truth or perfection from nothingness. But if we did not know that all truth and reality in us proceeds from a perfect and infinite being, then, however clear and distinct our ideas might be, we should have no reason to be certain that they had the perfection of truth.

Now when once the knowledge of God and the soul has made us certain of this rule, it is quite easy to see that the fancies we create in sleep should not make us doubt in any way the truth of the experiences (*pensées*) we have when awake. For if it happened even in sleep that one had some specially distinct idea; if, for instance, a geometer devised some new proof; then sleep would be no bar to its being true. The commonest delusion of dreams is that they represent various objects in the same manner as our external senses; but it does not matter that this gives us reason to doubt the truth of such ideas; for they are often capable of deceiving us even when we are not asleep; for instance, when men with jaundice see everything as yellow, or when the stars or other very remote bodies appear much smaller than they are. For, in conclusion, waking or sleeping, we should never let ourselves be convinced except by the evidence of our reason. Note that I say our reason, not our imagination or our senses. Although we see the sun 'very clearly', we must not therefore judge that it has only the size we see; and we can 'distinctly' imagine a lion's head on a goat's body, but we need not therefore conclude that a chimera exists in the world; for reason does not insist to us that what we thus see or imagine is real. But reason does insist that all our ideas or notions must have some basis of truth; for otherwise it would be impossible that God, who is all-perfect and all-truthful, should have placed them in us. And since our reasonings are never so evident nor so complete in sleep as in waking life, although sometimes our imagination then attains an equal or higher degree of force and detail, reason also insists that while our thoughts cannot all be true, because we are not wholly perfect, what truth they have must assuredly occur in those we have when awake rather than in our dreams.

(*Discourse*, Part Four, pp. 35—7)

Now it is to be noted, from the passage above:
'whatever we conceive very clearly and distinctly is true, is assured only because God is or exists . . . '.
In other words, the criteria for a true belief *were* criteria because the existence of God *guaranteed* that clear and distinct conceptions would lead to indubitable judgements.

But here we must pause. What has Descartes been saying? His argument has been:
I have a clear and distinct idea that I think and that I exist
This is indubitable, and therefore must be true.

Therefore clear and distinct ideas are the basis of knowledge – they are the criteria by which to test beliefs
I have a clear and distinct idea of a perfect being
Since the imperfect cannot cause the perfect, a perfect
being, i.e. God, must exist
A perfect being would not deceive, and the perfect being
gave me my powers of reasoning
Therefore any idea clearly and distinctly conceived must
be true

Put more shortly:

If I have a clear and distinct idea it must be true
I have a clear and distinct idea of God
Therefore God exists
God is no deceiver and this guarantees that clear and dis-
tinct ideas are true.

This is a patently circular argument – and indeed the circularity was pointed out by Father Arnauld, one of Descartes's
Roman Catholic friends:

My one remaining hesitation is about how it is possible to
avoid circularity when our author says that 'our only
guarantee that the things which we clearly and distinctly
conceive are true is the fact that God exists'. For, our only
guarantee that God exists is that we conceive very clearly
and very distinctly that he does exist; so before being convinced of the existence of God we need to be convinced
that everything which we clearly and distinctly conceive is
true.   (Quoted by A. Flew in *An Introduction
to Western Philosophy*, p. 330)

The error is there because Descartes's underlying assumption was that God existed. It may then be objected that the
Cartesian criteria are valueless since belief in the existence of
God has to be accepted and this cannot be proved. (Neither
the ontological argument nor further arguments produced by
Descartes are satisfactory, as Hume, Kant and others later
showed.) This is so; but as was stated in chapter 3 we must
accept that in order to know or to claim to know anything at
all, some assumptions must be made, some beliefs must be

accepted without proof. As Russell said 'we cannot have *reason* to reject a belief except on the ground of some other belief'. Today we might say that our fundamental beliefs are a belief that there is some order and regularity in the behaviour of events in the material world which we sense, and a belief that this material world exists independently of our perceptions. We also believe that deductive rules of inference and our own powers of reasoning are reliable (see also chapter 3). All these beliefs imply that there is some order in things and in ideas. Now it could be argued that in many important respects this assumption of order is analogous to belief in God. Neither can be *proved* to be true. The notion of there being order and regularity is a metaphysical assumption just as much as the notion of a governor of the cosmos.

Hence we may accept that Descartes's analysis of knowledge, his conclusion that the criteria for testing a belief were clear and distinct conceptions, has contributed to epistemology. He gave the necessary conditions for all knowledge and sufficient conditions for mathematical and abstract knowledge. These criteria do *not* depend on the *cogito* argument, but on the assumption that God exists and that *therefore* we can trust our powers of reasoning. Today we start from other assumptions, but they still involve the belief that we can trust our powers of reasoning.

Is the famous *cogito* relevant to epistemology? Of course it had helped Descartes and therefore it is historically interesting. Even though it is no longer of importance to epistemology today it is worth analysing the *cogito* philosophically. It will give another example of philosophical criticism and it will reveal how that which seems to be a self-evident truth can actually turn out to be either false or not very informative.

There are two possible ways of regarding the *cogito*, and it is not clear which way Descartes regarded it; perhaps he was ambivalent or perhaps he avoided analysing it. One way of treating the *cogito* is to treat it as an inference: 'I exist' is inferred from 'I think' — the proposition is 'I think *therefore* I am'. The other way is to regard both parts of the proposition as self-evident truths, so that the whole statement is simply two self-evident truths taken together; 'I think, I exist'. Descartes took both attitudes to the *cogito* in his writing.

A. J. Ayer holds that Descartes did regard the *cogito* as a logical inference and criticises it as such. He first states Descartes's case:

> He allowed it to be possible that a malignant demon should deceive him even with respect to those matters of which he was most certain. The demon would so work upon his reason that he took false statements to be self-evidently true. The hypothesis of there being such an arch-deceiver is indeed empty since his operations could never be detected: but it may be regarded as a picturesque way of expressing the fact that intuitive conviction is not a logical guarantee of truth. The question which Descartes then raises is whether, of all the propositions which we think we know, there can be any that escape the demon's reach.
>
> His answer is that there is one such proposition: the famous *cogito ergo sum*: I think therefore I am. . . . if I am thinking it is indubitable that I am thinking, then, Descartes argues, it is indubitable that I exist, at least during such times as I think.   (Ayer in Doney, p. 80)

Ayer says that Descartes was maintaining that not only was it physically impossible to doubt that one was thinking but that it was also logically impossible. Compare 'I cannot swim the Pacific ocean' (physically impossible — for me) with 'I cannot be in Exeter and London at the same time' (logically impossible). Now a logical impossibility involves a contradiction — something is stated both to be and not to be. But is it *contradictory* to doubt if one is thinking? It is a contingent fact that I exist (i.e. I might not have existed and it just happens to be the case that I do exist) and similarly it is a contingent fact that I think. The only *logical* truth is the inference 'If I think *then* I exist', but this does not tell us very much.

> If I start with the fact that I am doubting, I can validly draw the conclusion that I think and that I exist. That is to say, if there is such a person as myself, then there is such a person as myself and if I think, I think. Neither does this apply only to me. It is obviously true of anyone at all that if he exists he exists and if he thinks he thinks. What Descartes

> thought he had shown was that statements that he was
> conscious, and that he existed, were somehow privileged,
> that, for him at least, they were evidently true in a way
> which distinguished them from any other statements of
> fact. But this by no means follows from his argument. His
> argument does not prove that he or anyone, knows any-
> thing. It simply makes the logical point that one sort of
> statement follows from another.   (Ibid, p. 82)

Logical truths are tautologies, that is they are effectively
repetitions and empty of information. To say 'If I am conscious then I exist' is merely to emphasise that existence is
logically necessary for consciousness. As Ayer says this will
hold for *any* individual 'If X is conscious then X exists'. Of
course what made Descartes think that his *cogito* was indubitable was that *he* was expressing it. But then he had no need
to make an inference; he could simply have said 'I exist'. The
cogito

> is of interest only as drawing attention to the fact that
> there are sentences which are used in such a way that if
> the person who employs them ever raises the question
> whether the statements which they express are true, the
> answer must be yes.   (Ibid, p. 82)

So, if we claim to know that we are conscious can we claim
to know anything else, for instance that a clear and distinct
conception gives us a basis for judging truth? Ayer argues
that this is not so. But surely, it may be objected, the evidence
that anyone has that he exists is stronger (clearer and more
distinct) than any evidence for any other claim?

> How could I possibly have better evidence than I do for
> believing that I am conscious, let alone for believing that
> I exist? This question is indeed hard to answer, but mainly
> because it seems improper in these cases to speak of evi-
> dence at all. If someone were to ask me: How do you know
> that you are conscious? What evidence have you that you
> exist? I should not know how to answer him: I should not
> know what sort of answer was expected. The question

would appear to be a joke, a parody of philosophical cautiousness. If it were seriously pressed, I might become indignant: What do you mean how do I know that I exist? I am here, am I not, talking to you? If a 'philosophical' answer were insisted on, it might be said that I proved that I existed and that I was conscious by appealing to my experience. But not then to any particular experience. Any feeling or perception that I cared to instance would do equally well.   (Ibid, p. 83)

To have an experience of oneself is *not* a matter of introspection – we do not inspect some entity which is 'ourselves'. If we are conscious we are aware of present sensations and/or of rational thought processes. We can be self-conscious in that we can be aware of these experiences and can be aware of things happening to us: feeling cold, working out a problem, remembering some music, etc., but there is no special experience which is uniquely an experience of our self – *any* experience will do. So it is tempting to say that expressions such as 'I am conscious' or 'I exist' are not genuine propositions at all. Yet this is going too far.

All the same it is not difficult to imagine circumstances in which they would have a use. 'I am conscious' might be said informatively by someone recovering from a swoon.... On recovering consciousness after some accident or illness I might make this remark even to myself, and make it with a sense of discovery. ... But what information does this answer give? If I have occasion to tell others that I exist, the information which they receive is that there exists a man answering to some description, whatever description it may be that they identify me by; it would not be the same in every case. But when I tell myself that I exist, I do not identify myself by any description: I do not identify myself at all. The information which I convey to myself is not that there exists a person of such and such a sort, information which might be false if I were mistaken about my own identity or character. Yet I am in fact a person of such and such a sort. There is nothing more to me than what can be discovered by listing the totality of the descriptions which I satisfy. This is merely an expression of the tautology that if a description is complete there is nothing left to be described. But can it not be asked what it is that one is describing? The answer is that this question makes sense only as a request for further description: it implies that the description so far given is incomplete, as in fact it always will be. But then if, in saying that I exist, I am not saying anything about a description's being satisfied, what can I be saying? Again it is tempting to answer that I am saying nothing.   (Ibid, pp. 84–5)

If anything *more than* mere consciousness is claimed, i.e. the nature of the experience, or, even more open to doubt, the nature of the person making the claim, then the claim is *not* indubitable after all. I don't *know* (in the sense of knowing indubitably, which is what Descartes wanted) anything concrete when I say 'I exist' save that some entity exists. The statement is degenerate, it could be replaced by a gesture or a grunt.

To know that one exists is not, in this sense, to know anything about oneself any more than knowing that *this* exists is knowing anything about this.   (Ibid, pp. 86–7)

To say 'I exist' is analogous to saying 'I am here'. It is an empty statement. In certain special circumstances (e.g. lost in a fog on a mountain top) it can be informative but in those circumstances, *any* noise would do – the actual sentence is irrelevant.

Of course we are aware of our own existence in a way that others are not, but the way in which we *are* so aware does not allow us to make any further deductions about the world. The *cogito* is a valid inference and it is a logical truth; for that very reason it is not only useless as a basic premise but also useless for indicating criteria for knowledge. Descartes might claim that he had a clear and distinct idea of his own existence. But this was not to claim knowledge of any fact about himself; there was *no* proposition about this existent entity which was Descartes which could be known to be certainly true. Therefore he could not argue on the basis of the *cogito* that clarity and distinction were criteria by which real propositions could be judged.

The *cogito* is criticised in a different way by Hintikka. Ayer judged the inference to be true, but the 'I' was non-informative. Hintikka thinks that Descartes did indeed sometimes regard the *cogito* as an inference and that the 'I' did have some descriptive content. However, in that case the *cogito* is valueless as an inference because it already assumes what it sets out to prove, '*I* think' already assumes '*I* exist'. Hintikka says that Descartes only treated the *cogito* as a logical inference when he was writing popularly but even so, he did not appreciate that his argument was fallacious.

In the Meditations Descartes implied that he was not *deducing* 'I exist' from 'I think' but that he was perceiving it intuitively. The 'I think' of the *cogito* was needed to express the fact that rational thought was needed to grasp that 'I exist' is intuitively self-evident. We must bear in mind that for Descartes 'intuition' was not something irrational, but an act of a thinking rational mind. We need Cartesian rational intuition, i.e. thought, to appreciate that our existence is self-evident. Compare: 'I walk' and 'I do not walk' with 'I exist' and 'I do not exist'. The last statement shows what Hintikka calls 'existential inconsistency'. The absurdity of existentially inconsistent statements depends on a certain person's uttering them, i.e. performing the act of speech. If *I* say 'De Gaulle is dead' it is a perfectly ordinary statement, but this would not have been the case if *de Gaulle* had said it.

> Normally a speaker wants his hearer to believe what he says. The whole 'language-game' of fact-stating discourse is based on the assumption that this is normally the case. But nobody can make his hearer believe that he does not exist by telling him so; such an attempt it likely to have the opposite result.
> . . .
> The reason why Descartes's attempt to *think* that he does not exist necessarily fails is for a logician exactly the same as the reason why his attempt to tell one of his contemporaries that Descartes did not exist would have been bound to fail as soon as the hearer realized who the speaker was. (Hintikka in Doncy, p. 119)

Descartes could not mislead himself or anyone else, and therefor the truth of the *cogito* does not depend on introspection, it depends on the *act*, possibly accompanied by speech, i.e. on the *performance*.

> It is very misleading, however, to appeal to introspection in explaining the meaning of the Cogito, although there is likely to be a connection between the notion of introspection and the peculiarities of the Cartesian argument. We have seen that an existentially inconsistent sentence may also defeat itself through an 'external' speech act. The reason why Descartes could not doubt his own existence is in principle exactly the same as the reason why he could not hope to mislead anybody by saying 'I don't exist'. The one does not presuppose introspection any more than the other. What the philosophers who have spoken of introspection here are likely to have had in mind is often performatoriness rather than introspectiveness.
>
> The independence of Descartes' insight of introspection is illustrated by the fact that there is a peculiarity about certain sentences in the *second* person which is closely related to the peculiarities of Descartes' *ego sum, ego existo*. In the same way as it is self-defeating to say 'I don't exist', it is usually absurd to say 'You don't exist'. If the latter sentence is true, it is *ipso facto* empty in that there is no one to whom it could conceivably be addressed.
>
> (Ibid, p. 125)

But it is not surprising that we do connect the *cogito* with introspection for each one of us has to formulate his own *cogito*. The insight is not only non-generalisable, it is also a very momentary affair in so far as it is only indubitable *during* the performance. The word '*cogito*' doesn't just call attention to the fact that existence is known by *means of* thinking, so that once proved it is known from then on. No, the existence is known only *during* the thinking.

Descartes's insight is not comparable with one's becoming aware of the sound of music by pausing to listen to it but rather with making sure that music is to be heard by playing it oneself. Ceasing to play would not only stop one's hearing the music, in the way ceasing to listen could; it would put an end to the music itself. In the same way, it must have seemed to Descartes, his ceasing to think would not only mean ceasing to be aware of his own existence; it would put an end to the particular way in which his existence was found to manifest itself.   (Ibid, p. 128)

This meant that Descartes had to imply the broad meaning of *cogitare*, (*penser*) signifying feelings etc. as well as intellectual thought. But he is then guilty of confusing thinking (intellectual thought) with thinking (consciousness).[1] His argument started with an appeal to intuition (rational intellectual thought) and ended with the conclusion that he could be certain of his existence only whilst he was thinking, and this had to mean whilst he was conscious. He could indeed say 'I am cold, therefore I exist'. But he would not then have claimed that his nature was entirely and essentially 'feeling cold', it would have to be any and *all* possible forms of consciousness.

Hintikka says that Descartes's insight is clear but not distinct. Descartes failed to distinguish the various meanings of *cogitare* (penser). But the position is made worse because his argument depends on a transition from *cogitare*, signifying an intellectual process in the intuitive grasping of the connection between consciousness and existence and *cogitare* signifying consciousness itself. *Res cogitans* (a thinking thing) was a thing always conscious, but not necessarily always thinking intellectually.

Hence, the *cogito* does *not* lead us to conclude that an idea must be clear and distinct if it is to be judged as true. The criteria of clarity and distinctness are necessary if we are to judge an informative proposition but they are not sufficient. Their necessity can be shown if we start from the assumption that God exists and does not deceive us. (Or if we start from the assumption that there is a possibility of order in events and in ideas.) But pseudo-propositions like the *cogito* which only give information in so far as they are performances, cannot guide us to criteria for informative propositions.

FURTHER READING

W. Doney (ed.), *Descartes*.
Ibid., A. J. Ayer, 'I think, therefore I am'.
Ibid., J. Hintikka, *'Cogito, Ergo Sum:* Inference or Performance'.

NOTE

1. In the *Discourse* Descartes wrote in French, whereas in the *Second Meditation* he wrote in Latin and used the word *cogito* rather than *je pense*. Moreover, in the more erudite *Meditation* he did not write the relation of thinking to existence as an inference. He did not write 'I think *therefore* I am'. but: 'I . . . must at length conclude that this proposition 'I am', 'I exist', whenever I utter or conceive it in my mind is necessarily true'.

It should also be noted that *penser* and *cogitare* can signify more than the intellectual process of thinking. They could indicate any mental activity: emotions, volitions, imaginings etc. *'Res cogitans'*, commonly translated as 'thinking being' or 'thinking thing' is better translated as 'conscious being' or 'conscious thing'.

6

The British Empiricists:
Locke and Berkeley

In chapter 4 I said that Descartes held that sense perception could not be used as a basis for knowledge, since it could not provide indubitable premises. Rationalists maintain that the only propositions we can claim to know are firstly those which reason tells us are self-evident and secondly those whch may be logically deduced from self-evident premises. Empiricists hold that the basic premises must be provided by experience not by rational intuition. Experience may arise from sense perception of the external world (including our immediate feelings) or from reflecting on the inner activity of our mind: *all* our knowledge rests on this. As Locke said:

All those sublime thoughts, which tower above the clouds and reach as high as heaven itself, take their rise and footing here: in all that great extent wherein the mind wanders, in those remote speculations it may seem to be elevated with, it stirs not one jot beyond those *ideas* which sense or reflection have offered for its contemplation.
(*An Essay Concerning Human Understanding*, II, I, 24)

It is important to appreciate that empiricists did not reject reason as useless. On the contrary, reason was needed to interpret and bring out the implications of the data of experience, it was needed for the logical deductions to be made from the basic premises provided by experience. Similarly, rationalists do not reject experience as useless; as we have seen, Descartes regarded it as an important check on the conclusions arrived at by reason.

John Locke (1632—1704), was the son of a Somerset lawyer; his father was a supporter of Cromwell in the Civil War. Locke took a degree at Oxford and was elected to a senior studentship at Christ Church. But he took an active interest in public affairs and left the University. He travelled on the Continent and was in France from 1675—79 where he met many French philosophers who were disciples of Descartes. Locke had read Descartes's works when he was at Oxford, and, though he professed not to be impressed by Cartesian rationalism, his view of knowledge was much influenced by Descartes. He returned to England in 1689 and published all his major writings after that date. The one with which we shall be concerned is the Essay Concerning Human Understanding, which was published in 1690 when Locke was 58 years old.

Locke called the objects of experience *ideas*. This word did not have the same meaning for Locke as it does for us. Locke did not regard ideas as arising from the mind 'working on' something more basic so that the idea was a consequence of a train of thought. Ideas were 'given' in experience — there was, at any rate about simple *ideas* (see below) a certain passivity; the mind received them either from sense perception or inner reflection (introspection). In this chapter the word '*idea*' is to be taken in the sense that Locke used it.

> Let us then suppose the mind to be, as we say, white paper void of all characters, without any *ideas*. How comes it to be furnished? Whence comes it by that vast store which the busy and boundless fancy of man has painted on it with an almost endless variety? Whence has it all the materials of reason and knowledge? To this I answer, in one word, from *experience*; in that all our knowledge is founded, and from that it ultimately derives itself. Our observation, employed either about *external sensible*

objects, or about the internal operations of our minds per-
ceived and reflected on by ourselves, is that which supplies
our understanding with all the materials of thinking. These
two are the fountains of knowledge, from whence all the
ideas we have, or can naturally have, do spring.

(Ibid., II, I, 2)

Locke supposed that all *ideas* functioned as signs, representing the external world of objects and events or the inner
world of conscious experience to our minds. He held that the
words we used could only have meaning in so far as they stood
for *ideas*; if the *ideas* were vague, the words had little meaning
and the user could convey little, if any, sense:

words, in their primary or immediate signification, stand
for nothing but the ideas in the mind of him that uses them
. . . . Words being voluntary signs, they cannot be voluntary
signs imposed by him on things he knows not. That would
be to make them signs of nothing, sounds without signification.   (III, II, 2)

There were simple *ideas*, of which there were two kinds:

(1) Ideas of sensation — simple sense impressions, e.g. yel-
                          low, hard
                          immediate emotions, e.g. anger
(2) Ideas of reflection — imagined or remembered ideas of
                          sensation
                          awareness of remembering the
                          above
                          awareness of an emotion

First, *our senses*, conversant about particular sensible objects, do *convey into the mind* several distinct *perceptions*
of things according to those various ways wherein those
objects do affect them. And thus we come by those *ideas*
we have of *yellow, white, heat, cold, soft, hard, bitter,*
sweet, and all those which we call sensible qualities; which
when I say the sense convey into the mind, I mean, they
from external objects convey into the mind what produces

there those *perceptions*. This great source of most of the *ideas* we have, depending wholly upon our senses, and derived by them to the understanding, I shall call SENSATION.

(II, I, 3)

The ideas of reflection were parasitic on the ideas of sensation in that we could not reflect until we had some sensation to reflect *on*. Locke's account of ideas of reflection is complicated because he seemed to include not only memory and imagination but also awareness of the mental operation, i.e. remembering, as well as the memory, imagining as well as the image.

Secondly, the other fountain from which experience furnisheth the understanding with *ideas* is the *perception of the operations of our own minds* within us, as it is employed about the *ideas* it has got; which operations, when the soul comes to reflect on and consider, do furnish the understanding with another set of *ideas*, which could not be had from things without. And such are *perception, thinking, doubting, believing, reasoning, knowing, willing*, and all the different acting of our own minds; . . . This source of *ideas* every man has wholly in himself; and though it be not sense, as having nothing to do with external objects, yet it is very like it, and might properly be called internal sense. But as I call the other *sensation*, so I call this RE-FLECTION, the *ideas* it affords being such only as the mind gets by reflecting on its own operations within itself.

(II, I, 4)

From simple ideas complex ideas were built up; they were a continuation of the simple ideas. Again, there were two kinds:

(1) Complex ideas of sensation, e.g. physical objects
(2) Complex ideas of reflection, e.g. memories of physical objects
imagined objects
abstract concepts such as 'Man' and 'Justice'.

Locke said that a simple idea could not be explained, it had to be experienced in order to be understood, but a complex idea could be described and explained to another person:

> The simple *ideas* we have are such as experience teaches them us; but if, beyond that, we endeavour by words to make them clearer in the mind, we shall succeed no better than if we went about to clear up the darkness of a blind man's mind by talking, and to discourse into him the *ideas* of light and colours.
>
> (II, IV, 6)

It is worth noting here that Locke believed that the external world was *represented to* us by our ideas. In other words perception was not a matter of *directly* sensing the world, but was a matter of experiencing the *ideas* which the world stimulated us to produce. This was also Descartes's view of perception — the qualities we perceived were the result of the world acting on our sense organs.

> Whatsoever the mind perceives in itself, or is the immediate object of perception, thought or understanding, that I call *idea*; and the power to produce any *idea* in our mind, I call *quality* of the subject wherein that power is. Thus a snowball having the power to produce in us the *ideas* of *white*, *cold*, and *round*, the power to produce those *ideas* in us as they are in the snowball I call *qualities*; and as they are sensations or perceptions in our understandings, I call them *ideas*; which *ideas*, if I speak of sometimes as in the things themselves, I would be understood to mean those qualities in the objects which produce them in us.
>
> (II, VIII, 8)

Descartes had said that there were but two primary qualities: extension and motion. His corpuscular theory of matter (see chapter 4) was developed by British natural philosophers in the seventeenth century. Like Descartes, they held that matter was made up of minute particles which were responsible for the observed properties. But the particles were held to be indivisible (much more like our view of atoms) with empty space between them. The basic primary qualities of the corpuscles were extension, impenetrability, hardness, mobility and inertia. These were objective properties of the corpuscles and of the material bodies observed. Locke accepted this; his account of what the primary qualities *were* does vary a little however. He proposed solidity, extension, motion (and rest), and number (II, VIII, 9) and sometimes added 'texture' (see below). But we need not quibble about details; the point was that only relatively few qualities were completely objective and truly qualities of the material in itself; the others depended on interaction with a perceiver. Primary qualities were:

> such as are utterly inseparable from the body, in what state soever it be; such as in all the alterations and changes it suffers, all the force can be used upon it, it constantly keeps; and such as sense constantly . . . finds it every particle of matter which has bulk enough to be perceived.
>
> (II, VIII, 9)

Secondary qualities were:

> . . . *qualities* which in truth are nothing in the objects themselves but powers to produce various sensations in us by their *primary qualities*, i.e. by the bulk, figure, texture, and motion of their insensible parts, as colours, sounds, tastes, etc. These I call *secondary qualities*.
>
> (II, VIII, 10)

It is to be noted that, in Locke's terminology secondary so-called qualities are *powers* to produce sensations in us.

Locke stressed the objectivity of primary qualities; in contrast to secondary 'qualities' they did 'really exist'. It is worth considering the sense of 'real' in this context, in relation to the discussion in chapter 1.

> . . . the *ideas* of *primary qualities* of bodies *are resemblances* of them, and their patterns do really exist in the bodies themselves; but the *ideas produced* in us *by* these *secondary qualities have no resemblance* of them at all. There is nothing like our *ideas* existing in the bodies themselves.

They are, in the bodies we denominate from them, only a power to produce those sensations in us; and what is sweet, blue, or warm in *idea* is but the certain bulk, figure, and motion of the insensible parts in the bodies themselves, which we call so.   (II, VIII, 15)

The particular *bulk, number, figure* and *motion of the parts of fire or snow are really in them*, whether anyone's perceive them or not and therefore they may be called *real qualities*, because they really exist in those bodies. But *light, heat, whiteness,* or *coldness are no more really in them than sickness or pain is in* manna. Take away the sensation of them; let not the eyes see light or colours, nor the ears hear sounds; let the palate not taste, nor the nose smell; and all colours, tastes odours, and sounds, as they are such particular *ideas*, vanish and cease, and are reduced to their causes, i.e. bulk, figure and motion of parts.

(II, VIII, 17)

We shall return to consider the notion of primary and secondary qualities with Berkeley. But, before leaving Locke's account of perception we should note a problem which it produces. On his account we are not directly acquainted with the external world, we know only the representations it creates. *These* are what is 'before the mind' or 'present to the understanding'. Locke assumed that the meaning of these phrases was clear, for he does not discuss them. It would seem that he regarded the mind as inspecting the *ideas* which sense (or reflection) put before it. Now this leads to difficulties, for if an *idea* has to be inspected it must be inwardly perceived. It then follows that it should itself produce an *idea* in the inspecting mind, and then this new *idea* would have to be inspected by some inner part of that mind, and so on. What is called the representative theory of perception not only cuts us off from direct acquaintance with the world, by interposing a screen of ideas between us and the world, it also leads to an infinite regress, an infinite number of screens. A way of avoiding the regress is to propose that the inner inspection of *ideas* is different, and that the mind apprehends the *ideas* directly, not via another *idea*. But, if this is allowed, there

would seem no good reason not to allow the mind to apprehend the external world directly, and there would then be
no need for *any* intermediary *ideas*. This problem is one
which must be set aside to be considered along with other
problems posed by theories of perception in chapter 9. Here
I shall accept that Locke took perception to be the source of
knowledge and continue with his analysis. His purpose was:

> . . . to inquire into the original, certainty, and extent of
> human knowledge, together with the grounds and degrees
> of belief, opinion and assent: I shall not at present meddle
> with the physical consideration of the mind; or trouble
> myself to examine wherein its essence consists; or by what
> motions of our spirits or alterations of our bodies we come
> to have any sensation by our organs, or any *ideas* in our
> understandings; and whether those ideas do in their forma-
> tion, any or all of them, depend on matter or no. . . . It
> shall suffice to my present purposes to consider the dis-
> cerning faculties of a man, as they are employed about the
> objects which they have to do with.   (I, I, 2)

Locke was both reacting against and being influenced by
Descartes. Descartes *had* considered the physical changes in
the body and its sense organs when stimulated by light, touch
etc. and he had speculated on how the these changes might
affect the immaterial soul. Locke regarded such speculations
as irrelevant. On the other hand, Locke, like Descartes,
wished to inquire into the basis of original certainty. What is
our indubitable foundation to be? He was like Descartes in
holding that current beliefs must be subjected to critical
analysis and that a true belief could only rank as knowledge
if it were indubitable.

> May we not find a great number (not to say the greatest
> part) of men that think they have formed right judgements
> of several matters, and that for no other reason but because
> they never thought otherwise? That imagine themselves to
> have judged right only because they never questioned,
> never examined their own opinions? Which is indeed to
> think they judged right because they never judged at all;

and yet these of all men hold their opinions with the greatest stiffness, those being generally the most fierce and firm in their tenets who have least examined them. What we once know, we are certain is so; and we may be secure that there are no latent proofs undiscovered which may overturn our knowledge or bring it in doubt.

(IV, XVI, 3)

To have knowledge one had to be certain and one had to be able to justify that certainty conclusively. Locke could not free himself from the Greek and rationalist tradition that knowledge must be indubitable, nor from the rationalist doctrine that knowledge, apart from the basic first premises, could only be obtained by logical deduction from those premises. Locke argued, that to have knowledge of anything (mathematical entity or physical material) it was necessary to know its inner essential nature, its real essence. From this real essence observable properties could be logically deduced. Thus it would be shown what the observed properties *must*, as a matter of logical necessity, be. It is clear that this view is derived from the Aristotelian view of knowledge, described in chapter 3; the essential nature of anything was dependent on certain properties which coexisted in the substance, and which *necessarily* coexisted.

But since the *essences* of things are thought by some (and not without reason) to be wholly unknown, it may not be amiss to consider the *several significations of the word essence*.

First. Essence may be taken for the being of anything whereby it is what it is. And thus the real internal, but generally (in substances) unknown, constitution of things, whereon their discoverable qualities depend, may be called their *essence*. This is the proper original signification of the word, as is evident from the formation of it: *essentia*, in its primary notation, signifying properly *being*. And in this sense it is still used, when we speak of the *essence* of particular things, without giving them any name.

(III, III, 15)

Locke wrote of the essence of particular things, which might seem to contradict Aristotle's contention that particular things cannot be defined and therefore cannot be said to have an essential nature. But Locke was considering particular *kinds* of things, e.g. gold, silver and the essential nature of each kind.

Locke differed from Aristotle in an important way, for he stressed that the *real essence* was not necessarily the same as the *nominal essence*, the name, whereby the material (or object) was classified. Real essence signified the inner constitution of things and if it could be known it would be possible to deduce what observed properties (properties known through sense, or sense perception, and therefore sometimes called 'sensible properties') were the essence of each thing. By contrast nominal essence was simply the name given to the abstract idea by which we defined a material, and by which we classified it. Thus the word 'man' stood for an abstract idea, by which we define as *genus* 'animal' and *species* 'rational'. These, too, were abstract ideas but we have no guarantee that they gave the essential nature common to all men, i.e. the men who actually existed.

> *Secondly*, The learning and disputes of the Schools having been much busied about *genus* and *species*, the word *essence* has almost lost its primary signification and, instead of the real constitution of things, has been almost wholly applied to the artificial constitution of *genus* and *species*. It is true, there is ordinarily supposed a real constitution of the sorts of things, and it is past doubt there must be some real constitution on which any collection of simple *ideas* co-existing must depend. But, it being evident that things are ranked under names into sorts or *species*, only as they agree to certain abstract *ideas* to which we have annexed those names, the *essence* of each *genus* or sort comes to be nothing but that abstract *idea* which the general or *sortal* (if I may have leave so to call it from *sort*, as I do *general* from *genus*) name stands for. And this we shall find to be that which the word *essence* imports in its most familiar use. These two sorts of *essences*, I suppose, may not unfitly be termed the one the *real*, the other the *nominal essence*.　(III, III, 15)

> *Between the nominal essence and the name* there is so
> *near a connexion* that the name of any sort of things can-
> not be attributed to any particular being but what has this
> essence, whereby it answers that abstract *idea* whereof that
> name is the sign.   (III, III, 16)

Aristotle believed that the classifying scheme did show
an order which reflected the true order in nature and which
was therefore giving knowledge. Locke argued that classification by name did *not* give the real constitution of material
things. Some people, he said, did claim to know real essences
and regarded them as forms or moulds. But surely this was
incorrect: for example, if each individual man had to be cast
in the mould provided, how was it that deformed people
(monsters) could still be held to be men? Locke thought it
was more sensible for us to admit that we were ignorant. The
only real essences we could know were the essences of simple
ideas, e.g. yellow, where nominal and real essence were the
same, and the essence of mathematical entities where the abstract idea *is* the definition or essence. But we could know
nothing of the real essence of a material like gold, though we
could give the *name* 'gold' to anything which conformed to
our abstract idea of gold, as given by the genus and species
definition.

> Concerning the real essences of corporeal substance
> (to mention those only) there are, if I mistake not, two
> opinions. The one is of those who, using the word *essence*
> for they know not what, suppose a certain number of
> those essences, according to which all natural things are
> made and wherein they do exactly every one of them par-
> take, and so become of this or that *species*. The other and
> more rational opinion is of those who look on all natural
> things to have a real, but unknown, constitution of their
> insensible parts, from which flow those sensible qualities
> which serve us to distinguish them one from another,
> according as we have occasion to rank them into sorts,
> under common denominations. The former of these
> opinions, which supposes these *essences* as a certain number
> of forms or moulds wherein all natural things that exist are

cast and do equally partake, has, I imagine, very much perplexed the knowledge of natural things. The frequent productions of monsters in all the species of animals, and of changelings, and other strange issues of human birth carry with them difficulties not possible to consist with this *hypothesis*, since it is as impossible that two things partaking exactly of the same real *essence* should have different properties, as that two figures partaking of the same real *essence* of a circle should have different properties. But were there no other reason against it, yet the *supposition of essences that cannot be known* and the making them, nevertheless, to be that which distinguishes the species of things *is* so *wholly useless* and unserviceable to any part of our knowledge that that alone were sufficient to make us lay it by and content ourselves with such *essences* of the sorts of species of things as come within the reach of our knowledge: which, when seriously considered, will be found, as I have said, to be nothing else but those abstract complex *ideas* to which we have annexed distinct general names.

Essences being thus distinguished into *nominal and real*, we may further observe that, *in the species of simple* ideas *and modes*, they *are always the same*, but *in substances always quite different*. Thus, a figure including a space between three lines is the real as well as nominal *essence* of a triangle, it being not only the abstract *idea* to which the general name is annexed, but the very *essentia* or being of the thing itself, that foundation from which all its properties flow, and to which they are all inseparably annexed. But it is far otherwise concerning that parcel of matter which makes the ring on my finger, wherein these two *essences* are apparently different. For it is the real constitution of its insensible parts, on which depend all those properties of colour, weight, fusibility, fixedness, etc., which makes it to be *gold* or gives it a right to that name which is therefore its nominal *essence*, since nothing can be called *gold* but what has a conformity of qualities to that abstract complex *idea* to which that name is annexed. But this distinction of *essences* belonging particularly to substances, we shall, when we come to consider their names, have an occasion to treat of more fully.

(III, III, 17–18)

Mathematical entities provided us with good examples of real essences and this was because mathematical entities *were* abstract ideas; as Plato had said, we never knew a mathematical triangle, circle etc. but we had the *idea*. Hence in these cases we could know the essence, the essential nature.

> I doubt not but it will be easily granted that the *knowledge* we have *of mathematical truths is* not only certain, but *real knowledge*, and not the bare empty vision of vain, insignificant *chimeras* of the brain; and yet, if we will consider, we shall find that it is only of our own *ideas*. The mathematician considers the truth and properties belonging to a rectangle or circle only as they are in *idea* in his own mind. For it is possible he never found either of them existing mathematically, i.e. precisely true, in his life. But yet the knowledge he has of any truths or properties belonging to a circle, or any other mathematical figure, are nevertheless true and certain, even of real things existing; because real things are no further concerned, nor intended to be meant by any such propositions, than as things really agree to those *archetypes* in his mind. Is it true of the *idea* of a *triangle*, that its three angles are equal to two right ones? It is true also of a *triangle*, wherever it really exists. Whatever other figure exists, that is not exactly answerable to that *idea* of a *triangle* in his mind, is not at all concerned in that proposition. And therefore he is certain all his knowledge concerning such *ideas* is real knowledge: because, intending things no further than they agree with those his *ideas*, he is sure what he knows concerning those figures, when they have barely *an ideal existence* in his mind, will hold true of them also when they have a real existence in matter: his consideration being barely of those figures which are the same wherever or however they exist.

(IV, IV, 6)

Locke had no doubt that material substances *had* real essences; their real essences were the primary qualities coexisting in their constituent corpuscles. *If* these were known then it would be possible to deduce what observable properties must necessarily coexist. Unfortunately the inner nature could not be known, for it was not physically possible to know the primary qualities of the corpuscles. Hence we could not deduce the essential observable qualities, and hence we could never claim to know (in the sense of being logically certain of) the properties of material things. Now it was a great advance to concede that essential nature could not, in fact, be known. But Locke's conclusion was based on his opinion that there were impossible practical difficulties. He did not appreciate that even if the qualities of the corpuscles *were* discovered, the problem of what properties necessarily coexisted would have been then transferred to them.[1]

Let us consider his argument. He maintained that if the primary qualities of the corpuscles could be observed, then the perceptible properties of the material which was composed of those corpuscles could be deduced, and therefore truly *known*. The deduction of observed qualities from properties of the component microscopic corpuscles is perfectly acceptable; it is, after all, what scientists enable us to do. They say that a certain molecular structure will make a material with a certain hardness, elasticity, solubility etc. It is possible to suggest an as yet unformed molecular structure and then to deduce the properties which a material with this molecular structure would have; certain synthetic plastics have been conceived in molecular plan before a search for a way of producing them began. As Locke observed, if we knew the internal structure of a material, say gold, we could deduce what its properties would be even if no gold actually existed. This is analogous to deducing the properties of a triangle, knowing its definition (its real essence); the deduction is possible even though no perfect triangle is drawn.

> Had we such *ideas* of substances as to know what real constitutions produce those sensible qualities we find in them and how those qualities flowed from thence, we could, by the specific *ideas* of their real essences in our own minds,

more certainly find out their properties and discover what qualities they had or had not, than we can now by our senses; and to know the properties of *gold*, it would be no more necessary that *gold* should exist and that we should make experiments upon it than it is necessary, for the knowing of the properties of a triangle, that a triangle should exist in any matter: the *idea* in our minds would serve for the one as well as the other. But we are so far from being admitted to the secrets of nature that we scarce so much as ever approach the first entrance towards them.

(IV, IV, 11)

But whatever qualities were found to coexist in the corpuscles would just happen to be there; *their* coexistence would not be logically necessary, it would be a matter of what in fact happened to be the case. The association of certain properties is a contingent association, not a logical necessity — just as it is a contingent matter that someone has blue eyes and fair hair. If it is pointed out that these properties are related to the person having certain genes, we can say first, that it is a contingent matter that they have those genes, and second that it is a contingent matter that *those* genes give the individual the observed characteristics. And if the possession of the genes, or the relation of the genes to characteristics is related to another entity by a scientific law, then the properties of *that* entity and/or *that* law will be contingent or related to another law and so on. At bottom, what is the case in the world is just what is the case; we cannot say that it could not have been otherwise, which is what Aristotle, Locke and all those who seek logical certainty require.

But Locke's failure to appreciate that logical knowledge of materials was not even theoretically possible should not surprise us. Even today some scientists and philosphers (though they may concede that knowledge of atomic and molecular properties is not any more certain than knowledge of directly observable properties), are inclined to assert that the properties of component atoms and molecules are in some sense more real than directly observed properties. The quote from Bertrand Russell (chapter 4) shows this; according to Russell physics assures us that grass is not *really* green, snow not *really* cold in the sense we mean when we ordinarily speak of 'green' and 'cold'. He is implying that *really* 'green' ought to be related to the wavelengths of light, because *physics* tells us what the world is really like.

It was perhaps Locke's view of knowledge as something which must be indubitable, coupled with his desire to base knowledge on experience which led him to his position. He broke away from tradition in bringing out the importance of experience, but he could not free himself from the traditional rationalist view of knowledge. He did not want to accept that logical knowledge of the world was impossible in principle, though he did come far enough to acknowledge that it was impossible in practice. The same attitude can be seen in his treatment of the concept of substance. He followed the medieval tradition in believing that qualities in some sense 'inhered' in a basic and unknowable substratum. As interpreted by Locke, this would mean that the objective primary qualities of each corpuscle must inhere in the *substance* of the corpuscle. At least he was the first to acknowledge that this substance was unknowable:

> ... if anyone will examine himself concerning his *notion of pure substance in general*, he will find he has no other *idea* of it at all, but only a supposition of he knows not what support of such qualities which are capable of producing simple *ideas* in us; which qualities are commonly called accidents. If anyone should be asked what is the subject wherein colour or weight inheres, he would have nothing to say but, the solid extended parts; and if he were demanded what is it that solidity and extension adhere in, he would not be in a much better case than the *Indian* before-mentioned who, saying that the world was supported by a great elephant, was asked what the elephant rested on, to which his answer was, a great tortoise; but being again pressed to know what gave support to the broad-backed tortoise, replied, something, he knew not what. . . . The *idea* then we have, to which we give the general name substance, being nothing but the supposed, but unknown, support of those qualities we find existing.
>
> (II, XXIII, 2)

It was a step forward to acknowledge that we could not *know* substance; but it was only the beginning. Further progress was to come with Berkeley, who pointed out that we had no need for the concept of substance. George Berkeley (1685—1753), was born in Ireland and was a graduate and then a Fellow of Trinity College, Dublin. In 1724 Berkeley resigned his fellowship in order to become Dean of Derry; ten years later he became Bishop of Cloyne. He is often referred to as Bishop Berkeley, but his more influential writings were published before 1714, before he was 30 years old and before he had started his career in the Church.

Berkeley read Locke attentively and critically. Like Locke, he was an empiricist, believing that knowledge was founded on sense experience, arising from the *ideas* before the mind. But he developed certain consequences of this belief which led him to reject Locke's teaching on primary and secondary qualities, on substance, and on abstract ideas. For Berkeley, *all* 'qualities' were secondary qualities, i.e. *powers* of the spirit to produce *ideas*.

Berkeley suggested that if we could know all there was to know about material things through the *ideas* arising as a consequence of sense perception, then perhaps the *ideas* were all that there was to know. He argued that the very notion of some unknowable substratum, or substance, involved a contradiction. *All* qualities, both primary and secondary, were but *ideas* before the mind; there was no point in distinguishing colour (secondary) from extension, solidity (primary). He argued that *none* of them could exist without a perceiving entity, i.e. a perceiver. Thus matter itself existed only in the mind and there was *no* underlying substance — indeed there could not be because we had no *idea* (remember this means sense impression) which could correspond to it. Berkeley called this view of the external world *immaterialism*. It is the view that *things* are simply *ideas* before the mind. *Things* exist in virtue of being perceived; *spirits* (our own souls, angels and God) exist also, and their existence is shown by their capacity to perceive. So, existence consists either in perceiving or in being perceived.

. . . in this proposition, a die is hard, extended, and square;

they will have it (philosophers) that the word *die* denotes a subject or substance distinct from the hardness, extension, and figure, which are predicated of it, and in which they exist. This I cannot comprehend: (To me a die seems to be nothing distinct from those things which are termed its modes or accidents. And to say a die is hard, extended, and square, is not to attribute those qualities to a subject distinct from and supporting them, but only an explication of the meaning of the word *die*.)

(*Principles of Human Knowledge*, XLIX, p. 137)

By saying that *things* were but bundles of ideas Berkeley disposed of the difficulty of the representative theory of perception, namely that we could only know the representative of the external world (the *ideas*) not the world itself. Berkeley said these *ideas* were the world and so there was no screen between us and the world.

But this did not mean that he reduced the material world to insubstantial images. Many of his contemporaries ridiculed his immaterialism because they did not understand it. Dr Johnson was said to have remarked that if he stubbed his toe he was well aware that there was more than an *idea* of a stone. Dr Johnson missed Berkeley's point: the hardness and sharpness of the stone were *ideas* just as much as its visual appearance. Berkeley could further distinguish between *ideas* of the external world and images and dreams: the latter were less vivid and less coherent. Moreover the *ideas* of external objects were caused in us by God, whereas the *ideas* of dreams and images were caused by ourselves. We, as spiritual creatures, could 'have' our own *ideas*; we could cause our own dreams and images to exist; but we could also perceive God's ideas. Moreover, since God constantly perceived His own *ideas*, i.e. His own creation, ordinary material things did exist even when no human being was perceiving them.

> There once was a man who said 'God
> What seems most remarkably odd,
> Is the fact that this tree
> Continues to be,
> When there's no-one about in the quad.'

'Dear Sir,
Your astonishment's odd;
I am always about in the quad,
And that's why the tree
Will continue to be,
Since observed by
Yours faithfully,
God.'
(Quoted in Flew, *An Introduction to
Western Philosophy*, p. 343)

Berkeley argued that the coherence and consistency of our *ideas*, the fact that we could build up relations of cause and effect between certain sets of *ideas* and so produce laws of nature which were confirmed and established by the course of events, was a proof that God existed. There is a certain circularity in this argument which may remind us of Descartes: '*Ideas* about the external world are orderly and consistent Therefore they must be produced by God and so God exists. God is all-powerful and therefore ideas of the external world will be orderly and consistent.'

Berkeley's view of matter, namely that it is not an independent substance but simply a term which refers to the association of certain *ideas*, is a precursor of a well-known philosophical account of the nature of objects which is now called *phenomenalism*. Basically the phenomenalist position is that *any* description of a physical object is logically equivalent to a description of actual or possible *ideas* (today the term 'sense data' is used). Berkeley's immaterialism is not quite the same as phenomenalism because he held that physical objects were not only *produced* by God (and others) perceiving them but that God perpetually perceived them (see rhymes on previous page), and this is tantamount to saying that objects do exist independently of *our* (human) perceptions. Thus Berkeley's analysis makes objects independent of perception in the phenomenalist sense, since phenomenalists do imply that an object is a logical structure of human perceptions.

As we shall see later (chapter 9) it can be shown that there is a logical difference between statements about objects and statements about sense data (*ideas*) and if this accepted then it is not possible to support the phenomenalist view of objects; we cannot then argue that objects are logical constructs from percepts, i.e. from sense data or *ideas*.

Yet, if we are empiricists, we are relying on our perceptions. How then can we claim to *know* that physical objects, as opposed to sense data (*ideas*), have some sort of existence unless we do adopt a phenomenalist position? The problem was appreciated by David Hume long before phenomenalism had been explicitly formulated. At first it may seem puzzling that we should take our perceptions to go on existing when they are not before our mind. (Hume was reluctant to invoke God.) Hume suggested that we all, in the common course of life, take our perceptions to *be* the material objects. Now, we are quite happy to allow a given perception should leave our mind and yet that our mind should continue to exist in much the same condition as before; therefore we are happy to allow that a perception should continue to exist in much the same condition, whether it is 'before the mind' (as one of a bundle of perceptions) or whether not 'before the mind', and not a member of the bundle.

Now there being here an opposition betwixt the notion of the identity of resembling perceptions, and the interruption of their appearance, the mind must be uneasy in that situation, and will naturally seek relief from the uneasiness. Since the uneasiness arises from the opposition of two contrary principles, it must look for relief by sacrificing the one to the other. But as the smooth passage of our thought along our resembling perceptions makes us ascribe to them an identity, we can never without reluctance yield up that opinion. We must, therefore, turn to the other side, and suppose that our perceptions are no longer interrupted, but preserve a continu'd as well as an invariable existence, and are by that means entirely the same. But here the interruptions in the appearance of these perceptions are so long and frequent, that 'tis impossible to overlook them; and as the *appearance* of a perception in the mind and its *existence* seems at first sight entirely the same, it may be doubted, whether we can ever assent to so palpable a contradiction, and suppose a perception to exist without being present to the mind. In order to clear up this matter, and learn how the interruption in the appearance of a perception implies not necessarily an interruption in its existence, 'twill be proper to touch upon some principles, which we shall have occasion to explain more fully afterwards.

We may begin with observing, that the difficulty in the present case is not concerning the matter of fact, or whether the mind forms such a conclusion concerning continu'd existence of its perceptions, but only concerning the manner in which the conclusion is form'd, and principles from which it is deriv'd. 'Tis certain, that almost all mankind, and even philosophers themselves, for the greatest part of their lives, take their perceptions to be their only objects, and suppose, that the very being, which is intimately present to the mind, is the real body or material existence. 'Tis also certain, that this very perception or object is suppos'd to have a continu'd uninterrupted being, and neither to be annihilated by our absence, nor to be brought into existence by our presence. When we are absent from it, we say it still exists, but that we do not feel, we do not see it. When we are present, we say we feel, or see it. Here then may arise two questions; *First*, How can we satisfy ourselves in supposing a perception to be absent from the mind without being annihilated. *Secondly*, After what manner we conceive an object to become present to the mind, without some new creation of a perception or image; and what we mean by this *seeing*, and *feeling*, and *perceiving*.

As to the first question; we may observe, that what we call a *mind*, is nothing but a heap or collection of different perceptions, united together by certain relations, and suppos'd, tho' falsely, to be endow'd with a perfect simplicity and identity. Now as every perception is distinguishable from another, and may be consider'd as separately existent; it evidently follows, that there is no absurdity in separating any particular perception from the mind; that is, in breaking off all its relations, with that connected mass of perceptions, which constitute a thinking being.

The same reasoning affords us an answer to the second question. If the name of *perception* renders not this separation from a mind absurd and contradictory, the name of *object*, standing for the very same thing, can never render their conjunction impossible. External objects are seen, and felt, and become present to the mind; that is, they acquire such a relation to a connected heap of perceptions, as to influence them very considerably in augmenting their number by present reflexions and passions, and in storing the memory with ideas. The same continu'd and uninterrupted Being may, therefore, be sometimes present to the mind, and sometimes absent from it, without any real or essential change in the Being itself.

(Hume, *Treatise*, pp. 306—7)

Whether our reasoning was justified was another matter. As we shall see in chapter 7, Hume's empiricism was to lead him to the brink of scepticism; it was also to lead to a new way of judging what could rank as knowledge of objects and events in the external world.

Berkeley also criticised Locke's analysis of abstract ideas. In chapters 2 and 3 we considered the problem posed by Universals. Locke had another way of dealing with this. He argued that we had *ideas* which were arrived at by abstracting the general features from each particular; thus for the general word 'man' there was an *idea* which was arrived at by abstracting the general features (common to all men) from each particular man. We must remember that Locke did not think a word could have a meaning unless it did denote some *idea*.

. . . the mind makes the particular *ideas* received from particular objects to become general; which is done by considering them as they are in the mind such appearances, separate from all other existences and the circumstances of real existence, as time, place, or any other concomitant *ideas*. This is called ABSTRACTION, whereby *ideas* taken from particular beings become general representatives of all of the same kind; and their names, general names, applicable to whatever exists, conformable to such abstract ideas. . . . Thus the same colour being observed today in chalk or snow, which the mind yesterday received from milk, it considers that appearance alone, makes it a representative of all of that kind; and having given it the name *whiteness*, it by that sound signifies the same quality wheresoever to be imagined or met with; and thus universals, whether *ideas* or terms, are made.

(Essay, II, XI, 9)

Now Berkeley could not allow that an abstract idea existed for an abstract idea could not be perceived. He held that a general word could be applied to any member of its class (i.e. 'man' could be applied to any man) but that the general word did not name a special and peculiar *thing*. He very tellingly ridiculed the notion of abstracting; whatever sort of entity (*idea*) would one have?

VIII. *Of generalizing* — Again, the mind having observed that in the particular extensions perceived by sense, there is something *common* and alike in *all*, and some other things peculiar, as this or that figure or magnitude, which distinguish them one from another; it considers apart or singles out by itself that which is common, making thereof a most abstract idea of extension, which is neither line, surface, nor solid, nor has any figure or magnitude, but is an idea entirely prescinded from all these. So likewise the mind, by leaving out of the particular colours perceived by sense, that which distinguishes them one from another, and retaining that only which is *common to all*, makes an idea of colour in abstract, which is neither red, nor blue, nor white, nor any other determinate colour. And in like manner, by considering motion abstractedly not only from the body moved, but likewise from the figure it describes, and all particular directions and velocities, the abstract idea of motion is framed; which equally corresponds to all particular motions whatsoever that may be perceived by sense.

IX. *Of compounding* — And as the mind frames to itself abstract ideas of qualities or *modes*, so does it, by the same precision or mental separation, attain abstract ideas of the more compounded *beings*, which include several coexistent qualities. For example, the mind having observed that Peter,

James, and John resemble each other, in certain common
agreements of shape and other qualities, leaves out of the
complex or compounded idea it has of Peter, James, and
any other particular man, that which is peculiar to each,
retaining only what is common to all; and so makes an
abstract idea wherein all the particulars equally partake,
abstracting entirely from and cutting off all those circumstances and differences, which might determine it to any
particular existence. And after this manner it is said we
come by the abstract idea of *man*, or, if you please,
humanity or human nature; wherein it is true there is
included colour, because there is no man but has some
colour, but then it can be neither white, nor black, nor any
particular colour; because there is no one particular colour
wherein all men partake. So likewise there is included
stature, but then it is neither tall stature nor low stature,
nor yet middle stature, but something abstracted from all
these. And so of the rest. Moreover, there being a great
variety of other creatures that partake in some parts, but
not all, of the complex idea of *man*, the mind leaving out
those parts which are peculiar to men, and retaining those
only which are common to all the living creatures, frameth
the idea of *animals*, which abstracts not only from all particular men, but also all birds, beasts, fishes, and insects.
The constituent parts of the abstract idea of animal are
body, life, sense, and spontaneous motion. By *body* is meant,
body without any particular shape or figure, there being no
one shape or figure common to all animals, without covering,
either of hair or feathers, or scales, etc, nor yet naked: hair,
feathers, scales, and nakedness being the distinguishing properties of particular animals, and for that reason left out of
the *abstract idea*. Upon the same account the spontaneous
motion must be neither walking, nor flying, nor creeping;
it is nevertheless a motion, but what that motion is, it is
not easy to conceive.   (Introduction to *Principles*, p. 96)

Berkeley is making his point by inviting his readers to try
and perform the Lockean abstracting. But, he says, how can
you have an *idea* of an extension which is neither line, nor
surface, nor solid? What is the *idea* of colour which can be no

particular colour? What sort of creature is this abstract man
who is neither tall nor short, black nor white, fat nor thin? It
must, he says sarcastically, be a wonderful faculty, this faculty
of abstraction, but it is one which he does not possess.

X. *Two objections to the existence of abstract ideas* —
Whether others have this wonderful faculty of *abstracting
their ideas*, they best can tell; for myself I find indeed I
have a faculty of imagining, or representing to myself the
ideas of those particular things I have perceived, and of
variously compounding and dividing them. I can imagine a
man with two heads, or the upper parts of a man joined to
the body of a horse. I can consider the hand, the eye, the
nose, each by itself abstracted or separated from the rest
of the body. But then whatever hand or eye I imagine, it
must have some particular shape and colour. Likewise the
idea of man that I frame to myself, must be either of a
white, or a black, or a tawny, a straight, or a crooked, a
tall, or a low, or a middle-sized man. I cannot by any effort
of thought conceive the abstract idea above described. And
it is equally impossible for me to form the abstract idea
of motion distinct from the body moving, and which is
neither swift nor slow, curvilinear nor rectilinear; and the
like may be said of all other abstract general ideas whatsoever. To be plain [I own myself able to abstract *in one
sense*, as when I consider some particular parts or qualities
separated from others, with which though they are united
in some object, yet it is possible they may really exist
without them. But I deny that I can abstract one from
another, or conceive separately, those qualities which it is
impossible should exist so separated; or that I can frame a
general notion by abstracting from particulars in the manner aforesaid. Which two last are the proper accepta-
tions of *abstraction.*] And there are grounds to think most
men will acknowledge themselves to be in my case. The
generality of men which are simple and illiterate never pretend to *abstract notions.* [(1) It is said they are difficult,
and not to be attained without pains and study. We may
therefore reasonably conclude that, if such there be, they
are confined only to the learned.]   (Ibid, p. 112)

Berkeley says that he always has to imagine some *particular* man or some particular body. He admits that he can abstract in the sense that he can distinguish one quality or property of a thing, as separated or abstracted from the others, say the colour, or the shape, but that is not the sort of abstraction of which Locke speaks.

In the quotation below he discusses the view of Locke, the 'deservedly esteemed philosopher', that the biggest difference between humans and animals is in the human capacity to form abstract or general ideas. Locke argued that the fact that animals did not use words (or some non-verbal equivalent) showed that they had no general ideas and could not abstract. Locke did not deny that animals had some powers of reasoning (he disagreed with Descartes who thought that they were bare machines), but he argued that animals could reason only about particular ideas, their particular sense impressions. Berkeley fully agrees that animals are incapable of abstraction, but he thinks that if this is held to be the difference between humans and animals then a great many of the former must be reckoned among the latter, including Berkeley himself! He did not think that the power to use words, i.e. to have a language, showed that there must be a power to form abstract ideas. He thought that a word became general by being made a sign of several particular ideas, not of one abstract general idea.

Here Berkeley makes a very important point; a word does not *have* to stand for an *idea*. It *can* stand for an idea, e.g. 'blue' stands for the *idea* of blue, but it can also be a *sign* for several particular ideas of the same sort. The general terms are words of this kind. Take for instance the Newtonian law of motion (a very new law when Berkeley wrote):
'the change of motion is proportional to the impressed force', here the word 'motion' is a *sign* for whatever particular motion is to be considered:
'It is only implied that whatever motion I consider, whether it be swift or slow, perpendicular, horizontal, or oblique, or in whatever object, the axiom concerning it hold equally true.'

XI. I proceed to examine what can be alleged in *defence*

of the doctrine of abstraction, and try if I can discover
what it is that inclines the men of speculation to embrace
an opinion so remote from common sense as that seems to
be. There has been a late deservedly esteemed philosopher,
who, no doubt, has given it very much countenance by seeming to think that having abstract general ideas is what
puts the widest difference in point of understanding betwixt man and beast. 'The having of general ideas', saith he,
'is that which puts a perfect distinction betwixt man and
brutes, and is an excellency which the faculties of brutes
do by no means attain unto. For it is evident we observe
no footsteps in them of making use of general signs for
universal ideas; from which we have reason to imagine
that they have not the faculty of *abstracting*, or making
general ideas, since they have no use of words or any other
general signs'. And a little after: 'Therefore, I think, we
may suppose that it is in this that the species of brutes are
discriminated from men and it is that proper difference
wherein they are wholly separated, and which at last
widens to so wide a distance. For if they have any ideas at
all, and are not bare machines (as some would have them),
we cannot deny them to have some reason. It seems as
evident to me that they do some of them in certain instances reason as that they have sense, but it is only in particular ideas, just as they receive them from their senses.
They are the best of them tied up within those narrow
bounds, and have not (as I think) the faculty to enlarge
them by any kind of *abstraction*.' Essay on Hum. Underst.,
b. ii. ch. xi. sect. 10, 11. I readily agree with this learned
author, that the faculties of brutes can by no means attain
to *abstraction*. But then if this be made the distinguishing
property of that sort of animals, I fear a great many of
those that pass for men must be reckoned into their number. The reason that is here assigned why we have no
grounds to think brutes have abstract general ideas, is that
we observe in them no use of words or any other general
signs; (which is built on this supposition, to wit, that the
making use of words implies the having general ideas.)
From which it follows, that men who use language are able
to *abstract* or *generalize* their ideas. That this is the sense

and arguing of the author will further appear by his answering the question he in another place puts. 'Since all things that exist are only particulars, how come we by general terms?' His answer is, 'words become general by being made the signs of general ideas.' Essay on Hum. Underst., b. iii. ch. iii. sect. 6. But it seems that ((2) a word becomes general by being made the sign, not of an *abstract* general idea, but of several particular ideas, any one of which it indifferently suggests to the mind.) For example, when it is said *the change of motion is proportional to the impressed force*, or that *whatever has extension is divisible*; these propositions are to be understood of motion and extension in general, and nevertheless it will not follow that they suggest to my thoughts an idea of motion without a body moved, or any determinate direction and velocity, or that I must conceive an abstract general idea of extension, which is neither line, surface, nor solid, neither great nor small, black, white, nor red, nor of any other determinate colour. It is only implied that whatever motion I consider, whether it be swift or slow, perpendicular, horizontal, or oblique, or in whatever object, the axiom concerning it holds equally true. As does the other of every particular extension, it matters not whether line, surface, or solid, whether of this or that magnitude or figure.

(Ibid, p. 98)

So Berkeley does not wish to deny that we can have general ideas of things, what he denies is that we can have *abstract* general ideas. He argues that any idea is always an idea of a particular, but the idea becomes general by being made to represent or stand for every particular idea of the same sort. He takes an example of a line, drawn by a geometrician. It is a particular line but it can represent any line and therefore any argument or demonstration about it, *as a line*, will apply to any other line and so to lines in general.

Again he ridicules Locke's contention that it is not easy to form abstract ideas and that we know that children and the uneducated find it especially difficult. It is not difficult, says Berkeley, it is impossible! Can *anyone* imagine, for example, a triangle which is neither oblique, nor rightangled, not equilaterial, equicrural or scalenon, but all and none of these at once!

XII. *Existence of general ideas admitted* — By observing how ideas become general, we may the better judge how words are made so. And here it is to be noted that I do not deny absolutely there are general ideas but only that there are any *abstract general ideas*: for in the passages above quoted, wherein there is mention of general ideas, it is always supposed that they are formed by *abstraction*, after the manner set forth in Sects VIII and IX. Now if we will annex a meaning to our words, and speak only of what we can conceive, I believe we shall acknowledge, that an idea, which considered in itself is particular, becomes general, by being made to represent or stand for all other particular ideas of the *same sort*. To make this plain by an example, suppose a geometrician is demonstrating the method of cutting a line in two equal parts. He draws, for instance, a black line of an inch in length; this, which in itself is a particular line, is nevertheless with regard to its signification general, since, as it is there used, it represents all particular lines whatsoever; so that what is demonstrated of it, is demonstrated of all lines, or, in other words, of a line in general. And as that particular line becomes general, by being made a sign, so the name *line*, which taken absolutely is *particular*, by being a sign is made *general*. And as the former owes its generality, not to its being the sign of an abstract or general line, but of *all particular* right lines that may possibly exist; so the latter must be thought to derive its generality from the same cause, namely, the *various particular* lines which it indifferently denotes.

XIII. *Abstract general ideas necessary, according to Locke* — To give the reader a yet clearer view of the nature of abstract ideas, and the uses they are thought necessary to, I shall add one more passage out of the Essay on Human Understanding, which is as follows.

'Abstract ideas are not so obvious or easy to children or the yet unexercised mind as particular ones. If they seem to grown men, it is only because by constant and familiar use they are made so. For when we nicely reflect upon

them, we shall find that general ideas are fictions and con-
trivances of the mind, that carry difficulty with them, and
do not so easily offer themselves as we are apt to imagine.
For example, does it not require some pains and skill to
form the general idea of a triangle? (which is yet none of
the most abstract, comprehensive, and difficult;) for it
must be neither oblique nor rectangle, neither equilateral,
equicrural, nor scalenon, but *all and none* of these at once.
In effect, it is something imperfect that cannot exist, an
idea wherein some parts of several different and *inconsistent* ideas are put together. It is true the mind in this imperfect state has need of such ideas, and makes all the
haste to them it can, for the (1) *conveniency of communication* and (2) *enlargement of knowledge*, to both which it
is naturally very much inclined. But yet one has reason to
suspect such ideas are marks of our imperfection. At least
this is enough to show that the most abstract and general
ideas are not those that the mind is first and most easily
acquainted with, nor such as its earliest knowledge is conversant about.' Book iv. ch. vii. sect. 9. If any man has the
faculty of framing in his mind such an idea of a triangle as
is here described, it is in vain to pretend to dispute him out
of it, nor would I go about it. All I desire is, that the reader
would fully and certainly inform himself whether he has
such an idea or no. And this, methinks, can be no hard
task for any one to perform. What more easy than for any
one to look a little into his own thoughts, and there try
whether he has, or can attain to have, an idea that shall
correspond with the description that is here given of the
general idea of a triangle, which is, *neither oblique, nor
rectangle, equilateral, equicrural, nor scalenon, but all and
none of these at once?*

(Ibid)

In the extract below Berkeley argues that Locke's abstract
ideas are not necessary for communication to be possible.
For, if this were so, and since these abstract ideas are so difficult to grasp, children could not communicate – yet we all
can see that they do. Nor does he think that Lockean abstract
ideas are necessary for the enlargement of knowledge. We

come to knowledge of general properties without their help. We do not need to have a Lockean abstract idea of a line or a triangle in order to frame general propositions about triangles, nor do we need an abstract idea of men in order to propose general rules about men. All we need is to make sure that our proposition or rule refers to attribute(s) which are common to all triangles or to all men, i.e. that it does not depend on a property which is not shared; for example that we do not make a general proposition about triangles which only applies to equilateral triangles, or a general proposition about men which is only applicable to fat men.

> . . . a triangle is defined to be a *plain* [sic.] *surface comprehended by three right lines*; by which that name is limited to denote one certain idea and no other. To which I answer, that in the definition it is not said whether the surface be great or small, black or white, nor whether the sides are long or short, equal or unequal, nor with what angles they are inclined to each other; in all which there may be great variety (and consequently there is *no one settled idea* which limits the signification of the word *triangle*).
>
> XIV. *But they are not necessary for communication* — Much is here said of the difficulty that abstract ideas carry with them, and the pains and skill requisite to the forming them. And it is on all hands agreed that there is need of great toil and labour of the mind, to emancipate our thoughts from particular objects, and raise them to those sublime speculations that are conversant about abstract ideas. (From all which the natural consequence should seem to be, that so *difficult* a thing as the forming abstract ideas was not necessary for *communication*, which is so *easy* and familiar to *all sorts of men*). But we are told, if they seem obvious and easy to grown men, *it is only because by constant and familiar use they are made so.* (Now I would fain know at what time it is men are employed in surmounting that difficulty, and furnishing themselves with those necessary helps for discourse. It cannot be when they are grown-up, for then it seems they are not conscious of any such painstaking; it remains therefore to be the business of their childhood. And surely, the great

and multiplied labour of framing abstract notions will be found a hard task for that tender age.) Is it not a hard thing to imagine, that a couple of children cannot prate together of their sugar-plums, and rattles, and the rest of their little trinkets, till they have first tacked together numberless inconsistencies, and so framed in their minds *abstract general ideas*, and annexed them to every common name they make use of?

XV. *Nor for the enlargement of knowledge* — Nor do I think them a whit more needful for the *enlargement of knowledge* than for *communication*. It is, I know, a point much insisted on, that all knowledge and demonstration are about universal notions, to which I fully agree: but then it doth not appear to me that these notions are formed by *abstraction* in the manner premised; (*universality*, so far as I can comprehend, not consisting in the absolute, *positive* nature or conception of any thing, but in the *relation* it bears to the particulars signified or represented by it:) by virtue whereof it is that things, names, or notions, being in their own nature *particular*, are rendered *universal*. Thus when I demonstrate any propositions concerning triangles, it is to be supposed that I have in view the universal idea of a triangle; which ought not to be understood as if I could frame an idea of a triangle which was neither equilateral, nor scalenon, nor equicrural. But only that the particular triangle I consider, whether of this or that sort it matters not, doth equally stand for and represent all rectilinear triangles whatsoever, and is, in that sense, *universal*. All which seems very plain, and not to include any difficulty in it.

XVI. *Objection. — Answer* — But here it will be demanded, *how we can know any proposition to be true of all particular triangles, except* we have first seen it *demonstrated of the abstract idea of a triangle* which equally agrees to all? For, because a property may be demonstrated to agree to some one particular triangle, it will not thence follow that it equally belongs to any other triangle, which in all respects is not the same with it. For example, having demonstrated that the three angles of an isosceles rectangular triangle are equal to two right ones, I cannot therefore conclude this affection agrees to all other triangles, which have neither a right angle, nor two equal sides. It seems therefore that, to be certain this proposition is universally true, we must either make a particular demonstration for every particular triangle, which is impossible, or once for all demonstrate it of the *abstract idea of a triangle*, in which all the particulars do indifferently partake, and by which they are all equally represented. To which I answer, that though the idea I have in view whilst I make the demonstration, be, for instance, that of an isosceles rectangular triangle, whose sides are of a determinate length, I may nevertheless be certain it extends to all other rectilinear triangles, of what sort or bigness soever. (And that, because neither the right angle, nor the equality, nor determinate length of the sides, is at all concerned in the demonstration.) It is true, the diagram I have in view includes all these particulars, but then there is not the least mention made of them in the proof of the proposition. It is not said, the three angles are equal to two right ones, because one of them is a right angle, or because the sides comprehending it are of the same length. Which sufficiently shows that the right angle might have been oblique, and the sides unequal, and for all that the demonstration has held good. And for this reason it is, that I conclude that to be true of any obliquangular or scalenon, which I had demonstrated of a particular right-angled, equicrural triangle; and not because I demonstrated the proposition of the abstract idea of a triangle. (And here it must be acknowledged, that a man may consider a figure merely as triangular, without attending to the particular qualities of the angles, or relations of the sides. So far he may abstract: but this will never prove that he can frame an abstract general inconsistent idea of a triangle. In like manner we may consider Peter so far forth as man, or so far forth as animal, without framing the forementioned abstract idea, either of man or of animal, inasmuch as all that is perceived is not considered.)

XVII. *Advantage of investigating the doctrine of abstract general ideas* — It were an endless, as well as useless thing, to trace the *schoolmen*, those great masters of

abstraction, through all the manifold, inextricable laby-
rinths or error and dispute, which their doctrine of abstract
natures and notions seems to have led them into. What
bickerings and controversies, and what a learned dust have
been raised about those matters, and what mighty advantage hath been from thence derived to mankind, are things
at this day too clearly known to need being insisted on.
And it had been well if the ill effects of that doctrine were
confined to those only who make the most avowed profes-
sion of it. When men consider the great pains, industry,
and parts, that have, for so many ages, been laid out on the
cultivation and advancement of the sciences, and that notwithstanding all this, the far greater part of them remain
full of darkness and uncertainty and disputes that are like
never to have an end, and even those that are thought to
be supported by the most clear and cogent demonstrations,
contain in them paradoxes which are perfectly irreconcilable
to the understanding of men, and that, taking all together,
a small portion of them doth supply any real benefit to
mankind, otherwise than by being an innocent diversion
and amusement: I say, the consideration of all this is apt
to throw them into a despondency, and perfect contempt
of all study. But this may perhaps cease, upon a view of
the false principles that have obtained in the world,
amongst all which there is none, methinks, hath a more
wide influence over the thoughts of speculative men, than
this of abstract general ideas.

XVIII. (I come now to consider the *source of this pre-
vailing notion*, and that seems to me to be *language*. And
surely nothing of less extent than reason itself could have
been the source of an opinion so universally received.) The
truth of this appears as from other reasons, so also from
the plain confession of the ablest patrons of abstract ideas
(who acknowledge that they are made in order to naming;
from which it is a clear consequence, that if there had been
no such thing as speech or universal signs, there never had
been any thought of abstraction.) See book iii. ch. vi. sect.
39, and elsewhere, of the Essay on Human Understanding.
Let us therefore examine the manner wherein words have
contributed to the origin of that mistake. (Firstly, then, it is

thought that every name hath, or ought to have, *one only* precise and settled signification, which inclines men to think there are certain *abstract determinate ideas*, which constitute the true and only immediate signification of each general name. And that it is by the mediation of these abstract ideas, that a general name comes to signify any particular thing.) (Whereas, in truth, there is no such thing as one precise and definite signification annexed to any general name, they all signifying indifferently a great number of particular ideas.) All which doth evidently follow from what has been already said, and will clearly appear to any one by a little reflection. (To this it will be *objected*, that every name that has a definition, is thereby restrained to one certain signification.) For example, a *triangle* is defined to be a *plain surface comprehended by three right lines*; by which that name is limited to denote one certain idea and no other. To which I answer, that in the definition it is not said whether the surface be great or small, black or white, nor whether the sides are long or short, equal or unequal, nor with what angles they are inclined to each other; in all which there may be great variety (and consequently there is *no one settled idea* which limits the signification of the word *triangle*.) (It is one thing for to keep a name constantly to the same definition, and another to make it stand every where for the same idea: the one is necessary, the other useless and impracticable.)

(Ibid, p. 102)

We should note that Locke and Berkeley were both conceptualists. They both held that the defining qualities of, for example, 'man' or 'triangle' were abstracted from the qualities of particular men and particular triangles. Locke held that the process of abstraction resulted in the production of an abstract idea, and so the general term 'man' or 'triangle' signified the appropriate abstract idea. For Locke a word could not have meaning unless it did stand for an idea of some sort. But Berkeley could not allow abstract ideas, for he held that *ideas* only existed if they were perceived. It is quite clear that whatever one's view of general terms, be it realist, conceptualist or nominalist the *idea* (if there is one) could not be perceived because it could not affect the senses. So, for Berkeley, the process of abstraction could not lead to 'one settled idea.' As we have seen he had thereby indicated another function of words, for he had argued that a word need not stand for one idea, it could be a sign for many different ideas.

XIX. (*Secondly.* But to give a further account how *words* came to *produce the doctrine of abstract ideas*, it must be observed that it is a received opinion, that language has *no other end* but the communicating our ideas, and that every significant name stands for an idea.) This being so, and it being withal certain, that names, which yet are not thought altogether insignificant, do not always mark out *particular* conceivable ideas, it is straightway concluded that *they stand for abstract notions*. That there are many names in use amongst speculative men, which do not always suggest to others determinate particular ideas, is what nobody will deny. And a little attention will discover that it is not necessary (even in the strictest reasonings) significant names which stand for ideas should, every time they are used excite in the understanding the ideas they are made to stand for: (in reading and discoursing, names being, for the most part, used as letters are in *algebra*, in which, though a particular quantity be marked by each letter, yet to proceed right it is not requisite that in every step each letter suggest to your thoughts that particular quantity it was appointed to stand for.)

(Ibid, p. 107

But this very point indicates a weakness in the conceptualist account of general terms. If the word 'man' or 'triangle' can stand for any particular man or triangle (Locke) or be a sign of any particular man or triangle (Berkeley), how is it that we know when to apply it to a given entity? We may agree with Berkeley that a name 'marks' the man or triangle like a letter in algebra, 'marks' a given quantity, but how do we recognise what it marks? Each individual man has to be a rational animal, but how do we recognise rationality and the property of being an animal? Each individual triangle has to be a plane figure bounded by three straight lines, but how do we recognise planeness and lines?

These may seem ridiculous philosophical questions — we just know. Of course we *know*, but the interesting philosophical question is not answered. As stated in chapter 2, the conceptualist account of how we name and classify may well be correct: we classify by grouping things which resemble each other in certain ways, and thus have a concept. The general term is a term referring to the concept (Locke) or is a sign for any particular subsumed by the concept (Berkeley). But this conceptualist account does not answer the more basic question as to what is the nature of resemblance itself. If we say that the resemblance depends on all the particulars resembling the Universal then we have to account for the resemblance between the Universal and the particulars and we are in the infinite regress of the 'third man argument'. If we say that particulars have certain features in common which we can abstract from each one of them, we have done no more than say that the general resemblance depends on some specific resemblances. If we say that the particulars resemble each other because they are in the same group, the name simply being a short way of referring to any member of the group, we have not explained how the group was formed in the first place. As suggested in chapter 2 perhaps we must say that we seem to have a tendency to 'pick out' certain features in the external world and a tendency to mark 'same again'. The fact that we call this 'seeing resemblances' implies that there is some objective external order but it may really be a reflection of our own instincts and of an innate tendency to expect order, and therefore similarity and regularity.

Neither empiricist nor rationalist can give us grounds for claiming indubitable knowledge of the external world. Locke had shown that this was impossible in fact. Berkeley, like Descartes, argued that our scientific knowledge rested on the confidence we had in God remaining consistent. But both Locke and Berkeley accepted that knowledge was possible in principle. It was Hume who was the first to suggest that this was not so, that no knowledge of the world could be indubitable and that, therefore, we could not claim to *know*. Hume was resigned to scepticism but his work was to bring about a reassessment of the concept of knowledge.

FURTHER READING

G. Berkeley, *A New Theory of Vision and Other Writings.*
John Locke, *An Essay Concerning Human Understanding,* vols I and II.
D. J. O'Connor, *John Locke.*

NOTES

1. See also the discussion in chapter 3, and note 10 of that chapter.

7

Hume's Reappraisal and his Problem

David Hume (1711–1776) was born in Scotland. His father died when he was two years old and he was brought up by his mother. Althouth not rich, the family had a little property and Hume was able to live in moderate comfort even before he became known through his writings. In his twenties he went to France and visited the Jesuit College of La Flèche, where Descartes had been educated over a century earlier. Also, when in his twenties he published his 'Treatise of Human Nature'. It is the longer and more complex of his two major works on this subject. Over ten years later, in 1748, he published his 'Enquiries concerning Human Understanding'. This is written in a less involved style than his Treatise and Hume offered it in the hope that his ideas would become better known and understood. He said of the Treatise that it 'fell dead-born from the press without reaching such distinction as even to excite a murmur among the zealots'.

In this chapter we shall first discuss how Hume developed Locke's and Berkeley's empiricism, and then we shall consider his reappraisal of the nature of empirical knowledge. This reappraisal is of fundamental importance, and it places Hume among the greatest philosophers. His work has led us to appreciate that knowledge of relations of matters of fact, that is empirical knowledge, has a different status from mathematical and logical knowledge. It is based on a different kind of evidence and on a different kind of reasoning. Because of Hume's analysis, we have come to appreciate that claims to empirical knowledge must be assessed in a different way from claims to knowledge of relations of ideas.

Hume's Empiricism

Like Locke and Berkeley, Hume held that the foundation of any possible knowledge must be sense experience. He called direct experiences (which Locke had called *ideas of sensation*) *impressions*. There were two types:

(1)   Impressions of sensation — delivered by the senses (they could be simple or compound)
(2)   Impressions of reflection — feelings and emotions directly experienced

Hume called those experiences which arose from reflection on the impressions (which Locke had called *ideas of reflection*) *ideas*. There were, again, two types:

(1)   Ideas of sensation — memories and imaginings of sense impressions
(2)   Ideas of reflection — memories and imaginings of feelings.

As will be seen from the quotation below, Hume said that the difference between impressions and ideas was liveliness. But the impressions are more lively because they are direct and immediate and this is the basic distinction; ideas are always indirect and are parasitic on impressions.

> 12   Here therefore we may divide all the perceptions of the mind into two classes or species, which are distinguished by their different degrees of force and vivacity. The less forcible and lively are commonly denominated *Thoughts* or *Ideas*. The other species want a name in our language, and in most others; I suppose, because it was not requisite for any, but philosophical purposes, to rank them under a

general term or appellation. Let us, therefore, use a little freedom, and call them *Impressions*; employing that word in a sense somewhat different from the usual. By the term *impression*, then, I mean all our more lively perceptions, when we hear, or see, or feel, or love, or hate, or desire, or will. And impressions are distinguished from ideas, which are the less lively perceptions, of which we are conscious, when we reflect on any of those sensations or movements above mentioned.

13 Nothing, at first view, may seem more unbounded than the thought of man, which not only escapes all human power and authority, but is not even restrained within the limits of nature and reality. To form monsters, and join incongruous shapes and appearances, costs the imagination no more trouble than to conceive the most natural and familiar objects. And while the body is confined to one planet, along which it creeps with pain and difficulty, the thought can in an instant transport us into the most distant regions of the universe; or even beyond the universe, into the unbounded chaos, where nature is supposed to lie in total confusion. What never was seen, or heard of, may yet be conceived; nor is any thing beyond the power of thought, except what implies an absolute contradiction.

But though our thought seems to possess this unbounded liberty, we shall find, upon a nearer examination, that it is really confined within very narrow limits, and that all this creative power of the mind amounts to no more than the faculty of compounding, transposing, augmenting, or diminishing the materials afforded us by the senses and experience. When we think of a golden mountain, we only join two consistent ideas, *gold*, and *mountain*, with which we were formerly acquainted. A virtuous horse we can conceive; because, from our own feeling, we can conceive virtue; and this we may unite to the figure and shape of a horse, which is an animal familiar to us. In short, all the materials of thinking are derived either from our outward or inward sentiment: the mixture and composition of these belongs alone to the mind and will. Or, to express myself in philosophical language, all our ideas or more feeble perceptions are copies of our impressions or more lively ones.

14 To prove this, the two following arguments will, I hope, be sufficient. First, when we analyze our thoughts or ideas, however compounded or sublime, we always find that they resolve themselves into such simple ideas as were copied from a precedent feeling or sentiment. Even those ideas, which, at first view, seem the most wide of this origin, are found, upon a nearer scrutiny, to be derived from it. The idea of God, as meaning an infinitely intelligent, wise, and good Being, arises from reflecting on the operations of our own mind, and augmenting, without limit, those qualities of goodness and wisdom. We may prosecute this enquiry to what length we please; where we shall always find, that every idea which we examine is copied from a similar impression. Those who would assert that this position is not universally true nor without exception, have only one, and that an easy method of refuting it; by producing that idea, which, in their opinion, is not derived from this source.

(*Enquiry* I, Sec. II, paras 12–14)

Note how the opening of paragraph 14 repeats what Locke had said: however sublime the thought, however complex, it is always possible to trace its source to sense experience. Locke had said that this was so, even of those thoughts that 'reach as high as heaven itself'. Hume explicitly applies this to the thought of God. How far have we come from Descartes! There is no suggestion that the *thought* of a perfect being must of necessity be caused by a perfect being. No, it arises 'from reflecting on the operations of our own mind, and augmenting without limit, those qualities of goodness and wisdom'.

Since ideas are parasitic on impressions, it follows that abstract ideas must be parasitic on impressions. Therefore all general notions (abstract ideas), say of man, of triangles or of whiteness, must be derived from particular impressions of particular men, particular triangles and particular white objects. Any idea *has* to come from an impression:

All ideas, especially abstract ones, are naturally faint and obscure: the mind has but a slender hold of them: they are apt to be confounded with other resembling ideas; and when we have often employed any term, though without a distinct meaning, we are apt to imagine it has a determinate idea annexed to it. On the contrary, all impressions, that is, all sensations, either outward or inward, are strong and vivid: the limits between them are more exactly determined: nor is it easy to fall into any error or mistake with regard to them. When we entertain, therefore, any suspicion that a philosophical term is employed without any meaning or idea (as is but too frequent), we need but enquire, *from what impression is that supposed idea derived?* And if it be impossible to assign any, this will serve to confirm our suspicion. By bringing ideas into so clear a light we may reasonably hope to remove all dispute, which may arise, concerning their nature and reality.   (Ibid, para 17)

In this quotation it might appear that Hume was agreeing with Locke, and was treating abstract ideas as Lockean ideas of reflection, but in fact his view of abstract ideas was much closer to that of Berkeley.

The abstract idea of a man represents men of all sizes and all qualities; which 'tis concluded it cannot do, but either by representing at once all possible qualities, or by representing no particular one at all. Now it having been deemed absurd to defend the former proposition, as implying an infinite capacity in the mind, it has been commonly infer'd in favour of the latter; and our abstract ideas have been suppos'd to represent no particular degree either of quantity or quality. But that this inference is erroneous, I shall endeavour to make appear.

. . .

. . . 'tis a principle generally receiv'd in philosophy, that every thing in nature is individual, and that 'tis utterly absurd to suppose a triangle really existent, which has no precise proportion of sides and angles. If this therefore be absurd in *fact and reality*, it must also be absurd *in idea*; . . . . 'tis impossible to form an idea of an object, that is possest of quantity and quality, and yet is possest of no precise degree of either; it follows that there is an equal impossibility of forming an idea, that is not limited and confined in both these particulars. Abstract ideas are therefore in themselves individual, however they may become general in their representation. The image in the mind is only that of a particular object, tho' the application of it in our reasoning be the same, as if it were universal. . . . For this is one of the most extraordinary circumstances in the present affair, that after the mind has produc'd an individual idea, upon which we reason, the attendant custom, reviv'd by the general or abstract term, readily suggests any other individual, if by chance we form any reasoning, that agrees not with it. . . .

If ideas be particular in their nature and at the same time finite in their number, 'tis only by custom they can become general in their representation, and contain an infinite number of other ideas under them . . . *all ideas, which are different, are separable.* . . . if the figure be different from the body, their ideas must be separable as well as distinguishable; if they be not different; their ideas can neither be separable nor distinguishable. What then is meant by a distinction of reason, since it implies neither a difference nor a separation?

To remove this difficulty we must have recourse to the foregoing explication of abstract ideas. 'Tis certain that the mind wou'd never have dream'd of distinguishing a figure from the body figur'd, as being in reality neither distinguishable, nor different, nor separable; did it not observe, that even in this simplicity there might be contain'd many different resemblances and relations. Thus when a globe of white marble is presented, we receive only the impression of a white colour dispos'd in a certain form, nor are we able to separate and distinguish the colour from the form. But observing afterwards a globe of black marble and a cube of white, and comparing them with our former object, we find two separate resemblances, in what formerly seem'd, and really is, perfectly inseparable. After a little more practice of this kind, we begin to distinguish the figure from the colour by a *distinction of reason*; that is, we consider the figure and colour together, since they are in effect the same and undistinguishable; but still view them in different aspects, according to the resemblances, of which they are susceptible. When we wou'd consider only the figure of the globe of white marble, we form in reality an idea both of the figure and colour, but tacitly carry our eye to its resemblance with the globe of black marble: And in the same manner, when we wou'd consider its colour only, we turn our view to its resemblance with the cube of white marble. By this means we accompany our ideas with a kind of reflexion, of which custom renders us, in a great measure, insensible. A person, who desires us to consider the figure of a globe of white marble without thinking on its colour, desires an impossibility; but his meaning is, that we shou'd consider the colour and figure together, but still keep in our eye the resemblance to the globe of black marble, or that to any other globe of whatever colour or substance.

(*Treatise*, Book I, Sec. VII)

This is partly a restatement of Berkeley's exposition of the nature of abstract ideas: the idea itself must be an idea of a particular entity, but our attention is directed to certain positive features of the particular idea, e.g. its having three straight sides if it is a triangle, its being white, if it is a white sphere; so that its resemblance to other sorts of triangle or to other sorts of white objects is the predominant feature of the idea. Thus the general term is a sign for a group of particular ideas which all resemble each other in some particular respect. We should note that Hume's account still evades the problem of resemblance; he simply accepts that we do notice resemblances, but how we recognise them as resemblances is not discussed.

Hume's Reappraisal of Empirical Knowledge

Like Locke, Hume held that there were two types of informative statements: one expressing relations between ideas, i.e. mathematical and logical relations, and the other expressing relations between matters of fact, i.e. statements about objects and events in the world. But, unlike Locke, he came to the conclusion that it was not even theoretically possible to show the truth or falsity of any statements about any matters of fact by logical argument.

He discussed the nature of the evidence on which we base our knowledge of matters of fact: there was 'the present testimony of our senses' and 'the records of our memory'. The present testimony of the senses provided impressions, and the records of memory provided ideas and these were the foundations of empirical knowledge. But, of course, we make much greater claims to knowledge of the world than what we know from the deliverance of our senses and what we can remember of those deliverances.

As was implied in chapter 3 we claim to know that the objects we perceive have other properties which we do not, currently, perceive. For example, we look at a glass of water and *perceive* its colour and shape, but we claim to *know* that the glass is brittle and would break if we dropped it, that the water would quench our thirst, that it would boil if heated and would turn to ice if cooled, etc., etc. In addition, we claim to know that the glass of water would remain if we looked away, and that it would exist even if not perceived by anyone. In effect we claim, on the basis of transient impressions, that certain properties are regularly associated and therefore that terms such as 'glass' and 'water' stand for entities with an established set of properties. We assume that if we perceive some of the appropriate properties we can rely on the other properties being present, and that we are entitled to say that we *know* they are present. Moreover we claim more than knowledge of regular association of properties and the existence of entities unperceived. We claim that we know how objects will interact. We claim to know that if the glass was turned upside down the water would pour from it, we claim to know that if we threw it into the air it would come down again etc., etc. We claim to know that a very large number of common-sense generalisations and scientific laws about objects and events are true.

As we shall read in the extract below, Hume argued that no matter of fact could be demonstrated to be true. He said that if this were so, the denial of any matter of fact would be inconceivable. He is implying that it is inconceivable that any statement which can be demonstrated to be true should be denied by any rational person. For example, it is inconceivable that any rational person should deny '2 + 2 = 4', assuming that he or she is familiar with the notation. To deny this would be to talk nonsense. By contrast to deny 'It is raining' may be to make a false statement (for it may be raining), but it is not to talk nonsense. It is not nonsense because it is conceivable that it might not have been raining. The denial of a statement of fact is always conceivable because it is possible that the facts could be otherwise; the denial of a logical or mathematical truth is inconceivable because it is impossible that these truths could be otherwise.

In his recent book on Hume, Professor Ayer argues that Hume misleads us when he implies that the denial of a logical truth is inconceivable. For example, it happens that it is logically impossible to square the circle, but many rational people, among them the philosopher Hobbes (1588–1679) thought that it was possible. At present, we are able to conceive that the arithmetical theorem known as Goldbach's conjecture, namely that every even number greater than 2 is the sum of two primes, is true and that it is false; for we do not know whether it is true or false. As yet there has been no mathematical demonstration which has established it as true and there has been no example – of an even number greater than 2 which was *not* the sum of two primes – which would establish that the conjecture was false.

So, it is quite obvious that in one sense we can conceive the logically impossible. However, this is perhaps not quite the way to take Hume's view of the nature of the relations between ideas. He could counter that once such a relation has been *demonstrated* then it is inconceivable that any rational person should deny it. It was because Hobbes did not *understand* the mathematical arguments that he thought it was possible to square the circle, and, in respect of this particular matter, he was being irrational. In regard to Goldbach's conjecture anyone who proclaims that it is false, after its truth has been demonstrated (or vice versa) will also be irrational. Therefore we may say that Hume's assertion of the inconceivability of denying true relations between ideas is based on the assumption that the relation has been demonstrated to be true and that the argument is understood. It would have been less misleading if Hume had appealed, like Descartes, to clear and distinct ideas for if a demonstration is *understood* this is equivalent to saying that it is known clearly and distinctly and then it is inconceivable that any rational person should deny it.

We might of course argue that if someone stands out in the rain it is inconceivable that he or she should deny that it was raining (and still be regarded as a rational person). But this is to miss Hume's point: *it might not have been raining*, whereas there is no question that the circle might have been squared. So in the case of the circle, it is inconceivable that any informed and rational person should claim that it can be squared. What Hume did not make explicit is that the denial of a logical truth involves a contradiction and it is inconceivable that any rational person would support a contradiction (see also chapter 8). Nevertheless he certainly implied this, for he said in regard to *facts* 'No negation of a fact can involve a contradiction'.   (*Enquiry*, Sec. XII, Part III, 132)

We may note how Hume's view of knowledge is both like and unlike that of Descartes. He agreed with Descartes that if any statement was logically deduced, then it could not be otherwise and it would be absurd to deny it — inconceivable for a rational person to deny it. But, as we saw in chapter 4, Descartes thought that it would be possible to demonstrate empirical laws as well as relations between ideas. Hume rejected this completely and, in so doing, he founded a new approach to empirical knowledge. Since matters of fact cannot be demonstrated the question as to how we know anything about the nature of objects and the relations between them beyond what we directly observe and remember (and that is very little) remains to be answered. If we cannot demonstrate that the sun will rise tomorrow, if we cannot demonstrate that water will put out fire and that bread will nourish us, what grounds have we for claiming that we know that the sun will rise, that the water will put out the fire, that the bread will nourish us?

All the objects of human reason or enquiry may naturally

be divided into two kinds, to wit, *Relations of Ideas*, and *Matters of Fact*. Of the first kind are the sciences of Geometry, Algebra, and Arithmetic; and in short, every affirmation which is either intuitively or demonstratively certain. *That the square of the hypothenuse is equal to the square of the two sides*, is a proposition which expresses a relation between these figures. *That three times five is equal to the half of thirty*, expresses a relation between these numbers. Propositions of this kind are discoverable by the mere operation of thought, without dependence on what is anywhere existent in the universe. Though there never were a circle or triangle in nature, the truths demonstrated by Euclid would for ever retain their certainty and evidence.

Matters of fact, which are the second objects of human reason, are not ascertained in the same manner; nor is our evidence of their truth, however great, of a like nature with the foregoing. The contrary of every matter of fact is still possible; because it can never imply a contradiction, and is conceived by the mind with the same facility and distinctness, as if ever so conformable to reality. *That the sun will not rise to-morrow* is no less intelligible a proposition, and implies no more contradiction than the affirmation, *that it will rise*. We should in vain, therefore, attempt to demonstrate its falsehood. Were it demonstratively false, it would imply a contradiction, and could never be distinctly conceived by the mind.

It may, therefore, be a subject worthy of curiosity, to enquire what is the nature of that evidence which assures us of any real existence and matter of fact, beyond the present testimony of our senses, or the records of our memory. This part of philosophy, it is observable, has been little cultivated, either by the ancients or moderns; and therefore our doubts and errors, in the prosecution of so important an enquiry may be the more excusable; while we march through such difficult paths without any guide or direction. They may even prove useful, by exciting curiosity, and destroying that implicit faith and security, which is the bane of all reasoning and free enquiry. The discovery of defects in the common philosophy, if any such there be, will not, I presume, be a discouragement, but rather an incitement, as is usual, to attempt something more full and satisfactory than has yet been proposed to the public.   (*Enquiry* I, Sec. IV, p. 25)

What is the nature of the evidence which assures us of the existence of physical objects and of the truth of familiar generalisations?

In the quotation below, Hume considers the grounds for our beliefs in matters of fact and for belief in the existence of physical objects in particular. Note again the echo of Locke as Hume stresses that however our imagination ranges, we cannot advance one step beyond ourselves and our ideas.

Now since nothing is ever present to the mind but perceptions, and since all ideas are deriv'd from something antecedently present to the mind; it follows, that 'tis impossible for us so much as to conceive or form an idea of anything specifically different from ideas and impressions. Let us fix our attention out of ourselves as much as possible: Let us chace our imagination to the heavens, or to the utmost limits of the universe; we never really advance a step beyond ourselves, nor can conceive any kind of existence, but those perceptions, which have appear'd in that narrow compass. This is the universe of the imagination, nor have we any idea but what is there produc'd.

The farthest we can go towards a conception of external objects, when suppos'd *specifically* different from our perceptions, is to form a relative idea of them, without pretending to comprehend the related objects. Generally speaking we do not suppose them specifically different; but only attribute to them different relations, connexions and durations. But of this more fully hereafter.

(*Treatise*, Book I, Pt. II, Sec. VI)

We ought to examine apart those two questions, which are commonly confounded together, viz. Why we attribute a CONTINU'D existence to objects, even when they are not present to the senses; and why we suppose them to have an existence DISTINCT from the mind and perception. Under this last head I comprehend their situation as well as relations, their *external* position as well as the *independence* of their existence and operation. These two questions concerning the continu'd and distinct existence of body are intimately connected together. For if the objects of our senses continue to exist, even when they are not perceiv'd, their existence is of course independent of and distinct from the perception; and *vice versa*, if their existence be independent of the perception and distinct from it, they must continue to exist, even tho' they be not perceiv'd. But tho' the decision of the one question decides the other; yet that we may the more easily discover the principles of human nature, from whence the decision arises, we shall carry along with us this distinction, and shall consider, whether it be the *senses, reason* or the *imagination*, that produces the opinion of a *continu'd* or of a *distinct* existence. These are the only questions, that are intelligible on the present subject. For as to the notion of external existence, when taken for something specifically different from our perceptions, we have already shewn its absurdity.

To begin with the SENSES, 'tis evident these faculties are incapable of giving rise to the notion of the *continu'd* existence of their objects, after they no longer appear to the senses. For that is a contradiction in terms, and supposes that the senses continue to operate, even after they have ceas'd all manner of operation. These faculties, therefore, if they have any influence in the present case, must produce the opinion of a distinct, not of a continu'd existence; and in order to that, must present their impressions either as images and representations, or as these very distinct and external existences.

That our senses offer not their impressions as the images of something *distinct*, or *independent, and external*, is evident; because they convey to us nothing but a single perception, and never give us the least intimation of any thing beyond. A single perception can never produce the idea of a double existence, but by some inference either of the reason or imagination. When the mind looks farther than what immediately appears to it, its conclusions can never be put to the account of the senses; and it certainly looks farther, when from a single perception it infers a double existence, and supposes the relations of resemblance and causation betwixt them.   (Ibid, Sec. II)

If we are going to rely on sense experience as a basis for knowledge, and Hume did rely on this, then we can not be logically certain of any matter of fact, including the very existence of physical objects. According to Hume it is our imagination, prompted by the constancy and coherence of certain impressions, which is the basis of our confident *belief* that independent entities exist in the external world.

After a little examination, we shall find, that all those objects, to which we attribute a continu'd existence, have a peculiar *constancy*, which distinguishes them from the impressions, whose existence depends upon our perception. Those mountains, and houses, and trees, which lie at present under my eye, have always appear'd to me in the same order; and when I lose sight of them by shutting my eyes or turning my head, I soon after find them return upon me without the least alteration. My bed and table, my books and papers, present themselves in the same uniform manner, and change not upon account of any interruption in my seeing or perceiving them. . . .
This constancy, however, is not so perfect as not to admit of very considerable exceptions. Bodies often change their position and qualities, and after a little absence or interruption may become hardly knowable. But here 'tis observable, that even in these changes they preserve a *coherence*, and have a regular dependence on each other . . . . Having found that the opinion of the continu'd existence of body depends on the COHERENCE and CONSTANCY of certain impressions, I now proceed to examine after what manner these qualities give rise to so extraordinary an opinion. . . .
. . . the imagination, when set into any train of thinking, is apt to continue, even when its object fails it, and like a galley put in motion by the oars, carries on its course without any new impulse. . . . The same principle makes us easily entertain this opinion of the continu'd existence of

body. Objects have a certain coherence even as they appear to our senses; but this coherence is much greater and more uniform, if we suppose the objects to have a continu'd existence; and as the mind is once in the train of observing an uniformity among objects, it naturally continues, till it renders the uniformity as compleat as possible. The simple supposition of their continu'd existence suffices for this purpose, and gives us a notion of a much greater regularity among objects, than what they have when we look no farther than our senses.   (Ibid, Sec. II, p. 194)

But Hume did not disparage or dismiss propositions about the world as being useless just because we could not prove them or accept them as being logically true. Matters of fact and existence, moral reasonings and the various factual sciences might be supported by arguments appealing to relations of cause and effect. (It should be noted that, in the quotation below, Hume is referring to mathematics and geometry when he writes of 'the sciences properly so called'). Laws of regular relations between events were established by observation (experience) and though they could be denied without contradiction Hume did not therefore dismiss them as valueless. Nor did he dismiss aesthetic or moral judgements that depended on sentiment or faith if they also rested on an appeal to a standard set by the general tastes of mankind. This standard could also be regarded as a matter of fact. But, if an argument or a treatise contained neither abstract reasoning nor any basis of fact then it was indeed useless and should be put to the fire.

131 It seems to me, that the only objects of the abstract science or of demonstration are quantity and number, and that all attempts to extend this more perfect species of knowledge beyond these bounds are mere sophistry and illusion. As the component parts of quantity and number are entirely similar, their relations become intricate and involved; and nothing can be more curious, as well as useful, than to trace, by a variety of mediums, their equality or inequality, through their different appearances. But as all other ideas are clearly distinct and different from each

other, we can never advance farther, by our utmost scrutiny, than to observe this diversity, and, by an obvious reflection, pronounce one thing not to be another. Or if there be any difficulty in these decisions, it proceeds entirely from the undeterminate meaning of words, which is corrected by juster definitions. That *the square of the hypothenuse is equal to the squares of the other two sides*, cannot be known, let the terms be ever so exactly defined, without a train of reasoning and enquiry. But to convince us of this proposition, *that where there is no property, there can be no injustice*, it is only necessary to define the terms, and explain injustice to be a violation of property. This proposition is, indeed, nothing but a more imperfect definition. It is the same case with all those pretended syllogistical reasonings, which may be found in every other branch of learning, except the sciences of quantity and number; and these may safely, I think, be pronounced the only proper objects of knowledge and demonstration.

132 All other enquiries of men regard only matter of fact and existence; and these are evidently incapable of demonstration. Whatever *is* may *not be*. No negation of a fact can involve a contradiction. The non-existence of any being, without exception, is as clear and distinct an idea as its existence. The proposition, which affirms it not to be, however false, is no less conceivable and intelligible, than that which affirms it to be. The case is different with the sciences, properly so called. Every proposition, which is not true, is there confused and unintelligible. That the cube root of 64 is equal to the half of 10, is a false proposition, and can never be distinctly conceived. But that Caesar, or the angel Gabriel, or any being never existed, may be a false proposition, but still is perfectly conceivable. and implies no contradiction.

The existence, therefore, of any being can only be proved by arguments from its cause or its effect; and these arguments are founded entirely on experience. If we reason *a priori*, anything may appear able to produce anthing. The falling of a pebble may, for aught we know, extinguish the sun; or the wish of a man control the planets in their orbits. It is only experience, which teaches us the nature and bounds of cause and effect, and enables us to infer the existence of one object from that of another. Such is the foundation of moral reasoning, which forms the greater part of human knowledge, and is the source of all human action and behaviour.

Moral reasonings are either concerning particular or general facts. All deliberations in life regard the former; as also all disquisitions in history, chronology, geography, and astronomy.

The sciences, which treat of general facts, are politics, natural philosophy, physic, chemistry, &c. where the qualities, causes and effects of a whole species of objects are enquired into.

Divinity or Theology, as it proves the existence of a Deity, and the immortality of souls, is composed partly of reasonings concerning particular, partly concerning general facts. It has a foundation in *reason*, so far as it is supported by experience. But its best and most solid foundation is *faith* and divine revelation.

Morals and criticism are not so properly objects of the understanding as of taste and sentiment. Beauty, whether moral or natural, is felt, more properly than perceived. Or if we reason concerning it, and endeavour to fix its standard, we regard a new fact, to wit, the general tastes of mankind, or some such fact, which may be the object of reasoning and enquiry.

When we run over libraries, persuaded of these principles, what havoc must we make? If we take in our hand any volume; of divinity or school metaphysics, for instance; let us ask, *Does it contain any abstract reasoning concerning quantity or number?* No. *Does it contain any experimental reasoning concerning matter of fact and existence?* No. Commit it then to the flames: for it can contain nothing but sophistry and illusion. (*Enquiry*, Sec. XII Pt. III, p. 165)

Cause and Effect

We must now consider Hume's analysis of the relation of cause and effect which, he said, supported our reasoning about all matters of fact. We have already considered something of the concept of cause in discussing Aristotle (chapter 3). Aristotle's view of the cause and effect relation implied a certain animism in that the final cause, which was the ultimate explanation, was in terms of purpose and offered a teleological explanation. Today we accept teleological explanations of human actions and, indeed, we regard these as the most satisfying explanations of human actions and perhaps of certain types of animal behaviour.

But, in so far as physical events are concerned, causal explanations of effects are expected to be in terms of prior physical events. This view, as we saw in chapter 4, was established by Descartes. The relation between one physical event, the cause, with another, the effect, is accepted *as* a causal relation if it embodies some established common-sense or scientific law. For example, an explanation of why a car skidded may be that the road was wet, of why a man has a persistent cough may be because he is a heavy smoker, of why a vase broke may be because it was knocked over and fell to the ground. The wetness *caused* the skid, the smoking *caused*[1] the cough, the fall *caused* the break. (There will of course be other necessary conditions, but we can ignore these here.) These causes embody established common-sense and/or scientific laws; such laws may be based on observation of regularities or they may depend on further explanatory theories, e.g. wetness reduces friction, tobacco smoke contains irritants, bodies accelerate as they fall to the ground on account of gravitational attraction.

In this way the simple facts — the skid on the wet road etc. are made into reasoned facts. Aristotle held that if we had analysed the situation correctly we had scientific knowledge; the connection between cause and effect was a NECESSARY CONNECTION and IT COULD NOT BE OTHERWISE. Until the eighteenth century it was taken for granted that, if care was taken, it would be possible to find the true cause (or causes) of physical events, i.e. the true 'reason for the fact', and that this would give the logically *necessary* connection between cause and effect. Rationalists held that this must be deduced from intuitively self-evident first premises; empiricists that it could be inferred from carefully controlled observations.

Thus when Descartes formulated the laws of nature, although admittedly, he said that they were ultimately dependent on what God had decreed, he regarded them as embodying a necessary connection. Galileo, Newton and the seventeenth-century empiricists regarded the laws established by observation, and the theories which explained them, in particular the theory of gravitational attraction[2] as giving necessary truth.

With the introduction of Berkleyean idealism or immaterialism, we begin to see the first questioning of necessary connection. We have already seen that Berkeley held that the succession of *ideas*, what we call objects and events observed, was produced by an incorporeal spirit, namely God. (This was different from Descartes's view since Descartes did not regard objects and events as *ideas* but as corporeal substances of a totally different nature from ideas. Moreover, though they acted according to laws ordained by God, those laws had been laid down at the Creation.) A consequence of Berkeley's view was that no one *idea* could itself cause another *idea* for each *idea* was caused by God. Hence a prior *idea* could only act as a sign of a subsequent *idea*. However, because God was not a deceiver (cf. Descartes) we did in fact observe regular sequences of events regularities, which we called laws of nature. According to Berkeley these laws were merely the rules which God, the spirit causing our *ideas*, chose to adopt. It was a consequence of God's perfection that there were regularities; for any relation we observed between events were relations between God's *ideas* and the regularity depended on God being perfect and therefore consistent. Thus Berkeley anticipated Hume in so far as he did not advocate the *logical* necessity of the relation between cause and effect.

> . . . by a diligent observation of the phenomena within our view, we may *discover the general laws of nature, and from them deduce the other phenomena,* I do not say *demonstrate*; for all the deductions of that kind depend on the supposition that the Author of nature always operates uniformly, and in a constant observance of those rules we take for principles: *which we cannot evidently know.*
> (Berkeley, *Principles of Human Knowledge*, CVII, p. 167)

This is very close to Hume's view:

> When we look about us towards external objects, and con-
> sider the operation of causes, we are never able, in a single
> instance, to discover any power or necessary connection;
> any quality which binds the effect to the cause, and renders
> the one an infallible consequence of the other.
>
> (Hume, *Enquiry*, Sec. VII, Pt. I, 50, p. 63)

But Hume dismissed Berkeley's reliance on God:

> Thus, according to these philosophers, everything is full of
> God. Not content with the principle, that nothing exists
> but by his will, that nothing possesses any power but by
> his concession: They rob nature, and all created beings, of
> every power, in order to render their dependence on the
> Deity still more sensible and immediate.   (Ibid, p. 56[3])

> *First*, it seems to me that this theory of the universal energy
> and operation of the Supreme Being is too bold ever to
> carry conviction with it to a man, sufficiently apprized
> of the weakness of human reason, and the narrow limits to
> which it is confined in all its operations. Though the chain
> of arguments which conduct to it were ever so logical,
> there must arise a strong suspicion, if not an absolute
> assurance, that it has carried us quite beyond the reach of
> our faculties, when it leads to conclusions so extraordinary,
> and so remote from common life and experience. We are
> got into a fairy land, long ere we have reached the last steps
> of our theory; and *there* we have no reason to trust our
> common methods of argument, or to think that our usual
> analogies and probabilities have any authority.
>
> *Secondly*, I cannot perceive any force in the arguments
> on which this theory is founded. We are ignorant, it is true,
> of the manner in which bodies operate on each other: Their
> force or energy is entirely incomprehensible: But are we
> not equally ignorant of the manner of force by which a
> mind, even the supreme mind, operates either on itself or
> on body?   (Ibid, 57—8, p. 72)

Hume suggested that we came by the notion of causal connection between objects and events because we had *experience*
of the constant conjunction of certain events. It was experience alone which encouraged our imagination to expect the
second event after observing the first; but there was no *logical*
reason for this to happen. He did not deny that we did indeed
assume that there was a connection between cause and effect.
On the contrary, he asserted that all our empirical knowledge,
our knowledge of observed events in the world rested on our
confidence in this connection.

22 All reasonings concerning matter of fact seem to be
founded on the relation of *Cause and Effect*. By means of
that relation alone we can go beyond the evidence of our
memory and senses. If you were to ask a man, why he
believes any matter of fact, which is absent; for instance,
that his friend is in the country, or in France; he would
give you a reason; and this reason would be some other
fact; as a letter received from him, or the knowledge of his
former resolutions and promises. A man finding a watch or
any other machine in a desert island, would conclude that
there had once been men in that island. All our reasonings
concerning fact are of the same nature. And here it is constantly supposed that there is a connexion between the
present fact and that which is inferred from it. Were there
nothing to bind them together, the inference would be
entirely precarious. The hearing of an articulate voice and
rational discourse in the dark assures us of the presence of
some person: Why? because these are the effects of the
human make and fabric, and closely connected with it. If
we anatomize all the other reasonings of this nature, we
shall find that they are founded on the relation of cause
and effect, and that this relation is either near or remote,
direct or collateral. Heat and light are collateral effects of
fire, and the one effect may justly be inferred from the
other.   (Ibid, Sec. IV Pt. I, 22, p. 26)

But there was no logical necessity in this connection. We
arrived at the notion of the causal relation entirely through
experience, not through reason.

If we would satisfy ourselves, therefore, concerning the nature of that evidence, which assures us of matters of fact, we must enquire how we arrive at the knowledge of cause and effect.

I shall venture to affirm, as a general proposition, which admits of no exception, that the knowledge of this relation is not, in any instance, attained by reasonings *a priori*; but arises entirely from experience, when we find that any particular objects are constantly conjoined with each other. Let an object be presented to a man of ever so strong natural reason and abilities; if that object be entirely new to him, he will not be able, by the most accurate examination of its sensible qualities, to discover any of its causes or effects. Adam, though his rational faculties be supposed, at the very first, entirely perfect, could not have inferred from the fluidity and transparency of water that it would suffocate him, or from the light and warmth of fire that it would consume him. No object ever discovers, by the qualities which appear to the senses, either the causes which produced it, or the effects which will arise from it; nor can our reason unassisted by experience, ever draw any inference concerning real existence and matter of fact.

This proposition, *that causes and effects are discoverable, not by reason but by experience,* will readily be admitted with regard to such objects, as we remember to have once been altogether unknown to us; since we must be conscious of the utter inability, which we then lay under, of foretelling what would arise from them. Present two smooth pieces of marble to a man who has no tincture of natural philosophy; he will never discover that they will adhere together in such a manner as to require great force to separate them in a direct line, while they make so small a resistance to a lateral pressure. Such events, as bear little analogy to the common course of nature, are also readily confessed to be known only by experience; nor does any man imagine that the explosion of gunpowder, or the attraction of a loadstone, could ever be discovered by arguments *a priori.* In like manner, when an effect is supposed to depend upon an intricate machinery or secret structure of parts, we make no difficulty in attributing all our knowledge of it to experience. Who will assert that he can give the ultimate reason, why milk or bread is proper nourishment for a man, not for a lion or a tiger?

But the same truth may not appear, at first sight, to have the same evidence with regard to events, which have become familiar to us from our first appearance in the world, which bear a close analogy to the whole course of nature, and which are supposed to depend on the simple qualities of objects, without any secret structure of parts. We are apt to imagine that we could discover these effects by the mere operation of our reason, without experience. We fancy, that were we brought on a sudden into this world, we could at first have inferred that one Billiard-ball would communicate motion to another upon impulse; and that we needed not to have waited for the event, in order to pronounce with certainty concerning it. Such is the influence of custom, that, where it is strongest, it not only covers our natural ignorance, but even conceals itself, and seems not to take place, merely because it is found in the highest degree.

But to convince us all that all the laws of nature and all the operations of bodies without exception, are known only by experience, the following reflections may, perhaps, suffice. Were any object presented to us, and were we required to pronounce concerning the effect which will result from it, without consulting past observation; after what manner, I beseech you, must the mind proceed in this operation? It must invent or imagine some event, which it ascribes to the object as its effect; and it is plain that this invention must be entirely arbitrary. The mind can never possibly find the effect in the supposed cause, by the most accurate scrutiny and examination. For the effect is totally different from the cause, and consequently can never be discovered in it. Motion in the second Billiard-ball is a quite distinct event from motion in the first; nor is there anything in the one to suggest the smallest hint of the other. A stone or piece of metal raised into the air, and left without any support, immediately falls: but to consider the matter *a priori*, is there anything we discover in this situation which can beget the idea of a downward, rather than an upward, or any other motion, in the stone or metal?

(Ibid, Pt. IV, 23—5, p. 27)

Now this was a truly revolutionary idea. Hume was saying that if all we can know of the external world comes from our impressions, and each of these is separate, there is no way in which we can establish a logical connection between them. We can connect ideas (memories, thoughts and images) in a logical system and hence we can deduce relations between ideas, that is arithmetical and logical relations. But these relations are not relations of matters of fact, they are not empirical relations. Our knowledge of the world is based on the impressions which we receive from without, and it is we who relate them together and who expect the relationship to continue.

As far as Hume was concerned, it was simply a psychological fact about the way human beings thought that experience of constant association of impressions led them to infer some external causal relation. It led them to propose general laws of nature which they relied on when making predictions as to future events. Bertrand Russell was to call this 'animal faith'. Hume said it was the effect of custom. But both agree that it is not a reasoned belief, i.e. not one which can be established by logical argument.

Suppose a person, though endowed with the strongest faculties of reason and reflection, to be brought on a sudden into this world; he would, indeed, immediately observe a continual succession of objects, and one event following another; but he would not be able to discover anything farther. He would not, at first, by any reasoning, be able to reach the idea of cause and effect; since the particular powers, by which all natural operations are performed, never appear to the senses: nor is it reasonable to conclude, merely because one event, in one instance, precedes another, that therefore the one is the cause, the other the effect. Their conjunction may be arbitrary and casual. There may be no reason to infer the existence of one from the appearance of the other. And in a word, such a person, without more experience, could never employ his conjecture or reasoning concerning any matter of fact, or be assured of anything beyond what was immediately present to his memory and senses.

Suppose, again, that he has acquired more experience, and has lived so long in the world as to have observed familiar objects or events to be constantly conjoined together; what is the consequence of this experience? He immediately infers the existence of one object from the appearance of the other. Yet he has not, by all his experience acquired, any idea of knowledge of the secret power by which the one object produces the other; nor is it, by any process of reasoning, he is engaged to draw this inference. But still he finds himself determined to draw it: and though he should be convinced that his understanding has no part in the operation, he would nevertheless continue in the same course of thinking. There is some other principle which determines him to form such a conclusion.

This principle is Custom or Habit. For wherever the repetition of any particular act or operation produces a propensity to renew the same act or operation, without being impelled by any reasoning or process of the understanding, we always say, that this propensity is the effect of *Custom*. By employing that word, we pretend not to have given the ultimate reason of such a propensity. We only point out a principle of human nature, which is universally acknowledged, and which is well known by its effects. Perhaps we can push our enquiries no farther, or pretend to give the cause of this cause; but must rest contented with it as the ultimate principle, which we can assign, of all our conclusions from experience. It is sufficient satisfaction, that we can go so far, without repining at the narrowness of our faculties because they will carry us no farther. And it is certain we here advance a very intelligible proposition at least, if not a true one, when we assert that, after the constant conjunction of two objects — heat and flame, for instance, weight and solidity — we are determined by custom alone to expect the one from the appearance of the other. This hypothesis seems even the only one which explains the difficulty, why we draw, from a thousand instances, an inference which we are not able to draw from one instance, that is, in no respect, different from them. Reason is incapable of any such variation. The conclusions which it draws from considering one circle are the same which it would form upon surveying all the circles in the universe. But no man, having seen only one body move after being impelled by another, could infer that every other body will move after a like impulse. All inferences from experience, therefore, are effects of custom, not of reasoning.

Without the influence of custom, we should be entirely ignorant of every matter of fact beyond what is immediately present to the memory and senses. We should never know how to adjust means to ends, or to employ our natural powers in the production of any effect. There would be an end at once of all action, as well as of the chief part of speculation.

But here it may be proper to remark, that though our conclusions from experience carry us beyond our memory and senses, and asure us of matters of fact which happened in the most distant places and most remote ages, yet some fact must always be present to the senses or memory, from which we may first proceed in drawing these conclusions. A man, who should find in a desert country the remains of pompous buildings, would conclude that the country had, in ancient times, been cultivated by civilized inhabitants; but did nothing of this nature occur to him, he could never form such an inference. We learn the events of former ages from history; but then we must peruse the volumes in which this instruction is contained, and thence carry up our inferences from one testimony to another, till we arrive at the eyewitnesses and spectators of these distant events. In a word, if we proceed not upon some fact, present to the memory or senses, our reasonings would be merely hypothetical; and however the particular links might be connected with each other, the whole chain of inferences would have nothing to support it, nor could we ever, by its means, arrive at the knowledge of any real existence. If I ask why you believe any particular matter of fact, which you relate, you must tell me some reason; and this reason will be some other fact, connected with it. But as you cannot proceed after this manner, *in infinitum*, you must at last terminate in some fact, which is present to your memory or senses; or must allow that your belief is entirely without foundation.

What, then, is the conclusion of the whole matter? A simple one; though, it must be confessed, pretty remote from the common theories of philosophy. All belief of matter of fact or real existence is derived merely from some object, present to the memory or senses, and a customary conjunction between that and some other object. Or in other words; having found, in many instances, that any two kinds of objects — flame and heat, snow and cold — have always been conjoined together; if flame or snow be presented anew to the senses, the mind is carried by custom to expect heat or cold, and to *believe* that such a quality does exist, and will discover itself upon a nearer approach. This belief is the necessary result of placing the mind in such circumstances. It is an operation of the soul, when we are so situated, as unavoidable as to feel the passion of love, when we receive benefits; or hatred, when we meet with injuries. All these operations are a species of natural instincts, which no reasoning or process of the thought and understanding is able either to produce or to prevent.

At this point, it would be very allowable for us stop our philosophical researches. In most questions we can never make a single step farther; and in all questions we must terminate here at last, after our most restless and curious enquiries. But still our curiosity will be pardonable, perhaps commendable, if it carry us on to still farther researches, and make us examine more accurately the nature of this *belief*, and of the *customary conjunction*, whence it is derived. By this means we may meet with some explications and analogies that will give satisfaction; at least to such as love the abstract sciences, and can be entertained with speculations, which, however accurate, may still retain a degree of doubt and uncertainty.

(Ibid, Sec. V, Pt I, 35–8, p. 42)

Hume has presented us with what has come to be known as

Hume's problem, and sometimes as the problem of induction. Can we justify our belief that observation of regularities consistently occurring in similar circumstances, indicates that they are to continue to occur in the same pattern. For, if there is no *logical* necessity for the regularities to continue, i.e. no logical relation between cause and effect, what grounds do we have to claim knowledge of a connection?

When any natural object or event is presented, it is impossible for us, by any sagacity or penetration, to discover, or even conjecture, without experience, what event will result from it, or to carry our foresight beyond that object which is immediately present to the memory and senses. Even after one instance or experiment where we have observed a particular event to follow upon another, we are not entitled to form a general rule, or foretell what will happen in like cases; it being justly esteemed an unpardonable temerity to judge of the whole course of nature from one single experiment, however accurate or certain. But when one particular species of event has always, in all instances, been conjoined with another, we make no longer any scruple of foretelling one upon the appearance of the other, and of employing that reasoning, which can alone assure us of any matter of fact or existence. We then call the one object, *Cause*; the other, *Effect*. We suppose that there is some connexion between them; some power in the one, by which it infallibly produces the other, and operates with the greatest certainty and strongest necessity.

It appears, then, that this idea of a necessary connexion among events arises from a number of similar instances which occur of the constant conjunction of these events; nor can that idea ever be suggested by any one of these instances, surveyed in all possible lights and positions. But there is nothing in a number of instances, different from every single instance, which is supposed to be exactly similar; except only, that after a repetition of similar instances, the mind is carried by habit, upon the appearance of one event, to expect its usual attendant, and to believe that it will exist. This connexion, therefore, which we *feel* in the mind, this customary transition of the imagination from one object to its usual attendant, is the sentiment or impression from which we form the idea of power or necessary connexion. Nothing farther is in the case. Contemplate the subject on all sides; you will never find any other origin of that idea. This is the sole difference between one instance, from which we can never receive the idea of connexion, and a number of similar instances, by which it is suggested. The first time a man saw the communication of motion by impulse, as by the shock of two billiard balls, he could not pronounce that the one event was *connected*: but only that it was *conjoined* with the other. After he has observed several instances of this nature, he then pronounces them to be *connected*.   (Ibid, Sec. VII, Pt. II, 59, p. 74)

Hence, not only our common-sense 'knowledge', but our scientific laws did not have the firm foundation in demonstration, i.e. logical proof, which had been confidently assumed. We could not claim to *know* matters of fact in the same way as we could claim to know the demonstrations of mathematics.

And what stronger instance can be produced of the surprising ignorance and weakness of the understanding than the present? For surely, if there be any relation among objects which it imports to us to know perfectly, it is that of cause and effect. *On this are founded all our reasonings concerning matter of fact or existence.* By means of it alone we attain any assurance concerning objects which are removed from the present testimony of our memory and senses. The only immediate utility of all sciences, is to teach us, how to control and regulate future events by their causes. Our thoughts and enquiries are, therefore, every moment, employed about this relation. Yet so imperfect are the ideas which we form concerning it, that it is impossible to give any just definition of cause, except what is drawn from something extraneous and foreign to it. Similar objects are always conjoined with similar. Of this we have experience. Suitably to this experience, therefore, we may define a cause to be *an object, followed by another, and where all the objects similar to the first are followed by objects similar to the second.* Or in other words *where, if the first object had not been, the second never had existed.* The appearance of a cause always conveys the mind, by a customary transition, to the idea of the effect. Of this also we have experience. We may, therefore, suitably to this experience, form another definition of cause, and call it, *an object followed by another, and whose appearance always conveys the thought to that other.* But though both these definitions be drawn from circumstances foreign to the cause, we cannot remedy this inconvenience, or attain any more perfect definition, which may point out that circumstance in the cause, which gives it a connexion with its effect. We have no idea of this connexion, nor even any distinct notion what it is we desire to know, when we endeavour at a conception of it. We say, for instance, that the vibration of this string is the cause of this particular sound. But what do we mean by that affirmation? We either mean *that this vibration is followed by this sound, and that all similar vibrations have been followed by similar sounds:* Or, *that this vibration is followed by this sound, and that upon the appearance of one the mind anticipates the senses, and forms immediately an idea of the other.* We may consider the relation of cause and effect in either of these two lights; but beyond these, we have no idea of it. (Ibid, Pt IV, 60)

So must we be content with this psychological explanation of our trust in common-sense generalisations and scientific laws? We can and do appeal to explanatory theories, but *these* are themselves supported and must be supported by observation. The problem is simply pushed back a stage, it is not solved. The natural philosophers of Hume's day dismissed the problem; they asserted that Hume was denying that there were causal relations between events. But this was emphatically not the case; for Hume resemblance, contiguity and causation were the only ties to our thoughts, they were the cement of the universe. The *problem* was how to justify our confidence in this cement holding.

It was Kant who first appreciated Hume's problem, and this led him to propose a new approach to knowledge.

FURTHER READING

A. Flew, 'Hume', from O'Connor (ed.), *A Critical History of Western Philosophy.*
D. Hume, *An Enquiry concerning Human Understanding*, Sects II–V and VII.
—— *A Treatise of Human Nature*, Book I, Parts I, III and IV.
A. J. Ayer, *Hume*, chs 3 and 4.

NOTES

1. Here we have a statistical causal explanation: smoking *tends* to cause coughing in that smokers are more likely to be coughers than are non-smokers. Hence we may offer it as an explanation of a particular person's cough.

2. The French natural philosophers were not converted to Newton's theory of gravitational attraction until Voltaire championed it in the eighteenth century. But, once accepted, it was held to be indubitable.

3. Hume may have had other philosophers in mind, such as Malebranche and his theory of Occasionalism (see glossary).

8

Kant's Attempt to Solve Hume's Problem

In the previous chapter it was shown that Hume questioned our grounds for belief in the existence of physical objects, for belief in the regular association of properties and for belief in a regular sequence of events such that a given specific event, a cause, would necessarily be followed by another specific event, its effect. It is this last belief, the belief in necessary causal connection, which gives rise to what has become known as Hume's problem, namely the problem of justifying our belief in the existence of regularities, the problem of induction.

Kant (1724—1804) was one of the first philosophers to appreciate Hume's problem; he was born only 13 years after Hume, but his chief philosophical works did not begin to be published until 1780, i.e. after Hume had died. He was brought up in a strictly religious family and, unlike Hume, he always had great respect for religious faith. Most of his life he worked as a professor of logic and metaphysics at the University of Konigsberg, where he had been born, and he never travelled from his native province. He was far too intellectually honest and acute to deny the force of Hume's arguments, and he was concerned to resolve the problems that they revealed. He thought that unless they could be resolved there could be no firm foundation for science or for morality.

In this chapter we shall be concerned with his treatment of Hume's problem, the problem of causal connection. Like all of us, including Hume, he acknowledged the *feeling* that there seemed to be a necessary connection between cause and effect. Yet he saw that Hume had shown, quite conclusively, that there could be no logical connection.

Since LOCKE's and LEIBNIZ's Essays, or rather since the beginning of metaphysics as far as the history of it reaches, no event has occurred which could have been more decisive in respect of the fate of this science than the attack which DAVID HUME made on it. He brought no light into this kind of knowledge, but he struck a spark at which a light could well have been kindled, if it had found a receptive tinder and if the glow had been carefully kept up and increased.

HUME started in the main from a single but important concept in metaphysics, namely that of the *connection of cause and effect* (together with its consequential concepts of force and action etc.). He challenged Reason, who pretends to have conceived this concept in her womb, to give an account of herself and say with what right she thinks: that anything can be of such a nature, that if it is posited, something else must thereby also be posited necessarily; for that is what the concept of cause says. He proved irrefutably: that it is wholly impossible for reason to think such a conjunction *a priori* and out of concepts. For this conjunction contains necessity; but it is quite impossible to see how, because something is, something else must also necessarily be, and how therefore the concept of such an *a priori* connection can be introduced. From this he inferred that Reason completely deceives herself with this concept, in falsely taking it for her own child, whereas it is nothing but a bastard of the imagination fathered by experience. The imagination, having by experience brought certain representations under the law of association, passes off a subjective necessity arising out of this, namely custom, for an objective necessity from insight. From this he inferred: reason has no power to think such connections, not even only to think them universally, because its concepts would then be mere fictions, and all its ostensibly *a priori* Knowledge is nothing but falsely stamped ordinary experiences; which is as much as to say that there is no metaphysics at all, and cannot be any.   (*Prolegomena*, p. 5)

By 'metaphysics' Kant referred to those subjects which were independent of sense experience, and which could not be treated as part of a purely logical system. For example, the notion of necessary causal connection is a metaphysical notion: it cannot arise from sense experience and it cannot be shown to be logically necessary. Hume had 'challenged Reason, who pretends to have conceived this concept in her womb', and had shown that it was impossible for reason to demonstrate such a conjunction.

Kant was well aware that Hume's critics had not understood him, but he himself was not prepared to accept Hume's psychological explanation of our belief that there was a necessary connection between cause and effect. He wanted firmer ground than this.

He acknowledged, indeed, he stressed, that it was Hume who had revealed that there was a problem, and who had woken him from his 'dogmatic slumber'. It was Hume, Kant freely admitted, who had shown that it was essential to find a ground for that belief.

Hasty and incorrect as was his conclusion, it was at least founded on enquiry, and this enquiry surely made it worth while for the best brains of his time to have come together to solve the problem in the sense in which he expounded it, if possible more happily, and out of this a complete reform of the science must soon have arisen.

But fate, ever unkind to metaphysics, decreed that he should be understood by nobody. One cannot observe without feeling a certain pain, how his opponents REID, OSWALD, BEATTIE and finally PRIESTLEY, so entirely missed the point of his problem. By always taking for granted what he was doubting and on the other hand proving, with violence and often with great unseemliness, what it had never entered his mind to doubt, they so mistook his hint as to how to improve matters that everything remained as it was, as if nothing had happened. The question was not whether the concept of cause is correct, useful, and in respect of all knowledge of nature indispensable, for this HUME had never held in doubt: but whether it is thought *a priori* by reason, and in this way has an inner truth independent of all experience, and hence also has a more widely extended usefulness, not limited merely to objects of experience; this was the question on which HUME expected enlightenment. He was only talking about the origin of this concept, not about its indispensability in use; once the former were determined, the conditions of its use and the extent of its validity would have been settled automatically.

. . .

(Ibid, p. 7)

I freely admit: it was DAVID HUME's remark that first, many years ago, interrupted my dogmatic slumber and gave a completely different direction to my enquiries in the field of speculative philosophy. I was very far from listening to him in respect of his conclusions, which were merely the result of his not representing his problem to himself as a whole, and instead only lighting on part of it, which can give no information without taking the whole into account. When we begin from a thought well-grounded but not worked out which another has bequeathed to us, we may well hope through continued reflection to advance beyond the point reached by the sagacious man whom we have to thank for the first spark of this light.   (Ibid, p. 9)

Kant's attempt to solve Hume's problem was founded on a new assessment of the nature of empirical knowledge. But before we consider his proposal, we need to consider two distinctions he made: a distinction between two kinds of knowledge, and a distinction between two kinds of judgement.

A Priori *and* A Posteriori *Knowledge*

Kant said that there were two different kinds of knowledge: (1) *a priori* knowledge which was independent of sense experience; (2) *a posteriori* knowledge which was founded on sense experience and which, therefore, could only be attained after such experience.

Analytic and Synthetic Judgements

An analytic judgement is called 'analytic' because its truth can be known by analysing the terms, the predicate merely explicates the subject but does not add to it. Hence analytic judgements are always founded on logical truth and it is possible to demonstrate that a denial of the judgement would involve a contradiction. Kant makes explicit what Hume implied (see chapter 7). But he really says no more than did Descartes or Hume: if a logical truth is understood, it has to be accepted, its denial is inconceivable. The judgement depends on reason, and not on sense experience.

A synthetic judgement is called 'synthetic' because it adds something to our knowledge; the predicate does more than explicate the subject, it amplifies it. Synthetic judgements can always be denied without contradiction, because the predicate does not merely repeat the subject.

It should be noted that the essential difference between analytic and synthetic judgements is that analytic judgements do not amplify our knowledge whereas synthetic judgements do. It is a consequence of this essential difference that analytic judgements cannot be denied without contradiction whereas synthetic judgement can be denied without contradiction.

We may compare the analytic judgement

'This four-footed animal is a quadruped'

with the synthetic judgement

'This four-footed animal is a horse'.

We need no sense experience of the four-footed animal to judge that it is a quadruped; to deny it would involve a contradiction since 'quadruped' is equivalent to 'four-footed'. Thus

'This four-four-footed animal is a quadruped'

is equivalent to

'This four-footed animal is four-footed'

and

'It is not the case that this four-footed animal is a quadruped' is equivalent to

'It is not the case that this four-footed animal is four-footed'.
This is a contradiction, and is absurd. Thus the judgement
tells us no more about the animal than we already knew — it
simply explicates the terms 'four-footed' and 'quadruped'.

The second judgement, 'This four-footed animal is a horse',
does tell us something more about the animal, and it can be
denied without contradiction, for to say that a four-footed
animal is not a horse is not to make a senseless judgement.

In the extract below Kant compares analytic and synthetic
judgements:

> . . . But whatever origin judgements may have, or whatever
> they may be like as to their logical form, there is in them a
> distinction according to content, by virtue of which they
> are either merely *explicative* and add nothing to the con-
> tent of the knowledge, or *ampliative* and enlarge the given
> knowledge; the former can be called *analytic* judgements,
> the latter *synthetic* judgements.
>
> Analytic judgements say nothing in the predicate that
> was not already really thought in the concept of the subject,
> though not so clearly and with the same consciousness. If
> I say: all bodies are extended, I have not amplified my
> concept of body in the least, but only analysed it. Exten-
> sion, though not explicitly said of that concept, was already
> thought of it before the judgement. The judgement is thus
> analytic. On the other hand the proposition: some bodies
> are heavy contains something in the predicate that is not
> really thought in the universal concept of body. It thus
> enlarges my knowledge in that it adds something to my
> concept, and hence must be called a synthetic judgement.
> The common principle of all analytic judgements is the
> principle of contradiction.
>
> All analytic judgements rest wholly on the principle of
> contradiction, and it is in their nature to be knowledge *a
> priori*, whether the concepts that serve as matter for them
> are empirical or not. For because the predicate of an
> affirmative analytic judgement has already been thought in
> the concept of the subject, it cannot be denied of the sub-
> ject without contradiction. Similarly its contrary is neces-
> sarily denied of the subject in a negative analytic judgement,

also in consequence of the principle of contradiction. This is the case with the propositions: every body is extended, and no body is unextended (simple).

For the same reason all analytic propositions are judgements *a priori*, even though their concepts are empirical, e.g. gold is a yellow metal; for to know this I need no further experience outside my concept of gold, which contained that this body is yellow and metal; for this is what constituted my concept, and I needed to do nothing except analyse it, without looking round elsewhere outside it.

Synthetic judgements need a different principle from the principle of contradiction.

There are synthetic judgements *a posteriori*, which have an empirical origin; but there are also synthetic judgements which have *a priori* certainty, and have their origin in pure understanding and reason. Both agree in that they can never originate according to the principle of analysis alone, namely the principle of contradiction. They require another quite different principle, although whatever principle they are deduced from, they must always be deduced *in conformity with the* principle of contradiction. For nothing may be contrary to this principle, even though not everything can be deduced from it. I shall first classify the synthetic judgements.

Judgements of experience are always synthetic. For it would be absurd to ground an analytic judgement on experience, as I do not have to go outside my concept in order to make the judgement, and so have no need of the testimony of experience. That a body is extended is a proposition which holds *a priori*, and not a judgement of experience. For before I proceed to experience I already have in the concept of body all the conditions for my judgement. I have only to extract the predicate from it according to the principle of contradiction, and by so doing can at the same time become conscious of the *necessity* of the judgement — and that is what experience would never teach me.   (Ibid, pp. 16—17)

Kant contrasted 'A body[1] is extended', an analytic judgement, with 'A body is heavy', a synthetic judgement. The latter is synthetic because heaviness is not part of the concept of body and hence the judgement amplifies our knowledge of that particular body. It is a judgement we make from sense experience of the body, just as the judgement we make that a certain four-footed animal is a horse is based on sense experience, i.e. on observation, of the animal.

The judgements of experience, that is *a posteriori* judgements, are always synthetic. But Kant did not think that the converse was true; he did not think that all synthetic judgements were *a posteriori*, i.e. that they all had to depend on sense experience. He thought that some synthetic judgements were *a priori* judgements.

This was where he differed from Hume. Synthetic judgements amplify our knowledge of the world, and, for Hume, all such amplifications had to be matters of fact which could only be known through sense experience — they had to be *a posteriori*. Hume would have said 'All analytic judgements (relations of ideas) are *a priori* and all synthetic judgements (relations of matters of fact), are *a posteriori*'. Kant did not accept this simple dichotomy; he said:
'All analytic judgements are *a priori*, and many synthetic judgements are *a posteriori* but some synthetic judgements are *a priori*.'

He appreciated that unless he could show that *a priori* synthetic judgements were possible, that is unless we could know some facts about the world without appeal to experience, Hume's problem could not be solved. He agreed with Hume that our belief in necessary causal connection was not based on sense experience, but, as we have seen, he was not content with Hume's psychological explanation that it arose from custom and habit. Kant held that belief in necessary causal connection was a metaphysical belief, as was the belief in the existence of physical objects, and the belief in the regular association of properties. He desperately wanted to justify metaphysics and save it from the flames, because he thought that unless this could be done there could be no firm foundation for any empirical knowledge.

He realised that he had a difficult task, for he fully appreciated that it was easy to construct metaphysical systems which were empty of content, 'groundless philosophy and false wisdom', and so he understood why Hume had wished to deal with the subject so drastically. He argued that the question of the possibility of *a priori* synthetic judgements must be settled, if metaphysics was to be justified:

> Whether metaphysics is to stand or fall, and thus its existence, now entirely depends on the solving of this problem. A man may propound assertions in metaphysics as plausibly as he will, heaping conclusions on conclusions to suffocation; if he has not first been able to answer this question satisfactorily, I have the right to say: this is all vain groundless philosophy and false wisdom. You speak through pure reason and presume as it were to create cognitions *a priori*, not merely by analysing concepts but by giving out that you are making new connections which do not rest on the principle of contradiction, and you imagine you have insight into them independently of all experience; how do you arrive at all this and how will you justify your pretensions?
> (Ibid, p. 31)

So Kant set himself the task of justifying metaphysics by showing that there could be *a priori* synthetic propositions, that 'new connections' which did not rest on the principle of contradiction could be made.

His fundamental postulate was that our empirical knowledge was not knowledge of the world as it is in itself but knowledge of a world which we had constructed by processing ('synthesizing', as Kant put it) what was given to us in sensation. We could entertain the notion of a world 'in itself', independent of us and our sensations, but of such a world we could know nothing. It might as well not exist. All we could know were the objects we constructed out of sensations — the phenomena or appearances. All our empirical knowledge was knowledge of our own constructs, knowledge of phenomena (appearances).

Kant said that we had an innate tendency to 'place' our sensations in Euclidean space and to relate them in time. It was this power which enabled sensations to be subjectively appreciated, that is to become subjective experiences. The capacity was intuitive, not intellectual, and it did not give us objective experiences, we simply became subjectively aware of our sensation. Nevertheless, primary intuitions of space and time were the rock-bottom basis of any possible objective experience, and therefore of any objective knowledge. To get objective knowledge, the subjective experiences had to be subsumed under concepts. These were *a priori* concepts, in that they were prior to experience. They emerged as a result of an innate capacity to structure sensations and they had to be innate and prior to experience for they were needed in order for us to have objective experiences of any kind.

Examples of *a priori* concepts were the concept of causality, the concept of physical objects and the concept of the possibility of degrees of a quality. Kant disagreed with Hume's view that these must arise from impressions, and therefore come from experience. It was the other way round, experience came from the concepts:

> Experience rests on a synthesis according to concepts of an object of appearances in general. Apart from such a synthesis it would not be knowledge, but a rhapsody of perceptions.   (*Critique*, p. 193)

It is important to appreciate the originality of Kant's exposition. He was offering an entirely new assessment of empirical knowledge. He was not taking a Platonic view in regarding the world of sense experience as a shadow of ultimate reality. Nor was he merely insisting on the need for interpretation of sense, as Descartes had done. Descartes had held that, through reason, perception gave us knowledge of the world as it was in itself. Nor was Kant developing the empiricist view of knowledge based on impressions and ideas. He did not think that even the most simple impressions were 'given'; they had to be formed in accordance with our innate intuitions of space and time in order to be *experienced* at all. It was, he said, a Copernican revolution in philosophy: we didn't gain knowledge from objects in the world, our innate capacities created the world of objects:

> Instead of all our knowledge conforming to objects, let us suppose that all objects conform to our knowledge.
>
> (Ibid, p. 22)

Now how does this new view of empirical knowledge make *a priori* synthetic judgements possible? Kant argued that there were certain relations which could be known independently of any experience because they were imposed by the subject (the perceiver and thinker) himself. He thought that our perceptual and cognitive faculties imposed a certain form or structure on the sensations we received, somewhat as the wearing of blue spectacles imposes that colour on everything we see. Since the form or structure was imposed by us, it was independent of experience, and hence was the source of synthetic *a priori* knowledge.

Kant thought that all the propositions of pure mathematics were synthetic *a priori* judgements. They were synthetic because they gave extra information and therefore their truth could not be demonstrated by an appeal to the principle of contradiction — that is they could be denied without contradiction. Yet they were *a priori* because they *had* to be as they were, in order to conform with *a priori* intuition. For example, he argued that the concept of '7 + 5' did not contain the concept of '12', so that it was not possible to demonstrate that '7 + 5 = 12' by appeal to the principle of contradiction. He said that the reason why '7 + 5' *had* to be equal to '12' was that the fundamental intuition of time, through which we were able to understand arithmetic, necessitated that the proposition '7 + 5 = 12' be true.

It may be helpful here to appeal to inconceivability! We have seen that if the demonstration is understood, the denial of an analytic judgement is inconceivable — it would involve a contradiction. The denial of an *a priori* synthetic judgement is inconceivable because it would conflict with a fundamental intuition or concept. This inconceivability is perhaps more fundamental than the inconceivability of denying an analytic judgement, for it is denial of a basic requirement for the possibility of experience, not just denial of a logical principle.

Thus, for Kant, we could not deny that '7 + 5 = 12', nor could we deny any other true mathematical proposition not because such a denial would involve a contradiction but because we should have to reject a fundamental intuition, and this was truly inconceivable.[2]

One might indeed think at first that the proposition

7 + 5 = 12 is a merely analytic proposition, which follows according to the principle of contradiction from the concept of a sum of seven and five. But if we look more closely, we find that the concept of the sum of 7 and 5 contains nothing further than the unification of the two numbers into a single number, and in this we do not in the least think what this single number may be which combines the two. The concept of twelve is in no way already thought by merely thinking this unification of seven and five, and though I analyse my concept of such a possible sum as long as I please, I shall never find the twelve in it. We have to go outside these concepts and with the help of the intuition which corresponds to one of them, our five fingers for instance or five points, add to the concept of seven, unit by unit, the five given in intuition. Thus we really amplify our concept by this proposition 7 + 5 = 12, and add to the first concept a new one which was not thought in it.

What makes us commonly believe that the predicate of such apodictic judgements is already contained in our concept and that the judgement is therefore analytic, is merely the ambiguity of the term. We *are required* to join in thought a certain predicate to a given concept, and this necessity is inherent in the concepts themselves. But the question is not what we are *required* to join *in thought* to the given concept, but what we *really think* in it, even if only obscurely. It is then manifest that while the predicate is indeed attached to the concept necessarily, it is so, not immediately, but by means of an intuition which must also be present.

The essential difference of pure *mathematical* knowledge from all other knowledge *a priori* is that it must *never* proceed *from concepts*, but always only by construction of concepts . . . . In its propositions pure mathematics must therefore go beyond the concept to what the corresponding intuition contains; hence its propositions can and should never originate from analysis of concepts, i.e. analytically, and are therefore without exception synthetic.

(*Prolegomena*, p. 19)

Judgements bringing observations under *a priori* concepts are synthetic *a priori* judgements. They can be regarded as principles by which we make sense of particular observed experiences:

> *Natural science (Physica)* contains in itself synthetic judgements *a priori* as principles. I will only cite a few propositions as examples: the propositions that in all changes in the corporeal world the quantity of matter remains unchanged, or that in all communication of movement action and reaction must always be equal. Both, it is clear, are not only necessary and *a priori* in origin, but also synthetic. For in the concept of matter I do not think its permanence but only its presence in space by occupying it. Thus I really go beyond the concept of matter in order to add to it *a priori* in thought something which I did not think in it. The proposition is therefore not analytic but synthetic, but yet thought *a priori*, and so are the other propositions of the pure part of natural science.
>
> (Ibid, p. 22)

'In all changes in the corporeal world the quantity of matter remains unchanged'.

Kant has argued that this proposition is synthetic because the attribute of the permanence of the *quantity* of matter throughout any chemical or physical change, is not part of the definition of matter. Matter is defined as 'that which occupies space'. Hence the proposition could not be found by analysis; therefore it is not analytic, it is synthetic.

On the other hand it is *a priori* because we can only think about matter as subsumed under the *a priori* concept of material objects. Material objects are things which do not and cannot appear from nothing or disappear into nothing; they have an objective permanence.

> *Properly metaphysical* judgements are without exception synthetic. Judgements *belonging to metaphysics* must be distinguished from properly *metaphysical* judgements. Very many among the former are analytic, but they only form the means to metaphysical judgements which are the whole aim of this science, and which are always synthetic.

For if a concept, e.g. that of substance, belongs to meta-physics, judgements which originate in mere analysis of this concept also belong necessarily to metaphysics, e.g. substance is that which only exists as subject etc. By means of several such analytic judgements we try to arrive at the definition of a concept. But as the analysis of a pure con-cept of the understanding (such as metaphysics contains) does not proceed in any other way than the analysis of all other concepts, empirical included, that do not belong to metaphysics (e.g. air is an elastic fluid, the elasticity of which is not suspended by any known degree of cold), the analytic judgement is not peculiarly metaphysical, even though the concept is. For this science has something special and peculiar to itself in the generation of its cognitions *a priori*, and this generation must therefore be distinguished from what the science has in common with all other know-ledge by the understanding; thus for example the propo-sition: everything that is substance in things is permanent, is a synthetic and peculiarly metaphysical proposition.

When the concepts *a priori* which constitute the matter of metaphysics and its building-stones have been collected according to certain principles, the analysis of these con-cepts is of great value. It can also be expounded separately from all the synthetic propositions which constitute meta-physics itself, as a distinct part (as it were as *philosophia definitiva*) containing nothing but analytic propositions belonging to metaphysics. For these analyses have in fact no appreciable utility anywhere else than in metaphysics, i.e. with a view to the synthetic propositions that are to be generated out of the concepts *a priori* when they have been analysed.   (Ibid, p. 22)

In the extract above, Kant has considered metaphysical judgements, that is judgements which are not subject to the test of physical observation. Some of these he says are not properly metaphysical but *belong to* metaphysics: for example, logical relations, and definitions. They are not properly meta-physical because, as he points out they are judgements about physical things. Thus a definition such as: 'Air is an elastic fluid, however low the temperature' is merely part of the definition of air. It is metaphysical, because its truth need not be subject to test by observation, but not 'properly metaphysical'. We now know that this proposition is false, air will liquefy at very low temperatures, (oxygen is separated from nitrogen because the two gases liquefy at different temperatures). But this was not known by Kant. He took it to be part of the definition of 'air' (just as before the discovery of the duckbill platypus, part of the definition of 'mammal' was that their young were born viviparously). For Kant the proposition about air was analogous to 'All bachelors are unmarried').

The value of these propositions, *belonging* to metaphysics, though not properly metaphysical, is that they can help us to generate properly metaphysical judgements, which are *a priori* synthetic judgements, from the *a priori* concepts. For example, as we have seen, mathematical relations are *a priori* and synthetic; they are properly metaphysical judgements because they do not refer to physical entities. But of course many mathematical judgements are derived by logical deduction and so make use of the metaphysical judgements which are not dependent on the *a priori* concepts but on deduction or definition.

Today we would say that no mathematical proposition is an *a priori* synthetic judgement. It was the hope of Russell and others to show that mathematics was a branch of logic (see below p. 195) but, though this has not been demonstrated, it is now accepted that mathematical propositions cannot be taken as *a priori* synthetic judgements, as Kant had supposed.

Thus the conclusion that Kant came to, namely that knowledge can be generated *a priori* by arriving at *a priori* synthetic propositions by analysis from *a priori* intuitions and concepts cannot be accepted. Nevertheless we shall find it profitable to consider the development of his argument.

The conclusion of this paragraph is therefore: that metaphysics has to do properly with synthetic propositions *a priori*, and these alone constitute its end, for which it does indeed require many analyses of its concepts and many analytic judgements, in which the procedure is no different from that in every other kind of knowledge when we merely try to clarify our concepts by analysis. But the *generation* of knowledge *a priori*, both according to intuition and according to concepts, and finally the generation of synthetic propositions *a priori* in philosophical knowlledge, constitutes the essential content of metaphysics.

(Ibid, p. 22)

Though the intuitions and concepts enabled us to make synthetic *a priori* judgements about the phenomena we perceived, it did not follow that our knowledge of the world was completely independent of experience.

Notwithstanding the independence of our pure concepts of the understanding and principles from experience, notwithstanding indeed the apparently greater extent of their use, nothing can be thought through them outside the field of experience, because they can do nothing but merely determine the logical form of the judgement in respect of given intuitions; and as there is no intuition whatever outside the field of sensibility, these pure concepts have no meaning whatever, for there is no means of exhibiting them *in concreto* ... our understanding is not a faculty of intuition but merely a faculty of the connection of given intuitions in experience. Hence experience must contain all the objects for our concepts, but beyond it all concepts will be without meaning as no intuition can be subsumed under them.

(Ibid, pp. 77–8)

For example, the concept of causality would have no meaning unless we had sense intuitions, subjective experiences which could be subsumed under that concept. In the *Critique of Pure Reason* Kant says:

Without sensibility no object could be given to us, without understanding no object could be thought. Thoughts without content are empty, intuitions without concepts are blind.   (*Critique*, p. 93)

Synthesis is general ... is the mere result of the power of

the imagination, a blind but indispensable function of the soul, without which we should have no knowledge whatsoever, but of which we are scarcely conscious. To bring this synthesis to concepts is a function which belongs to the understanding, and it is through this function of the understanding that we first obtain knowledge properly so called.

(*Prolegomena*, p. 112)

It must not be forgotten that, in respect of knowledge derived from perception, Kant always intends knowledge of phenomena. Scientific knowledge, just like common-sense knowledge, is knowledge of phenomena, not knowledge of things-in-themselves. He held that there was absolutely no reason to suppose that the limits of scientific knowledge were the limits of knowledge of reality. The latter was an indefinitely vast field.

Therefore, though Kant can be regarded as an empiricist in that he held that objective knowledge demanded sense experience, he parted company from the older empiricists in two ways:

(1)   He postulated an *a priori* element in all sense experience; not innate ideas, but an innate and essential *capacity* to structure sensations,

(2)   He did not claim knowledge of reality; he accepted that we could only know the world as we structured it, and this was a world of phenomena.

Now there are important and indeed lethal criticisms of Kant's approach to knowledge. Firstly, though he says that we can know nothing of things-in-themselves, and indeed implies that they might as well not be there, he does not deny that they are there, i.e. that there is a reality which transcends our experience. Yet, if he denies that we can know that things-in-themselves can affect us, and produce sensations in us, it is difficult to understand his grounds for affirming that they exist. Secondly Kant assumed that the basic intuition of space, one of the *a priori* intuitions needed even for subjective experience, had to be an intuition of Euclidean space. His premise is that we could not structure a world in any other sort of space so that objects (including geometrical ideal objects and figures) must conform to Euclidean geometry to be subjectively experienced. We now know that this is a false assumption; not only can we conceive of objects in non-Euclidean space, we hold that such space actually exists. Thirdly, even if we accept Kant's view that we must organise our percepts as physical objects linked by causal relations (i.e. in order that the sensations we have shall make sense that we should hold that every event has a cause), this can tell us nothing about the logical connection between specific events. We cannot say that any observed event (cause) is logically related to another event (its customary effect).

Kant assumed that the laws of Newtonian mechanics were necessarily true, that phenomena *had* to behave in accordance with these laws because we could not apprehend a world where this was not so. We *made* phenomena such that they did conform to those laws, and we would not have been able to understand a world where these laws did not hold. Again, this assumption is false; not only can we conceive a different mechanics, we believe that the actual world does not conform to the laws of Newtonian mechanics.

Lastly, the whole notion of synthetic *a priori* truth, with mathematics as the supreme example of such truth is rejected today. At the end of the nineteenth century Peano and Frege, followed by Russell and Whitehead, tried to show that mathematics could be treated as a branch of deductive logic. They failed but, nevertheless, it was apparent that mathematical propositions could not be regarded as synthetic *a priori* propositions. An indefinitely large number of mathematical propositions such as '7 + 5 = 12' can be regarded as analytic statements which can be shown to be true by logical analysis. The concept of '12' *is* contained in the concept of '7 + 5' and to deny the proposition '7 + 5 = 12' will involve a contradiction in the same way as the denial of the proposition 'This four-footed animal is not a quadruped' involves a contradiction.

Similarly geometrical theorems are simply the logical consequences of the axioms of the particular geometry from which they are derived. A geometrical system, such as the Euclidean system, is indeed *a priori*, but the system is constructed by us and there is no logical necessity for the world to conform to it. As Einstein said:

> As far as the laws of mathematics refer to reality, they are
> not certain; and as far as they are certain, they do not
> refer to reality.   (*Sidelights of Relativity*, p. 27)

Nevertheless, although it failed in its purpose, Kant's analysis has given us much greater insight into the nature of sense experience and much greater understanding of the complex assumptions which underly the most simple and commonplace observations. Warnock says:

> We are no doubt inclined to think of space and time as
> being simply 'given' features of the world. It is just the
> case that we find ourselves in a space of three dimensions,
> and that events occur successively in a single and irreversible
> time order. But Kant points out that there are further
> considerations which seem to be inconsistent with the idea
> that all this is a mere fact about the world. For one thing,
> we seem to find it inconceivable that space and time might
> have been, or might become, fundamentally different from
> what they are.   (*Crit. Hist. West. Phil.*, p. 301)

There are simple facts about the world, such as ravens being black, or pigs not flying which are 'what is the case'; but it is quite easy to imagine a world where ravens were rainbow coloured and pigs did fly. There is no logical difficulty about this. What we call contingent facts always could have been otherwise. Sometimes it is more difficult to imagine that a particular contingent fact could be otherwise, and we may then be tempted to say that it is a necessary fact. For example Kant held that it was necessary for space to be Euclidean space. It is only relatively recently that we have come to appreciate not only that this is a contingent fact but that it is possible to conceive, and indeed to observe, a non-Euclidean space. But when we come to imagine a space of more than three dimensions there does seem to be some at least quasi-logical barrier.

If it were similarly just a fact about the world that space

has three dimensions, it ought to be no less easy to suppose that it might have had two, or four or seven, but can we really make head or tail of such alleged possibilities? Do we know what a world of seven dimensions would be like? For another thing, we are evidently prepared to make assertions about space and time for which, if these are merely assertions of fact, we surely have not the necessary evidence. We are prepared to assert, without any qualification, that there is only *one* space; what evidence have we for so vast a claim? We take it to be certain that in any part of the universe the nature of temporal sequence will be the same as it is in our vicinity; but by what right . . . ? It appears, then . . . that we do not really treat assertions about space and time as ordinary assertions of fact — as assertions to which alternatives are perfectly conceivable and for which we require the warrant of empirical observation. . . . it appears rather that we approach the universe with the postulate that whatever it may anywhere contain, its contents *shall* be in a three-dimensional space, and that whatever events may at any time occur, they *shall* all have their places in a single time series; and it appears also that this postulate is for us the only one that is fully and genuinely intelligible.   (Ibid, p. 301)

Now, of course, it may be that there will come a day when we *can* conceive of different multi-dimensional spaces in the world, and, perhaps with the development of relativity theory, our notions of time sequence are already being modified to a set of time series. But two points made by Kant still stand: first we need to have some metaphysical framework and, secondly, our sensations can only give us intelligible experiences if they conform to our conceptual framework. Where we differ from Kant is in holding that there is one and only one possible framework. Where we agree, and this is far more important, is in acknowledging that Kant showed the necessity for some framework. At any time, only a certain *kind* of world, the world that conforms to our conceptual frame, can be understood. Our world, the world we experience through our senses, is, to a much greater extent than was appreciated before Kant's time, constructed by us.

It seems to be a contingent fact that our fundamental meta-physical presuppositions — that space is three dimensional, that physical objects exist, that there are causal relations — have remained unchanged. In the next chapter we shall see that it does not seem logically impossible for our world to be a world of ever-changing sensory qualities, rather than a world of objects. But, if we grant that our experiences emerge from our current metaphysical framework, then we can accept that we have the foundations for being certain of a certain *type* of empirical knowledge.

Our present metaphysical framework makes it *a priori* certain that there are physical objects and that there are regularities in the sequence of events. What it does not justify is any *a priori* certainty about specific synthetic judgements. Thus, though we may say it is certain that physical objects exist and that there are causal connections we cannot say *a priori* 'This particular physical object exists' or 'This particular event (a cause) will be followed by this other particular event (the effect)'.

Kant did not show that empirical knowledge can be as certain as logical knowledge. He did not resolve Hume's problem, and we have to accept Hume's dichotomy[3] between *a priori* relations of ideas (analytic judgements) and *a posteriori* relations of matters of fact (synthetic judgements). The quest for an empirical certainty, analogous to a logical certainty, about the course of events is impossible; but it does not follow that, as Kant feared, we can have no scientific knowledge. Although we are not justified in claiming that experience teaches us that things cannot be otherwise, we may be justified in appealing to evidence provided by experience. We may be justified as long as we do not insist that our knowledge be incorrigible.

Kant's analysis is not worthless, for it has shown us the limitations of empiricism and the necessity for metaphysical assumptions. It shows that reason and sense are not enough to give even the limited knowledge to which we can aspire. We have to accept some metaphysical assumptions in order to make sense of our sensations. Metaphysical speculation must be controlled, but it cannot be consigned to the flames.

FURTHER READING

I. Kant, *Prolegomena*, trans. P. Lucas.
W. H. Walsh, 'Categories', from R. P. Wolff (ed.), *Kant*.
G. J. Warnock, 'Kant', from O'Connor (ed.), *A Critical History of Western Philosophy*.

NOTES

1. Kant used the term 'body' to denote any physical object.

2. We assume that the proposition is understood; mistakes in mathematics are certainly conceivable.

3. In fact the dichotomy has been questioned, see Quine, *From a Logical Point of View* (1953) but we shall not discuss this here.

9

Knowledge and Perception

At the end of the last chapter it was stated that we may be justified in claiming knowledge of matters of fact by appealing to evidence provided by experience, that is evidence provided by sense perception. In this chapter we shall discuss the reliability of that evidence, and whether it does indeed justify a claim to knowledge of matters of fact.

Common sense relates perception directly to the world: 'I know, I was there', 'I saw it with my own eyes', 'I heard the very words', 'I actually touched it', 'I smell bacon for breakfast'. Common sense leads us to believe that we know about the external world directly through our senses. It supports the view that, in general, the world about us is as it appears to be, i.e. as it appears to us. Reflecting common sense will modify this rather crude belief, in that, on reflection, we will come to acknowledge that sensations have been interpreted, and that what we experience is not merely a passively received stimulation. But, in general, it is held that most interpretation demands little effort. In addition, reflecting common sense will acknowledge that there can be perceptual mistakes, but these are thought to be infrequent and almost always easily corrected. Thus common sense tells us that, as a rule, our senses give clear and direct information about the outside world. This common-sense position is the position of the naive realist, the position of that mythical animal, the man in the street.

We have already seen that the common-sense position has

been attacked by philosophers. Philosophy is not infrequently criticised as an absurd activity because it urges us to question our common-sense beliefs and assumptions. But, by now, we should be aware that it is not absurd to pose such questions; it is the critics of philosophy who are at fault. Indeed, in regard to the evidence offered by perception, natural science as well as philosophy, will tell us that common sense can be a misleading guide — a guide which is liable to bring us to false conclusions and untenable positions. Common sense said that the earth was flat, that the sky was an arched dome and that the sun moved across the sky. Science as well as philosophy, teaches us that things are not always what they seem. Nevertheless, all of us start from common-sense assumptions and beliefs, and any starting point must be treated with respect. We do have to start from somewhere if we are going to progress. Therefore it is up to those who wish to correct common sense, to establish their case and to show the defects of the common-sense position. It is also up to them to provide and to justify an alternative account.

The philosopher, like the scientist, starts by asking questions, and the two groups of philosophical questions about perception are:

(1) How far can the senses be trusted to reveal the nature of the external world?[1] Can perception give us knowledge of the world, and, if so, to what extent? Are things as they seem? Is appearance reality?

(2) How can we explain the action of the senses as intermediaries between us and the external world? How do physiological processes lead to conscious awareness? What is the nature of perceptual consciousness?

In relation to epistemology, we can set the problem of perceptual consciousness aside. It is a philosophical question which must be considered when discussing the problem of the relation between mind and body. All the same, we must accept that any answer to the first group of questions must not be incompatible with the fact there is perceptual consciousness and that there are sense organs and physiological events (chemical and physical changes in our bodies) involved in perception.

There may be some objection to the question 'Is appearance

reality?', for, in chapter 1, it was argued that general questions about reality were suspect. 'Real' is a word which needs to be attached to a subject in order to be significant — it is substantive-hungry. In addition it is a trouser-word, and must be contrasted with the non-real.

Our question implies that 'reality' is the reality of everything perceivable — the substantive is the perceivable cosmos. But then we have nothing non-real to provide a comparison. Hence we may be tempted to conclude that questions such as 'Is appearance reality?' are meaningless. If there is doubt as to whether the cosmos we perceive is the real cosmos we may counter by saying that it will do very well for us until we become acquainted with the real one.

In effect this will be the counter that is offered in this chapter, so that we shall not arrive at a judgement as to the reliability of perception which is markedly different from the judgement of common sense. But there will be some differences. In this context to say that appearance *is* reality is to say that things are as they seem. But that is misleading for things are not *always* what they seem. Therefore in this context we must be able to draw a distinction between appearance and reality.

But first we should remind ourselves that there is a philosophical position which contrasts the perceivable world of appearances with another kind of world, a world which is apprehended by the mind. In chapter 2 we read that Plato contrasted the changing world of sense perception with the immutable world of Universals. In his view, the world of appearances could not be truly real because it was always changing and therefore could not be an object of knowledge. He held that the empirical world which was presented in sense perception was but a pale shadow of the intelligible world which could come to be apprehended through mental contemplation. Sense perception was not entirely useless, because it could remind us of the world of Universals and could stimulate us to try to apprehend this world. But sense perception could never give knowledge because it gave no direct access to the reality of the world of Universals.

Belief in the existence of a world of Universals is a metaphysical belief, one which cannot be justified by appeal to sense perception or deduced by logical analysis. We are only concerned with metaphysics in so far as it provides us with assumptions. If we reject Plato's metaphysics, and his view of the nature of reality, we must be concerned with the appearances delivered by sense perception. But even if we are disposed to accept Plato's view that ultimate reality is not in the world of sense perception, we can still be concerned with the extent to which perception gives us true opinion of the shadowy empirical world. Here, we shall take 'the world' to be the empirical world and we shall not debate the metaphysical question of some ultimate reality beyond the world of sense perception. Hence we are bound to offer some interpretation of a question such as 'Is appearance reality?' for the only world we admit is the world available to us through our senses.

The interpretation offered is elaborated by Professor Ayer in a quotation towards the end of this chapter. Here it is only necessary to point out that the question 'Is appearance reality?' is not intended to imply that our senses may always deceive us, but rather to imply that our access to the external world may always be indirect. We are asking whether we *perceive* things, or whether we receive sensations, on the basis of which we *infer* what things are like. We are asking whether there is always a gap between the appearances (what we sense) and the reality (what is actually there). This does have a bearing on the question of the possibility of knowledge through perception for, if the senses give us direct and immediate access to the world, we shall be more confident that they give grounds for knowledge, than if we must infer from what they deliver. In the latter case there is a possibility of mistaken inferences, and our claim to know the external world from sense perception is not so well-supported.

In chapter 4 we saw that Descartes held that all perception involved some inference, and also that some of the qualities which we sensed were not intrinsic properties of the objects perceived, but were due to the action of those objects on us. These were the *secondary* qualities, such qualities as colours, tastes and smells. On the other hand, *primary* qualities, such as extension and motion were not just the result of an interaction with perceivers, they were 'really' properties of the objects perceived.

In chapter 6 we saw that the notion of primary and secondary[2] qualities was developed by Locke, and led to what is called the representative theory of perception. Berkeley and Hume also held that only *ideas* (called *impressions* by Hume) could be directly known. At first, the suggestion that we can only have *direct* knowledge of our own sensations or representations is appealing but, as was explained in chapter 6, this can lead to difficulties. Again, as we saw in chapter 6, one development of Berkeley's immaterialism (the view that nothing but perceivers [who were immaterial] and what they perceived [i.e. *ideas*] existed, so that talk of physical objects was equivalent to talking of *ideas*), is the modern philosophical account of perception called phenomenalism. Both these views are to be criticised in this chapter.

But, though neither view will be accepted, the fact that both merit serious attention, and, indeed that they raise questions which require an answer, shows us that the naive realist view (the common-sense view) of perception, needs to be justified.

Leaving aside, for the moment, the fact that there are perceptual mistakes, such as illusions and hallucinations (and it is fair to leave this aside since it can be accommodated to the common-sense account without great difficulty), we have to accept that *all* we can learn about the external world must depend on our senses and our interpretation of what they deliver. This is not to say that we acquire knowledge from sensations alone. All that is being asserted is that knowledge of the world is not possible without sensations, i.e. without consciously appreciated sense experiences.

We are then faced with three specific questions, which are elaborations of our first main question:
(a) Is there an external world at all and are there objects in it?
(b) If it does exist do we have direct access to it?
(c) If we do have direct access how much can we claim to know?

One answer to (a) (which is such that it answers all the others) is given by the sceptic. The sceptic asserts that we cannot claim to know that anything exists apart from our own percepts, and the extreme sceptic is the solipsist who asserts that the only things he or she can claim to know are his or her own experiences. This, as we saw when considering the Cartesian *cogito* is to claim very little indeed, and Descartes himself did not of course use the *cogito* to support scepticism but to reject it. However a diehard sceptic cannot be refuted by argument: though I personally *know* that any sceptic is wrong in claiming that the only certainty is that he or she exists, because *I know* that I exist, I have to concede that the sceptic is not logically compelled to accept my claim. But, though it is not possible to demonstrate that the sceptic is wrong it does not follow that the sceptic is right. Russell says:

In one sense it must be admitted that we can never *prove* the existence of things other than ourselves and our experiences. No logical absurdity results from the hypothesis that the world consists of myself and my thoughts and feelings and sensations, and that everything else is mere fancy. In dreams a very complicated world may seem to be present, and yet on waking we find it was a delusion; that is to say, we find that the sense-data in the dream do not appear to have corresponded with such physical objects as we should naturally infer from our sense-data. (It is true that, when the physical world is assumed, it is possible to find physical causes for the sense-data in dreams: a door banging, for instance, may cause us to dream of a naval engagement. But although, in this case, there is a physical *cause* for the sense-data, there is not a physical object *corresponding* to the sense-data in the way in which an actual naval battle would correspond.) There is no logical impossibility in the supposition that the whole of life is a dream, in which we ourselves create all the objects that come before us. But although this is not logically impossible, there is no reason whatever to suppose that it is true; and it is, in fact, a less simple hypothesis, viewed as a means of accounting for the facts of our own life, than the common-sense hypothesis that there really are objects independent of us, whose action on us causes our sensations.

The way in which simplicity comes in from supposing that there really are physical objects is easily seen. If the cat appears at one moment in one part of the room, and at another in another part, it is natural to suppose that it has moved from the one to the other, passing over a series of intermediate positions. But if it is merely a set of sense-data, it cannot have ever been in any place where I did not see it; thus we shall have to suppose that it did not exist at all while I was not looking, but suddenly sprang into being in a new place. If the cat exists whether I see it or not, we can understand from our own experience how it gets hungry between one meal and the next; but if it does not exist when I am not seeing it, it seems odd that appetite should grow during non-existence as fast as during existence. And if the cat consists only of sense-data, it cannot be *hungry*, since no hunger but my own can be a sense-datum to me. Thus the behaviour of the sense-data which represent the cat to me, though it seems quite natural when regarded as an expression of hunger, becomes utterly inexplicable when regarded as mere movements and changes of patches of colour, which are as incapable of hunger as a triangle is of playing football.

But the difficulty in the case of the cat is nothing compared to the difficulty in the case of human beings. When human beings speak — that is when we hear certain noises which we associate with ideas, and simultaneously see certain motions of lips and expressions of face — it is very difficult to suppose that what we hear is not the expression of a thought as we know it would be if we emitted the same sounds. Of course similar things happen in dreams, where we are mistaken as to the existence of other people. But dreams are more or less suggested by what we call waking life, and are capable of being more or less accounted for on scientific principles if we assume that there really is a physical world. Thus every principle of simplicity urges us to adopt the natural view, that there really are objects other than ourselves and our sense-data which have an existence not dependent upon our perceiving them.

Of course it is not by argument that we originally come by our belief in an independent external world. We find this belief ready in ourselves as soon as we begin to reflect: it is what may be called an *instinctive* belief. We should never have been led to question this belief but for the fact that, at any rate in the case of sight, it seems as if the sense-datum itself were instinctively believed to be the independent object, whereas argument shows that the object cannot be identical with the sense-datum. This discovery, however — which is not at all paradoxical in the case of taste and smell and sound, and only slightly so in the case of touch — leaves undiminished our instinctive belief that there *are* objects *corresponding* to our sense-data. Since this belief does not lead to any difficulties, but on the contrary tends to simplify and systematize our account of our experiences, there seems no good reason for rejecting it. We may therefore admit — though with a slight doubt derived from dreams — that the external world does really exist, and is not wholly dependent for its existence upon our continuing to perceive it.   (*The Problems of Philosophy*, ch. 2)

So, if we grant that there is an external world, and that there are physical objects existing independently, and that there are people like ourselves, then we have to consider whether our senses give us direct knowledge of this world and its inhabitants. We have seen that many philosophers, Locke, Berkeley, Hume and Kant, thought that they did not. Russell also contends that we have no direct access to the world, so that all we can know directly, and for certain, are our own experiences. These consist of inner thoughts and feelings and of consciously appreciated sensations; it is the latter which may be called sense data.

The notion of sense data has been developed from Locke's and Berkeley's account of *ideas* and from Hume's account of *impressions*. Sense data are sensations: colours, shapes, sounds, smells, tastes and 'feels' of which we are directly aware when we are perceiving. Examples of each kind of sense experience are given by Descartes in his account of the wax (see chapter 4) but it will be remembered that Descartes did *not* think that these sense experiences gave knowledge. By contrast, sense-data theorists hold that sense experiences provide the only certain and indubitable knowledge that we can have of the external world. They say that the only things of which any person can be sure of are his or her experiences, and, in regard to the external world, the relevant information comes from those experiences which are sense data.

It might seem that they were thereby encouraging a form of solipsism or, at the very least, an alarmingly subjectivist view of knowledge from perception; for sense data are of necessity private to each person. They are private in the sense that each person can only experience his or her own experiences; for instance I cannot have your experiences and you cannot have mine. But, though it is a logical truth that my experiences are mine and no-one else's, and yours are yours and no-one else's, it does not follow that others cannot have similar experiences. The fact that we seem to communicate is very good evidence that we do have similar experiences. No-one can prove that this is so, just as no-one can refute the sceptic, but, in this text, we shall assume that there is genuine communication between people and that they can and do have similar experiences.

On any given occasion, differences between perceptual experiences may be accounted for as being due to differences of position (in space and also in time) and to physiological and psychological differences, among the individuals concerned. For example, if two people look at a table they will have different visual experiences, i.e. different visual sense data, because they will be looking from different angles; if two people look at a sunset, from the same place but one after the other, they will have different visual sense data; if a tone-deaf person and a musician listen to a symphony they will have different auditory sense data; if someone with a cold and someone who is healthy eat roast beef they will have different taste and smell sense data; a person who is frightened of heights will have sense data different from a person who is not so frightened when they are both on the battlements of a castle. But, though in these and in all other circumstances, each person's sense data will be unique, there will be enough common ground, at least in the vast majority of cases, for there to be a large measure of agreement as to the nature of the external world.

For the sense-data theorist, knowledge of the nature of the external world depends on the information provided by sense data. It follows that, for them, all entities, and in particular all physical objects: stars, sunsets, rivers, tables and atoms, must be regarded as inferences from sense data.

Now there are two ways of treating these inferences. One is the phenomenalist treatment which, as indicated earlier, can be regarded as a development of Berkeley's immaterialism. Phenomenalists hold that since sense data are all that we can know, it must be possible to give a complete description of any physical object entirely in terms of actual and potential sense data. They hold that any statement about a physical object will be translatable into a statement about sense data, without any loss of significance. It follows that physical objects must be regarded as *logical* constructs from sense data, and that the concept of any given physical object is logically equivalent to the concept of a specified collection of sense data.

This view has been opposed by Professor Ayer. We shall consider Ayer's views of perception; he is the first contemporary philosopher to be discussed, and we shall discuss this aspect of his work because, like many other aspects, it has had and is having a great influence on current thought. Ayer was born in 1910 and became known very early, after the publication of his book *Language Truth and Logic*, in 1936. There he championed an approach to knowledge which was called logical positivism. Logical positivisits were anxious to establish a criterion of meaning, so that they could distinguish genuine empirical propositions such as 'It is raining', from metaphysical statements such as 'The universe is eternal'. They held that metaphysical propositions were meaningless — like Hume they thought they might as well be thrown into the flames! The criterion adopted was that of the possibility of verification by observation: if a proposition was verifiable by observation then it could be regarded as a genuine empirical proposition which had meaning and significance. It did not follow that the proposition had to be *true*; after all 'It is raining' might be false, but it did follow that it had a meaning because observation could establish whether it was true or false. There was a distinction drawn between 'strong' and 'weak' verifiability: 'A proposition is said to be verifiable in the strong sense . . . if and only if, its truth could be conclusively established by experience. But it is verifiable in the weak sense, if it is possible for experience to render it probable.'

(*Language Truth and Logic*, p. 37)

Unfortunately the criterion of weak verifiability is not satisfactory: either it excludes propositions that our intuition tells us should be included, propositions such as 'All ravens are black', for instance, or it includes the very propositions that we had wanted to exclude, such as 'The universe is infinite', and, indeed, all metaphysical propositions. Although logical positivism has been abandoned by Ayer, it does raise very interesting and important philosophical questions, but we shall not consider these here. The quotations from Ayer's works are from *The Problem of Knowledge* (1956) and *The Central Questions of Philosophy* (1973). As we saw, the phenomenalist[3] position is that any statements about any physical object can be completely satisfactorily 'translated' into statements about sense-data. In the extract below Ayer argues that this is not the case.

In the sense in which it is compatible with naive realism, the causal theory is compatible also with phenomenalism; that is, with the thesis that physical objects are logical constructions out of sense-data, or, in other words, that the sceptic's gap is to be bridged by a reduction of the way things are to the way they seem. The phenomenalist need not deny that the manner in which sense-data occur can be explained in terms of entities which are not themselves observable; he will, however, add that to talk about such unobservable entities is, in the end, to talk about sense-data. For the position which he takes is that every empirical statement about a physical object, whether it seems to refer to a scientific entity or to an object of the more familiar kind that we normally claim to perceive, is reducible to a statement, or set of statements, which refer exclusively to sense-data.

The first difficulty which the phenomenalist has to meet is that physical objects, unlike sense-data, can exist without being perceived. To say this is not to beg the question against Berkeley. It is simply that we so define our terms that unless a thing has the ability to exist unperceived it is not counted as a physical object. This is not in itself to say that anything satisfies this condition, and one might interpret Berkeley as maintaining that nothing except minds did satisfy it; that there were in fact no physical objects, or rather, that there could not be. I doubt, however, if this interpretation would be altogether just to him. He did allow that things that commonly pass for physical objects could continue to exist when only God perceived them: and to say of something that it is perceived only by God is to say that it is not, in any ordinary sense, perceived at all. But, whatever Berkeley's position may have been, the phenomenalist does not deny that there are physical objects. His contention is just that, if there are any, they are constituted by sense-data. Whether there are any is a matter of empirical fact, which as such does not concern him. It is enough for him that there could be physical objects; his problem is then to analyse the statements which refer to them. And here the fact that it is possible for physical objects to exist when they are not perceived introduces a complication into his analysis. It obliges him to hold that the statements about sense-data, into which, according to his programme, statements about physical objects are to be translated, are themselves predominantly hypothetical. They will for the most part have to state not that any sense-data are actually occurring, but only that in a given set of circumstances certain sense-data would occur. In other words, the majority of the statements will not describe how things actually do seem to anyone, but only how they would seem if the appropriate conditions were fulfilled.

. . .

John Stuart Mill, who held a phenomenalist position, summarized it by describing physical objects as 'permanent possibilities of sensation'. But a permanent possibility of sensation is not something that can very well be pictured. In Plato's myth, the shadows on the wall of the cave, which are all that the prisoners can see, are contrasted with substantial objects outside. Phenomenalism seems to leave us with nothing but the shadows.

But while this may account for the psychological resistance with which phenomenalists so very often meet, it does not show that their thesis is false. However hard they may make it for us to construct an imaginative picture of the physical world, they may still be right in claiming that

statements about physical objects are reducible to statements about sense-data, that to talk about the way things
are comes down in the end to talking about the way they
would seem. The character of their thesis is, in a broad
sense, logical, and it must be submitted to a logical examination. Even so, I do not think that it succeeds.

Let us begin by remarking one of the more obvious difficulties. In the most common case, where it is not implied
that a physical object is actually being perceived, to describe
it is supposed to be wholly a matter of saying how it would
appear, that is, what sense-data there would be if certain
conditions were fulfilled. Roughly speaking, the conditions
are those which are required for the object, if it exists, to
be perceptible. But how are these conditions to be specified? It is not enough for the phenomenalist to make such
vague assertions as that what he means by saying that there
is a table in the next room is that if he were there he would
perceive it. For his being there is a matter of a physical
body's being in a certain spatial relationship to other physical objects, and, on the assumption that the talk about physical objects is always to talk about sense-data, this situation
must itself be described in purely sensory terms. But it is
not at all easy to see how this could be done. One may
avoid a part of the difficulty simply by eliminating any
reference to an observer. This does not imply that there
could be sense-data without observers: it must be remembered that we have not so far succeeded in giving any
meaning to speaking of sense-data except as a way of
describing how things seem to people; so that, in any talk
of this kind, some reference to an observer remains implicit.
But the point is that it need not be explicit. There is no
need to bring in a description of any particular person. It
would, indeed, be incorrect to do so except in the cases
where a particular person is actually mentioned in the
statement to be analysed. The hypothetical observer must
be, as it were, outside the picture. Otherwise we should
have to reckon with the possibility that his presence would
somehow affect the situation: and clearly this would falsify
the analysis.

But even if one need not mention the observer, one has

still to 'place' the situation in which the observations are supposed to be made. One has to describe the setting in which the occurrence of certain sense-data is to be taken as establishing the existence of the physical object in question; and this description must be purely sensory. But it would seem hardly possible to find a set of sensory descriptions which would sufficiently distinguish one place from another. And when it comes to times the difficulty is even more obvious. Suppose, for example, that the problem were to give a phenomenalist translation of such a statement as that Julius Caesar crossed the Rubicon in 49 BC. How would one set about rendering '49 BC' in purely sensory terms? To this the phenomenalist may reply that we do in fact succeed in identifying places and times by making observations; we note features of the landscape, look at watches and calendars, and so forth; and these performances in the end consist in our sensing sense-data. It does not follow, however, that any description of these sense-data would be sufficient to identify the place or time uniquely; and so long as no such description is found the phenomenalist's reduction has not been carried out.

I do not dwell upon this point because it is only a special case of a more general difficulty, which is, I think, fatal to phenomenalism. If the phenomenalist is right, the existence of a physical object of a certain sort must be a sufficient condition for the occurrence, in the appropriate circumstances, of certain sense-data; there must, in short, be a deductive step from descriptions of physical reality to descriptions of possible, if not actual, appearances. And conversely, the occurrence of the sense-data must be a sufficient condition for the existence of the physical object; there must be a deductive step from descriptions of actual, or at any rate possible, appearances to descriptions of physical reality. The decisive objection to phenomenalism is that neither of these requirements can be satisfied.

. . .

At the present moment there is indeed no doubt, so far as I am concerned, that this table, this piece of paper, this pen, this hand, and many other physical objects exist. I know that they exist, and I know it on the basis of my sense-experiences. Even so, it does not follow that the assertion of their existence, or of the existence of any one of them, is logically entailed by any description of my sense-experiences. The fuller such a description is made, assuming all the evidence to be favourable, the more far-fetched becomes the hypothesis that the physical object in question does not in fact exist; the harder it is, in short, to explain the appearances away. But this is still not to say that the possibility of explaining them away is ever *logically* absent. At what precise point would the suggested explanation cease to be merely fanciful and become formally incompatible with the evidence? For the phenomenalist to succeed, he must be able to produce a specimen set of statements, describing the occurrence in particular conditions of certain specified sense-data, from which it follows logically that a given physical object exists. And I do not see how this is to be achieved.

But it is doubtful whether the occurrence of a given series of sense-data can ever be a sufficient condition for the existence of a physical object, it is, I think, even more doubtful whether the existence of the physical object can be a sufficient condition for the occurrence of the sense-data. Those who think that it may be sufficient are assuming that with respect to any physical object which is capable of being perceived, it is possible to specify a set of conditions such that if any observer satisfies them he must perceive it. This point of view is expressed in a rough way by Berkeley when he claims that to say, for example, that the earth moves is to say that 'if we were placed in such and such circumstances, and such or such a position and distance, both from the earth and the sun, we should perceive the former to move'. But, setting aside the difficulty, which we have already noticed, of describing the circumstances in purely sensory terms, it might very well happen that when we were placed in them we did not perceive the earth to move at all, not because it was not moving, but because we were inattentive, or looking in the wrong direction, or our view was in some way obscured, or because we were suffering from some physiological or psychological disorder. It might indeed be thought that such obstacles could be provided for. Thus we might attempt to rule out the possibility of the observer's suffering from a physiological disorder by adding a further hypothetical to the effect that if a physiologist were to examine him, or rather, were to seem to be examining him, it would seem to the physiologist that his patient's vision was unimpaired. But then we should require a further hypothetical to guard against the possibility that the physiologist himself was undergoing an illusion: and so *ad infinitum*. This is not to say that the fact that some physical object fails to be observed is never to be counted as a proof that it does not exist. On the contrary, it is, under certain conditions, the very best proof obtainable. But it is not a demonstrative proof. From the fact that in the specified conditions the requisite sense-data do not occur, it does not follow logically that the physical object in question does not exist, or that it does not have the properties it is supposed to have. In many cases this is the obvious, indeed the only reasonable, explanation of the facts; but the possibility of an alternative explanation must always remain open.

It may still be thought that this difficulty can be met by stipulating that the test for the presence or absence of the physical object is to be carried out in normal conditions by a normal observer: this is, indeed, the assumption that is tacitly made by those who maintain that to speak of any such object as existing unperceived is to imply that if one were in the appropriate situation one would be perceiving it. But this is merely a way of concealing the difficulty, not of resolving it. If we are to understand by 'normal' conditions those conditions that permit an observer to perceive things as they really are, and by a 'normal' observer one who in such conditions does perceive things as they really are, then certainly it will follow, from the fact that there is a physical object in such and such a place, that if a normal observer were there he would under normal conditions be perceiving it. But it will follow just because it is made to follow by our definition of normality. And the difficulty which we are trying to avoid will reappear immediately as the difficulty of making sure that the conditions and the observer really are, in this sense, normal.

We may try to make sure by stipulating that if tests were made for every known source of abnormality, their results would all appear to be negative. But there again we shall need an infinite series of further hypotheticals to guarantee the tests themselves. Neither is it necessarily true that the sources of abnormality that are known to us are all the sources that there are. It follows that the step from descriptions of physical reality to descriptions of possible appearances cannot by this method be made formally deductive: nor, as far as I can see, can it be made so by any other.

We must conclude then, if my reasoning is correct, that the phenomenalist's programme cannot be carried through. Statements about physical objects are not formally translatable into statements about sense-data. In itself, indeed, this conclusion is not startling. It is rather what one would expect if one reflected merely on the way in which sentences which refer to physical objects are actually used. That phenomenalism has commanded so strong an allegiance has been due not to its being intrinsically plausible but rather to the fact that the introduction of sense-data appeared to leave no other alternative open. It has been assumed that since statements about physical objects can be verified or falsified only through the occurrence of sense-data, they must somehow be reducible to statements about sense-data. This is a natural assumption to make, but the result of our examining it has been to show that it is false.

(*The Problem of Knowledge*, ch. 3, p. 118 *et seq*)

Ayer has argued, convincingly in my view, that the existence of any physical object is not logically entailed by any description of a person's actual or potential sense data. For phenomenalism to be acceptable, it would have to be possible to produce a set of statements of the occurrences of sense data from which it would follow *logically* that a given physical object existed; it would also be necessary to show that the existence of any physical object was a *logically* sufficient condition for the occurrence of sense data. This cannot be done.

But, as already stated, there is a second way of approaching the relation of sense data to physical objects. Physical objects can be regarded as theoretical constructs from sense data, rather than as logical constructs. The statement that there are physical objects, can be taken as a hypothesis to explain and account for the fact that we have the sense data which we do have. It is then perfectly acceptable to say that physical objects have properties which transcend the sense data that provide evidence for their existence. Just as we can say that the theory of gravitational attraction implies more than the fact that bodies fall to the earth with approximately constant acceleration and that the planets have approximately elliptical orbits, so we can say that the existence of physical objects implies more than the possibility of their being observed. If we take physical objects to be theoretical constructs we can say that the existence and the nature of the external world and of physical objects in that world is *inferred* from the evidence provided by sense data. It might seem that this view is clearly right; it seems almost perverse to deny that there is and must be inference. Indeed it can be argued that common-sense realists do infer and that the flaw in their account of perception is that, because the inference is so spontaneous, it is overlooked.

We can grant that there is a spontaneous inference as to the existence of an external world — Russell called it an instinctive belief — and that the common-sense realist is at fault in overlooking this, but it is arguable whether this inference arises as a result of the evidence provided by sense data. It is arguable that sense data are more fundamental than are physical objects.

Ayer concedes that it would not be impossible to describe our experiences meaningfully in terms of sense data. Indeed he says that it may be merely a contingent fact, i.e. it may just happen to be the case, that this is *not* the way we do describe the world. It may be a contingent psychological fact about human nature or a contingent sociological fact about the human groups which have emerged, that we take physical objects as our basic data, save in exceptional circumstances. Our claim to knowledge from perception is based on the assumption that we do have direct access to physical objects. These objects are held to be 'public' because they are accessible to all observers who are suitably placed. They are, as explained above, a source of similar sense data for different observers. The sense data remain private, but the objects are public and these are taken as fundamental.

We can appreciate how basic is our perception of physical objects, if we consider the meaning of the term 'sense datum'. Sense data have been described as consciously appreciated sensations, but, as will be seen in the quotation from Ayer below, it is a matter of convention as to what we take to be a single sense datum. Moreover, whatever we decide, the account we give will seem meaningful because the sense data selected are related to physical objects. Sense data, as Ayer puts it, are given the status of 'seeming objects'.

For example, if I look out of the window and see a cow, I would normally say 'There is a cow outside'. But, if asked to produce a statement which was indubitable, I might say 'It seemed to me that there was a cow outside'. I can be certain that it seemed to me that there was a cow, even if I admit that there is a chance that really no cow was there. As Ayer points out, all that sense-data theorists are doing is proposing an alteration in the way we describe our experiences. They propose that instead of saying 'It seemed to me that there was a cow outside' I should say 'I experienced a cow-sense-datum' or 'I saw a seeming-cow'. The noun 'seeming-cow' does the work of the verb 'it *seemed to be* a cow'. In one sense this is purely a matter of convention, but, as Ayer points out, we have replaced a public object, the cow, by a private object, the seeming-cow, and this could lead us back to solipsism.

Even so there is something suspect about their procedure. The transition from 'it now seems to me that I see *x*' to 'there is seeming-*x* which I now see' may be defended on the ground that the second sentence is merely a reformulation of the first, a reformulation which it is convenient to make because it is simpler and neater, in the contexts for which such sentences might be required, to make nouns do the work of verbs, to talk of sense-data rather than of how things seem to people. But, if this is allowed, one must be careful to say nothing about sense-data that cannot be translated back into the terminology of seeming. The danger is that these private objects, which have been brought into existence as a matter of literary convenience, become independent of their origin. Questions arise about the criteria for the self-identity of these objects, the means of distinguishing one of them from another, the possibility of their changing, the duration of their existence; and one may think that mere inspection of them will provide the answers. But the position is rather that until such questions have been answered there are no objects to inspect. It is from the way in which we *decide* to answer them that the term 'sense-datum' acquires a more definite use. But how are these decisions to be reached? How, for example, are we to determine what is to count as one sense-datum? At the present moment it seems to me that I see the walls of a house, covered with virginia creeper, and a rose tree climbing to an open window, and two dogs asleep upon a terrace, and a lawn bespeckled with buttercups and clover, and many other things besides; and it seems to me that I hear, among other things, the buzzing of insects and the chirruping of birds. How many visual or auditory sense-data am I sensing? And at what point are they replaced by others? If one of the dogs seems to stir in its sleep does this create a new sense-datum for me or merely transform an old one? And if it is to be new, do all the others remain the same? Clearly the answers to these questions will be arbitrary; the appearance of the whole frontage of the house may be treated as one sense-datum, or it may be divided into almost any number. The difficulty is to find a rule that would be generally applicable. It might be suggested, for example, that we should say that there were, for a given observer at any given moment, as many visual sense-data as there were features that he could visually discriminate: but this again raises the question of what is to count as a single feature. And similar objections may be made to any other ruling that I can think of. The correct reply may, therefore, be that these questions do not admit of a definite answer, any more than there is a definite answer to the question how many parts a thing can have, or how much it can change without altering its identity. That is to say, there are no general rules from which the answers to such questions can be derived; but this does not mean that they cannot be given answers in particular cases. In the present instance, I can choose to speak of there being a sense-datum of the rose tree, or a sense-datum of one of its roses, or of one of the petals of the rose, or even just a sense-datum of something red; the only condition is that I in every case refer to something which it now seems to me that I see. And if it be asked whether my present contemplation of the rose tree yields me one sense-datum of it, or a series, and if it is a series, how many members it has, the answer once again is that there can be as many as I choose to distinguish. No single sense-datum can outlast the experience of which it helps to make up the content; but then it is not clear what is to count as one experience. I can distinguish the experience I am having now from those that I have had at different times in the past, but if I were asked how many experiences I had had, for example, during the last five minutes, I should not know what to answer: I should not know how to to set about counting. The question would appear to have no meaning. It does not follow, however, that I cannot at any given moment delimit some experience which I am then having: the boundaries may be fluid, but I can say confidently of certain things that they fall within the experience, and of others that they do not. And for our present purposes this may be all that is required.

It must then be admitted that the notion of a sense-datum is not precise. Moreover, it appears to borrow what little precision it has from the way in which we talk about physical objects. If I can pick out my present sense-datum of a rose it is because roses are things for which there are established criteria of identity. It is, in fact, only by the use of expressions which refer to the perception of physical objects that we have given any meaning to talking of sense-data at all. And it is hard to see how else we could have proceeded if we were to have any hope of being intelligible. This seems to me, however, to be a matter of psychology rather than of logic. If one has to describe the use of an unfamiliar terminology, the description, in order to be informative, must be given in terms of what is already understood; and we are all brought up to understand a form of language in which the perception of physical objects is treated as the standard case. But this is a contingent fact: it is surely not inconceivable that there should be a language in which sense-experiences were described by the use of purely qualitative expressions which carried no reference to the appearances of physical objects. Such a language would not be very useful, but it could be adequate for the description of any given experience. Neither do I see any reason *a priori* why someone who had devised it as a means of recording his own experiences should not succeed in teaching it to others.

(Ibid, ch. 3)

Ayer does not dismiss the sense-data account of perception, but he does not regard it as a practical substitute for the realist account. In *The Central Questions of Philosophy* he discusses the question of *what* we perceive, in the light of the sense-data theory. Sense-data theorists assert that we perceive sense data, that is our own sensations, and that it is a mistake to say that we perceive physical objects. Ayer points out that this cannot be an ordinary sort of mistaken identification, because ordinary mistakes of identification must be contrasted with situations in which there is no such mistake. We can admit that we have mistakenly identified a piece of Monopoly paper as a pound note because we can compare it with a genuine pound note. We detect ordinary mistakes by comparing them with situations where there is no mistake; ordinary mistakes are detectable, and may be corrigible. But if *all* our percepts are of sense data and not of objects, then there can be no possibility of detecting or correcting the mistake. It must be a different sort of mistake, a mistake about the nature of the information provided by perception:

The suggestion is that when I look, or at any rate believe myself to be looking, at the table in front of me, what I primarily see is not the table at all but something else, which has the impermanence and perhaps also the subjectivity of a mental image. In general, this view has been advanced as if it were an empirical discovery, with the implication that the naive realist who thinks that he does see the table is simply mistaken on a question of empirical fact. Thus, Professor Prichard, who thought it correct to say that we see colours, is supposed to have remarked of the ordinary man that when he sees a colour he 'straight off mistakes it for a body'. In this way, all our ordinary judgements of perception are assimilated to the cases in which we misidentify what we perceive. It is as if we were constantly like the Eskimos who when they were first shown Flaherty's film about their lives rushed to harpoon the seals which they saw on the screen. But surely this is not a fair analogy. In the ordinary way, the ground for thinking that an object has been misidentified is that one's identification of it is not borne out by further observations. The Eskimos soon discovered that they were not destroying animals but defacing images. But what experience could reveal that we had constantly been mistaking colours, of ideas, or sense-data, for bodies? If bodies are not directly perceptible, there can be no chance for our senses to detect the masquerade. It follows that if the ordinary man is making any mistake at all when he thinks that he perceives physical objects without the mediation of other entities, it is a mistake of a different kind; a purely theoretical error. He must be misinterpreting not just some particular item but the general character of his perceptual experiences. But then what grounds do we have for thinking that this is so?

(*The Central Questions of Philosophy*, ch. IV)

Sense-data theorists would say that their grounds are not only established by the fact that mistakes can be made, i.e. that things are not always what they seem (appearance is not always a guide to reality) but also by the fact that appearances *in general* are always the end-product of a chain of physiological and psychological events. Appearances are causally dependent on external conditions (light, distance, etc.) and on the physiological and psychological state of the observer. Now Ayer argues that we have direct access to objects. It is true that conditions make a *difference* to appearances, but we can stipulate what 'normal' conditions are to be. This is to some extent an arbitrary matter but we can justify our ruling by taking those conditions as normal which give us the greatest possibility of describing how objects would appear under *other* conditions. For example, if we say that a carpet looks dark blue in daylight we can predict that it will look black in artificial light. But if we are told that a carpet is black in artificial light we shall not be able to predict what colour it will be in daylight. Hence it is more convenient to stipulate that the 'real' colour shall be the colour it appears in daylight.

But, says Ayer, Russell and sense-data philosophers generally do at least draw attention to the fact that perception involves inference. By denying that there is any gap between appearance and reality (the question of *mistakes* can be set aside here), the naive realist ignores the task of explaining how it is that the *same* object can present different appearances. Now clearly there *is* a gap between the way things seem and the way they are and we do need to be able to make a distinction between appearance and reality; naive realism must be modified.

All the same, we do not need to abandon *realism*, though we shall have to substitute sophisticated realism for naive realism. We have to accept that what we take to be the real properties of an object is a matter of convention. But, having adopted a convention, we can then describe real properties and compare them with appearances. In addition we have to concede that our belief in the existence of physical objects is based on conjecture. Nevertheless, if we *do* believe that there are physical objects (i.e. we accept the theory or conjecture) then we can claim that we have direct access to them by perception.

Apart from appealing to the different appearances which objects may present (an appeal which we can now dismiss) Russell wants to abandon realism because of the findings of science. He argues that the primary qualities of objects are those revealed by science, and that these are the *true* or *real* qualities of objects (see chapter 4, p. 84). We start with common sense (naive realism) but it leads us to the scientific view and scientific inquiry shows that our original common sense or naive realist view is false. Russell says:

Naive realism leads to physics and physics, if true, shows

that naive realism is false. Therefore naive realism, if true, is false; therefore it is false.

(*An Inquiry into Meaning and Truth*, p. 15)

The argument can be set out less concisely but perhaps more understandably as follows:

Common sense (naive realism) inquiry leads to (sophisticated) scientific inquiry.
Scientific inquiry has yielded us the conclusions of physics as to the structure of materials.
These conclusions tell us that the ordinary common-sense view of materials is false.
Therefore, common sense is misleading and naive realism is false.

N.B. If we hold that physics (and the findings of scientific inquiry generally) is not correct then common sense misleads us from the start and naive realism is false from the start.

Now this argument is valid and, if we wish to reject the conclusion we must reject one or both the premises. First of all must we accept that scientific inquiry tells us that our common-sense view of materials is false? We can argue that what science does is to offer us an *alternative* account of materials and objects, and this does *not* mean that the scientific and the common-sense accounts are incompatible. A table may be described as a solid brown wooden object of a certain size and shape or it may be described as a collection of very small and very complex particles (molecules) but the one description need not exclude the other, they can be complementary. Secondly we can criticise the framework of Russell's complete argument. In the note above I said that if physics was not correct then common sense misleads from the start, *but* if common sense is considered to have been proven false *by* physics how is it that we can rely on physics, which it is admitted must arise from common sense? It is of course possible for true conclusions to be obtained from false premises and assumptions, but we certainly cannot claim to prove that a conclusion is true if a premise of the argument is false! Russell's argument seems to saw off the conclusion as if it were a branch from the tree of premises to which it is attached.

All our scientific theories are justified by evidence which is interpreted on the assumption that we do perceive physical objects correctly. If we end up by doubting our common-sense interpretations of sense experience, we destroy the evidence which supported our theories. For what is the evidence that we have to justify our belief that matter is composed of molecules? Only that we can observe the behaviour of common-sense objects which we can locate and identify in what is taken as directly perceptible space. But if we are going to say that the only real objects are the imperceptible scientific entities (whose existence is inferred from our experiences of our own private sense data) then there *is* no objective perceptible space. We cannot then talk about objects being responsible for our sensations (be they inferred common-sense objects or inferred scientific entities such as molecules) for these objects cannot be located — there is no space in which to locate them. Ayer regards this as a decisive objection:

> Put succinctly, the decisive objection to the version of the causal theory which turns physical objects into unobservable occupants of an unobservable space is that if this were so we should have no means of identifying them, and if we had no means of identifying them, we should have no reason to believe that they played any part in the production of our sensations, or even that they existed at all. The point which the advocates of this position have overlooked is that physical objects cannot be identified in the first instance as the causes of our sensations: they have to be independently identified before we can have any right to say that the causal relation holds. It is only because I can, through perception, independently establish the fact that the table is there in front of me, that I can subsequently explain my seeing it in terms of its effects upon me.
>
> It follows that there must be a primitive account of perception which makes no reference to any casual relation between the percipient and the objects which he perceives. We do, indeed, have reason at some point to insert a causal clause into our analysis of perceptual judgements. For instance, if someone had been induced by post-hypnotic

suggestion, or by the artificial stimulation of his optic nerves, to believe that he saw such and such an object, whether it was really there or not, then the fact that it happened really to be there would not be thought sufficient in these circumstances to entail that he genuinely saw it, just because the requisite causal relation between them would be lacking. Even so, this causal requirement can be laid down only at a later stage when we have already established our claim to have some knowledge of the physical world. It cannot operate from the start, because the objects to which it relates must be independently identified, and since they can be identified, at least in general, only through our perceiving them, there must be earlier stages in the analysis of perception in which it does not figure.

What then becomes of the argument that the causal conditions of perception make it improbable that we ever perceive things as they really are? The answer is that it too is out of order: it has no standing at the primitive level. Our criteria of reality have in the first instance to be framed in terms of the way things appear to us. We have nothing else to go by. Only when we have constructed at least an elementary picture of the physical world, can we theorize about it in a way that may make such an argument acceptable. If we do accept it, we should, to use Wittgenstein's simile, be throwing away the ladder up which we have climbed.

(*Central Questions of Philosophy*, ch. IV)

'Our criteria of reality have in the first instance to be framed in the way things appear to us. We have nothing else to go by.' Common sense *must* come into its own. Our philosophical analysis has shown that the common-sense view needs to be modified but not rejected. What we should appreciate is that our world can be described in different ways, first as coloured shapes, sounds, smells, etc, which is the rock-bottom level from which we all start. Very soon our innate capacities lead us to construct a world of physical objects and this becomes our normal external world. It is related to the world of shapes and sounds and, in certain special circumstances, say if we are puzzled or if we are artists painting a picture, we may return to that more primitive and fundamental world. For most of us to a limited extent, and for a few of us to a greater extent, there is a third world, the more sophisticated world of science inhabited by scientific entities. All these worlds are equally real, but the 'lower' worlds are more firmly based than those above them. A scientific theory may change and thereby alter that third world of science, and yet leave the world of physical objects unaltered. For example, our scientific account of combustion has changed since the eighteenth century but the description of flames, regarded as physical objects, is unchanged; a description of flames regarded as varying coloured shapes is also unchanged. Or, to take another example at the second level, our description of an object as a fresh apple will alter when we find, on closer inspecton, that it is made of wax, but a first-level account in terms of shape, colour and size would remain unchanged.

Hence the answers to our questions are:

(a) There is good though not logically conclusive reason to suppose that there is an external world containing physical objects, i.e. objects which exist independently of our perceiving them.
(b) We have direct access to that world via our senses.
(c) Our senses provide us with information which justifies our saying that we can know (or at least have true opinion) about those features of the world which affect us.

Now our major question was:
'How far can the senses be trusted to reveal the nature of the external world, does perception give us knowledge and, if so to what extent? Is appearance reality?'

The answers are that, if we accept that there is an external world then appearance *must* in general be reality, for appearance is all we have to go on. But appearances emerge as the result of the deliverance of our senses, interpreted by our minds. According to the mode of interpretation different aspects of reality are revealed to us. Nevertheless such knowledge as we may acquire can hardly be all that the external world has to offer. We are limited in what we can hope to know by our senses and by our minds. We do not directly sense magnetic fields, there are 'sounds' of too high and too low a pitch for us to hear, there are electromagnetic radiations which we sense neither as light nor as heat, there are almost certainly other phenomena which we cannot conceive of. Had we a wider range of our present senses and *a fortiori* had we extra senses, our world would be very different. In addition, those phenomena which do impinge are interpreted by our minds. Kant held that we constructed our world, and, even if we do not accept the details of Kant's account, we must accept that the significance of sense impressions must depend on our mental activities. Thus the external world is as it is to us because we are as we are — to a very large extent it is *our* world.

But given this limitation, and it is a limitation which we have no way of overcoming, we can say that perception informs us. Even if we cannot say we have knowledge (and we shall discuss this in chapter 10) we can say that it is possible to have true opinion.

FURTHER READING

J. L. Austin, *Sense and Sensibilia*.
A. J. Ayer, *The Central Questions of Philosophy*, chs IV and V.
—— *The Problem of Knowledge*, ch 3.
Bertrand Russell, *The Problems of Philosophy*, chs 1, 2 and 3.
G. M. Wyburn, R. W. Pickford, R. J. Hirst, *Human Senses and Perception*, Part III, chs 12—16.

NOTES

1. In relation to perception, the external world consists of all that is perceivable by the senses, but which exists independently of any perceiver. *In this context* it is identical with the empirical world.

2. Secondary qualities are 'nothing in the objects themselves but powers to produce various sensations in us by their primary qualities'. Locke, *Essay*, II, VIII, 10; also quoted in chapter 6, p. 114.

3. See chapter 6.

10

Knowledge and Belief

In chapter 2 we saw that Plato made an absolute distinction between knowledge and belief, in that it was only possible to have knowledge of necessary truths. The sole objects of knowledge were Universals (mathematical entities being lower orders of Universals, see p. 28) whose necessary and essential attributes were apprehended through recollection and ratiocination. Knowledge of objects accessible to sense perception was not possible since such objects had no permanent and therefore no necessary attributes. In this chapter we shall consider whether it is desirable to draw a sharp distinction between knowledge and belief and between objects of knowledge and objects of belief.

Here, and indeed throughout this book, understanding and belief are taken as primitive and therefore as undefinable concepts. They are taken to be *simple ideas* (in Locke's sense) which must be apprehended by direct experience. Locke said:

> The simple *ideas* we have are such as experience teaches them us; but if, beyond that, we endeavour by words to make them clearer in the mind, we shall succeed no better than if we went about to clear up the darkness of a blind man's mind by talking, and to discourse into him the *ideas* of light and colours.
>
> (*Essay*, II, IV, 6, quoted in chapter 6, p. 113)

We can use these primitive concepts to analyse more sophisticated concepts and we shall analyse knowledge in terms of belief and understanding.

All our claims to knowledge presuppose belief, for if we claim to know that some statement is true we have to believe that it is true. (We are assuming throughout this discussion that there is no intention to deceive.) But, apart from certain fundamental and instinctive beliefs, (for example the belief in the existence of physical objects etc., see chapter 9 p. 217) which we accept as needing no justification, we must produce evidence for a belief if it is to be rated as knowledge.

At this point it may be helpful to make clear the kind of knowledge with which we are concerned. We are concerned with claims to know that certain statements are true. We are *not* concerned with knowing how to do certain things. In other words, we are concerned with 'knowing that' as opposed to 'knowing how'.

'Knowing how' is a very important kind of knowing, but, as Aristotle[1] pointed out, it is related to desire rather than to belief, and it is judged by overt performance. For example, if a person claims to know how to ride a bicycle or how to play chess, the claim is justified by the way he or she performs. The knowledge of how to do things does not preclude conscious beliefs as to the truth of relevant statements, but such beliefs are not required. The proof given by competent performance is entirely adequate.

Here we are concerned with two types of statements. First we are concerned with logical and mathematical statements, that is analytic judgements. Second we are concerned with statements which purport to describe states of affairs in the world; these are synthetic judgements. Various criteria have been suggested to help in assessing whether a claim to know that a statement is true or false is justified. The criteria adopted here[2] are:

(1) The statement must be understood and the claimant must believe that the statement is true.
(2) The claimant must be able to produce objective evidence which supports the claim; the evidence is objective in the

sense that it satisfies other appropriately qualified people, as well as the claimant.

(3) The statement must in fact be true.

With reference to criterion (1) we have no great difficulty. To claim knowledge that some statement is true, and we shall throughout this discussion assume rationality as well as sincerity, it is obvious that the claimant must understand what is claimed and must believe that this is indeed true. Criterion (2) is a little less straightforward. The claimant must be able to produce objective evidence which satisfies not only himself or herself but any rational person who is capable of understanding the statement and understanding the evidence. Now, in the case of logical and mathematical statements, the evidence consists of other statements[3] and the relations between these and the statement claimed to be known to be true. As we have seen (chapter 4) a claimant who understands clearly and distinctly will also *know* that the statement is true. The evidence will be completely satisfying and will convince anyone else who is capable of understanding the argument. But, in the case of empirical synthetic statements, the evidence can never give this kind of *logical* certainty. Hence there is and has been much argument over whether any kind of factual statement can be *known* to be true, and if some kinds of factual statement *can* be known to be true, what kinds they are.

This brings us to criterion (3), namely that if a statement is *known* to be true it *must* (logically 'must', since it is involved in the definition of 'know') be true. It is this which has led many philosophers, from Plato onwards, to the view that knowledge cannot be claimed unless the truth of the statement is *logically* indubitable (i.e. it is, in Hume's terms, inconceivable that it should be false). This is the rationalist view, and it leads rationalists to assert that only mathematical and logical statements can be known to be true[4]. In their view knowledge of the world and states of affairs in the world is only possible if it can be logically deduced from indubitable premises. Descartes rejected the possibility of knowing even logical and mathematical truths *at first* (see chapter 5) and said that the only thing he could know was that he existed as a thinking thing. But he was able to argue that he could then show that God existed, and, since God, being perfect, would not deceive us, it would follow that mathematical and logical statements that we apprehended clearly and distinctly, could be known to be true.

But, if we do not accept the Cartesian reliance on God, and concede that there is always a logical possibility that our calculations or ratiocinations are incorrect, then we cannot even claim to know that mathematical and logical statements are true. So, if we do not permit appeal to the beneficence of God, we cannot claim to know that any statement is true, and then we have no use for the word 'know', in the sense of 'knowing that'. It would be impossible for us ever to claim that we had knowledge that any statement whatever was true. We have got ourselves into a ridiculous position; for we use 'know' to make a distinction between what we regard as well-justified belief and semi-justified and unjustified beliefs. We do not want to adopt a criterion for the use of the word 'know' which will make it inapplicable to any situation involving belief.

Therefore we must be more circumspect in applying our criteria. Although for a claim to knowledge to be correctly made, the statement claimed to be known to be true must indeed *be* true, we do not insist that the claim cannot be made unless the truth of the statement is beyond any conceivable doubt. Here we shall take the view that, as long as we are satisfied that the evidence places the truth of the statement beyond reasonable doubt (i.e. so that any competent jury would regard it as completely adequate), we are justified in claiming to know that the statement is true. A consequence of this is that there will be times when we will have to admit that we were wrong to make a particular claim. We thought that we knew but we were mistaken for the statement we claimed to know was true has turned out to be false.

However we do not expect this admission to be made very often because we adopt high standards for the evidence we accept as putting the truth of a statement beyond reasonable doubt. What sort of evidence can we accept? First we postulate that we will accept evidence based on reasoning. This does not mean that we will rely on our own reasoning alone.

But, if we, along with others, check our steps in a logical argument and find no mistake then we can claim to know that the conclusion *is* validly derived. There remains the possibility that we are all mistaken, but we are prepared to assert that we *know* that the conclusion is a logical consequence of the premises in spite of the logical possibility that there is still some flaw in the deductive argument.

Secondly we postulate that we will accept the direct evidence of our own senses. For example, 'I am in pain', 'I am not hungry', 'I see a red patch'. There is a sense (excluding the possibility of a purely verbal mistake) in which these sentences might be said to be less possible to doubt than logical and mathematical truths. We may be more confident that we know our own sense experiences than that we can calculate correctly! But care is needed here. If the sentences are taken as expression of subjective feeling, they are not statements and therefore they cannot be said to be true or false. They are like the expressions 'Oh', 'Ah', 'Ooh'; they do not directly provide information. But surely it may be said, if a child cries out and/or if it says 'I am in pain' she gives information to her mother? Indeed this is so, but in such cases, i.e. when the expression is providing *information* it is no longer *logically* indubitable.

For example, if I say that I am in pain (and sincerely believe this), that I am not hungry, or that I see a red patch, the objective *information* can be doubted even though no one doubts that I am expressing my subjective *feelings*. Others may think that I am not really suffering, I am over-reacting to something mildly unpleasant; they may think that I do require food but due to my emotional state I do not appreciate that I am hungry, and really do require food.

Thirdly we postulate that any statements about currently observed objects and events can be objects of knowledge. We can often claim to know that 'The cat is on the mat', 'The telephone is ringing', 'The milk is sour', 'The plate is hot' and so on. Of course we do not *invariably* claim to *know* such statements are true and then we may well express the statement with an implied reservation 'That looks like the cat on the mat', 'Surely that is the telephone ringing' and so on. But if we *do* claim to know, then we are prepared to submit further evidence based on further observation and description. Others will judge whether we are justified: whether the conditions for perception are adequate and/or whether we have properly functioning sense organs and the capacity to interpret our sense experiences. In general, if we are held to be competent observers, then the evidence we offer will be judged good enough to allow us to claim knowledge.

Fourthly we may claim to know the truth of many statements which we do not observe ourselves, or which we remember, or which are recorded by others: 'The sun rose at 6.0 a.m.', 'I have two kidneys', 'I posted that letter yesterday', 'Hitler was the German leader in 1939', 'Columbus sailed for America in 1492' and so on. These types of statements can also be regarded as possible objects of knowledge even though the evidence is based neither on pure reason nor on direct perception. If more evidence is demanded it too must be indirect and it has to be assessed more carefully than direct evidence to see whether it warrants a claim to knowledge. There may well be disagreement and, if knowledge is claimed, it will be what Professor Malcolm would call knowledge in the weak sense (see passage below).

Fifthly we may claim to know empirical generalisations 'Cream is at the top of milk', 'Ice floats on water', 'Dead men tell no tales', 'Copper is a good conductor of electricity', 'Hydrogen is explosive' 'Men and apes have common ancestors' and so on. In everyday life we claim to know that well-attested common-sense and scientific generalisations are true. Our evidence may be based on observation (our own and that of others) and/or may be derived from theories which we regard as established beyond reasonable doubt. Strictly speaking our claim to know even the best attested generalisations is questionable; for such generalisations are supported by inductive inferences based on observation of particular instances,[5] and, as we saw in chapter 7, inductive inference cannot be rationally justified. On the other hand, just as with the evidence offered by memory and testimony, we wish to distinguish confidence amounting to practical certainty from reasonable confidence, probability and possibility. If we are practically certain we judge it justifiable to claim knowledge, though again it must be knowledge in the weak sense.

These considerations might seem to imply that objects of knowledge in the weak sense are always empirical statements but, as we shall see, Professor Malcolm argues that certain mathematical propositions might also be rated as known in the weak rather than the strong sense.

In the passage below Professor Malcolm considers the case for degrees of knowledge.[6] He suggests that there is a strong sense of 'know' which implies that the knowledge is indubitable in that he who claims to know would admit *no* evidence as capable of refuting the claim. By contrast a claim to know in the weak sense implies that the claimant concedes the possibility of refutation. In this case the claimant does not, of course believe that refuting evidence will be forthcoming (if that were so he could not claim knowledge), but he concedes that if it were produced it would have to be accepted. Malcolm deliberately chooses the bizarre example of claiming to know that one has a heart in one's body. It would seem that this was something which we could claim to know in the strong sense, but he argues that *if* enough evidence were forthcoming we should be forced to accept that we had no heart. Therefore a present claim to know that we have a heart is a claim to know in the weak sense.

Malcolm opens by disputing a point made by H. A. Prichard. Prichard argued that knowing was a condition which could be intuitively apprehended to be a condition of knowing. He said that, by inner reflection, we could tell whether our condition was one of knowing, or merely one of believing. Malcolm begins with a quotation from Prichard:

'We must recognize that when we know something we either do, or by reflecting, can know that our condition is one of knowing that thing, while when we believe something, we either do or can know that our condition is one of believing and not of knowing: so that we cannot mistake belief for knowledge or vice versa.'

This remark is worthy of investigation. Can I discover *in myself* whether I know something or merely believe it?

Let us begin by studying the ordinary usage of 'know' and 'believe'. Suppose, for example, that several of us intend to go for a walk and that you propose that we walk in

Cascadilla Gorge. I protest that I should like to walk beside a flowing stream and that at this season the gorge is probably dry. Consider the following cases:

(1) You say 'I believe that it won't be dry although I have no particular reason for thinking so'. If we went to the gorge and found a flowing stream we should not say that you *knew* that there would be water but that you thought so and were right.

(2) You say 'I believe that it won't be dry because it rained only three days ago and usually water flows in the gorge for at least that long after a rain'. If we found water we should be inclined to say that you knew that there would be water. It would be quite natural for you to say 'I knew that it wouldn't be dry'; and we should tolerate your remark. This case differs from the previous one in that here you had a *reason*.

(3) You say 'I know that it won't be dry' and give the same reason as in (2). If we found water we should have very little hesitation in saying that you knew. Not only had you a reason, but you *said* 'I know' instead of 'I believe'. It may seem to us that the latter should not make a difference — but it does.

(4) You say 'I know that it won't be dry' and give a stronger reason, e.g., 'I saw a lot of water flowing in the gorge when I passed it this morning'. If we went and found water, there would be no hesitation at all in saying that you knew. If, for example, we later met someone who said 'Weren't you surprised to see water in the gorge this afternoon?' you would reply 'No, I *knew* that there would be water; I had been there earlier in the day'. We should have no objection to this statement.

(5) Everything happens as in (4), except that upon going to the gorge we find it to be dry. We should not say that you knew, but that you *believed* that there would be water. And this is true even though you declared that you knew, and even though your evidence was the same as it was in case (4) in which you did know.

I wish to make some comments on the usage of 'know', 'knew', 'believe', and 'believed', as illustrated in the preceding cases:

(a) Whether we should say that you knew, depends in part on whether you had grounds for your assertion and on the strength of those grounds. There would certainly be less hesitation to say that you knew in case (4) than in case (3), and this can be due only to the difference in the strength of the grounds.

(b) Whether we should say that you knew, depends in part on how *confident* you were. In case (2), if you said 'It rained only three days ago and usually water flows in the gorge for at least that long after a rain; but, of course, I don't feel absolutely sure that there will be water', then we should *not* have said that you knew that there would be water. If you lack confidence that p is true then others do not say that you know that p is true, even though *they* know that p is true. Being confident is a necessary condition for knowing.

(c) Prichard says that if we reflect we cannot mistake belief for knowledge. In case (4) you knew that there would be water, and in case (5) you merely believed it. Was there any way that you could have discovered by reflection, in case (5), that you did not know? It would have been useless to have reconsidered your grounds for saying that there would be water, because in case (4), where you *did* know, your grounds were identical. They could be at fault in (5) only if they were at fault in (4), and they were not at fault in (4). Cases (4)' and (5) differ in only one respect – namely, that in one case you did subsequently find water and in the other you did not. Prichard says that we can determine by reflection whether we know something or merely believe it. But where, in these cases, is the material that reflection would strike upon? There is none.

There is only one way that Prichard could defend his position. He would have to say that in case (4) you did *not* know that there would be water. And it is obvious that he would have said this. But this is false. It is an enormously common usage of language to say, in commenting upon just such an incident as (4), 'He knew that the gorge would not be dry because he had seen water flowing there that morning'. It is a usage that all of us are familiar with.

We so employ 'know' and 'knew' every day of our lives. We do not think of our usage as being loose or incorrect — and it is not. As philosophers we may be surprised to observe that it *can* be that the knowledge that *p* is true should differ from the belief that *p* is true *only* in the respect that in one case *p* is true and in the other false. But that is the fact.

There is an argument that one is inclined to use as a proof that you did not know that there would be water. The argument is the following: It could have turned out that you found no water; if it had so turned out you would have been mistaken in saying that you would find water; therefore you could have been mistaken; but if you could have been mistaken then you did not know.

Now it certainly *could* have turned out that the gorge was quite dry when you went there, even though you saw lots of water flowing through it only a few hours before. This does not show, however, that you did not know that there would be water. What it shows is that *although you knew you could have been mistaken*. This would seem to be a contradictory result; but it is not. It seems so because our minds are fixed upon another usage of 'know' and 'knew'; one in which 'It could have turned out that I was mistaken', implies 'I did not know'.

Malcolm is arguing against the view that we can know that we know through inner reflection because inner reflection will tell us whether there is any possibility that we could be mistaken. Those supporting this view, such as Prichard argue that if there *is* such a possibility then we know that we don't *know*, at best we *believe*. Malcolm agrees that if, as a result of inner reflection, we do conclude that it is impossible for us to be mistaken then we can indeed know that we know and he says, this is because we are asserting that *nothing* could or will count as evidence against the statement.

When is 'know' used in this sense? I believe that Prichard uses it in this sense when he says that when we go through the proof of the proposition that the angles of a triangle are equal to two right angles we *know* that the proposition is true . . . . He says that if we put to ourselves the question: Is our condition one of knowing this, or is it only one of being convinced of it? then 'We can only answer "Whatever may be our state on other occasions, here we are knowing this." And this statement is an expression of our *knowing* that we are knowing; for we do not *believe* that we are knowing this, we know that we are' . . . . He goes on to say that if someone were to object that we might be making a mistake 'because for all we know we can later on discover some fact which is incompatible with a triangle's having angles that are equal to two right angles, we can answer that we *know* that there can be no such fact, for in knowing that a triangle must have such angles we also know that nothing can exist which is incompatible with this fact' . . . .

It is easy to imagine a non-philosophical context in which it would have been natural for Prichard to have said 'I know that the angles of a triangle are equal to two right angles'. Suppose that a young man just beginning the study of geometry was in doubt as to whether that proposition is true, and had even constructed an ingenious argument that appeared to prove it false. Suppose that Prichard was unable to find any error in the argument. He might have said to the young man: 'There must be an error in it. I know that the angles of a triangle are equal to two right angles'.

When Prichard says that 'nothing can exist which is incompatible with' the truth of that proposition, is he prophesying that no one will ever have the ingenuity to construct a flawless-looking argument against it? I believe not. When Prichard says that 'we' *know* (and implies that *he* knows) that the proposition is true and *know* that nothing can exist that is incompatible with its being true, he is not making any *prediction* as to what the future will bring in the way of arguments or measurements. On the contrary, he is asserting that *nothing* that the future might bring could ever count as evidence against the proposition. He is implying that he would not *call* anything 'evidence' against it. He is using 'know' in what I shall call its 'strong' sense. 'Know' is used in this sense when a person's statement 'I know that *p* is true' implies that the person who makes the statement would look upon nothing whatever as evidence that *p* is false.

Malcolm does not think that claims to know mathematical truths are claims to know in the strong sense in every case. For, in the case of a truth involving more complicated deductions we should be prepared to entertain evidence which suggested that we were mistaken.

It must not be assumed that whenever 'know' is used in connexion with mathematical propositions it is used in the strong sense. A great many people have *heard* of various theorems of geometry, e.g., the Pythagorean. These theorems are a part of 'common knowledge'. If a schoolboy doing his geometry assignment felt a doubt about the Pythagorean theorem, and said to an adult 'Are you *sure* that it is true?' the latter might reply 'Yes, I know that it is'. He might make this reply even though he could not give proof of it and even though he had never gone through a proof of it. If subsequently he was presented with a 'demonstration' that the theorem is false, or if various persons reputed to have a knowledge of geometry soberly assured him that it is false, he might be filled with doubt or even be convinced that he was mistaken. When he said 'Yes, I know that it is true', he did not pledge himself to hold to the theorem through thick and thin. He did not absolutely exclude the possibility that something could prove it to be false. I shall say that he used 'know' in the 'weak' sense.

Consider another example from mathematics of the difference between the strong and weak senses of 'know'. I have just now rapidly calculated that 92 times 16 is 1472. If I had done this in the commerce of daily life where a practical problem was at stake, and if someone had asked 'Are you sure that 92 x 16 = 1427? I might have answered 'I *know* that it is; I have just now calculated it'. But also I might have answered 'I know that it is; but I will calculate it again to *make sure*'. And here my language points to a distinction. I say that I *know* that 92 x 16 =

1472. Yet I am willing to *confirm* it — that is, there is something that I should *call* 'making sure'; and, likewise, there is something that I should *call* 'finding out that it is false'. If I were to do this calculation again and obtain the result that 92 x 16 = 1372 and if I were to carefully check this latter calculation without finding any error, I should be disposed to say that I was previously mistaken when I declared that 92 x 16 = 1472. Thus when I say that I know that 92 x 16 = 1472, I allow for the possibility of a *refutation*, and so I am using 'know' in its weak sense.

Now consider propositions like 2 + 2 = 4 and 7 + 5 = 12. It is hard to think of circumstances in which it would be natural for me to say that I know that 2 + 2 = 4, because no one ever questions it. Let us try to suppose, however, that someone whose intelligence I respect argues that certain developments in arithmetic have shown that 2 + 2 does not equal 4. He writes out a proof of this in which I can find no flaw. Suppose that his demeanour showed me that he was in earnest? Suppose that several persons of normal intelligence became persuaded that his proof was correct and that 2 + 2 does not equal 4. What would be my reaction? I should say 'I can't see what is wrong with your proof; but it *is* wrong, because I *know* that 2 + 2 = 4'. Here I should be using 'know' in its strong sense. I should not admit that any argument or any future development in mathematics could show that it is false that 2 + 2 = 4.

The propositions 2 + 2 = 4 and 92 x 16 = 1472 do not have the same status. There *can* be a demonstration that 2 + 2 = 4. But a demonstration would be for me (and for any average person) only a curious exercise, a sort of *game*. We have no serious interest in proving that proposition. It does not *need* a proof. It stands without one, and would not fall if a proof went against it. The case is different with the proposition that 92 x 16 = 1472. We take an interest in the demonstration (calculation) because that proposition *depends* upon its demonstration. A calculation may lead me to reject it as false. But 2 + 2 = 4 does *not* depend on its demonstration. It does not depend on anything! And in the calculation that proves 92 x 16 = 1472, there are steps that do not depend on any calculation (e.g., $2 \times 6 = 12$; $5 + 2 = 7$; $5 + 9 = 14$).

There is a correspondence between this dualism in the logical status of mathematical propositions and the two senses of 'know'. When I use 'know' in the weak sense I am prepared to let an investigation (demonstration, calculation) determine whether the something that I claim to know is true or false. When I use 'know' in the strong sense I am not prepared to look upon anything as an *investigation*; I do not concede that anything whatsoever could prove me mistaken; I do not regard the matter as open to any *question*; I do not admit that my proposition could turn out to be false, that any future investigation *could* refute it or cast doubt on it.

When we consider factual propositions, i.e. empirical propositions about what is the case and what we have called synthetic statements, there is the same distinction to be drawn. Sometimes we use 'know' in the strong sense and sometimes in the weak sense. It may, of course, be hard to draw the line and, the bizarre case (ii) already noted is used to illustrate this.

We have been considering the strong sense of 'know' in its application to mathematical propositions. Does it have application anywhere in the realm of *empirical* propositions — for example, to propositions that assert or imply that certain physical things exist? Descartes said that we have a 'moral assurance' of the truth of some of the latter propositions but that we lack a 'metaphysical certainty'. Locke said that the perception of the existence of physical things is not 'so certain as our intuitive knowledge, or the deductions of our reason' although 'it is an assurance that deserves the name of knowledge'. Some philosophers have held that when we make judgements of perception such as that there are peonies in the garden, cows in the field, or dishes in the cupboard, we are 'taking for granted' that the peonies, cows, and dishes exist, but not knowing it in the 'strict' sense. Others have held that all empirical propositions, including judgements of perception, are merely hypotheses.

The thought behind this exaggerated mode of expression is that any empirical proposition whatever *could* be refuted by future experience — that is, it *could* turn out to be false. Are these philosophers right?

Consider the following propositions:

(i)   The sun is about ninety million miles from the earth.
(ii) There is a heart in my body.
(iii) Here is an ink-bottle.

In various circumstances I should be willing to assert of each of these propositions that I know it to be true. Yet they differ strikingly. This I see when, with each, I try to imagine the possibility that it is false.

(i) If in ordinary conversation someone said to me 'The sun is about twenty million miles from the earth, isn't it?' I should reply 'No, it is about ninety million miles from us'. If he said 'I think that you are confusing the sun with Polaris', I should reply, 'I *know* that ninety million miles is roughly the sun's distance from the earth'. I might invite him to verify the figure in an encyclopedia. A third person who overheard our conversation could quite correctly report that I knew the distance to the sun, whereas the other man did not. But this knowledge of mine is little better than hearsay. I have seen that figure mentioned in a few books. I know nothing about the observations and calculations that led astronomers to accept it. If tomorrow a group of eminent astronomers announced that a great error had been made and that the correct figure is twenty million miles, I should not insist that they were wrong. It would surprise me that such an enormous mistake could have been made. But I should no longer be willing to say that I *know* that ninety million is the correct figure.

Although I should *now* claim that I know the distance to be about ninety million miles, it is easy for me to envisage the possibility that some future investigation will prove this to be false.

(ii) Suppose that after a routine medical examination the excited doctor reports to me that the X-ray photographs shows that I have no heart. I should tell him to get a new machine. I should be inclined to say that the fact that I have a heart is one of the few things that I can count on as absolutely certain. I can feel it beat. I know it's there. Furthermore, how could my blood circulate if I didn't have one? Suppose that later on I suffer a chest injury and undergo a surgical operation. Afterwards the astonished surgeons solemnly declare that they searched my chest cavity and found no heart, and that they made incisions and looked about in other likely places but found it not. They are convinced that I am without a heart. They are unable to understand how circulation can occur or what accounts for the thumping in my chest. But they are in agreement and obviously sincere, and they have clear photographs of my interior spaces. What would be my attitude? Would it be to insist that they were all mistaken? I think not. I believe that I should eventually accept their testimony and the evidence of the photographs. I should consider to be false what I now regard as an absolute certainty.

(iii) Suppose that as I write this paper someone in the next room were to call out to me 'I can't find an ink-bottle; is there one in the house?' I should reply 'Here is an ink-bottle'. If he said in a doubtful tone 'Are you sure? I looked there before', I should reply 'Yes, I know there is; come and get it'.

Now could it turn out to be false that there is an ink-bottle directly in front of me on this desk? Many philosophers have thought so. They would say that many things could happen of such a nature that if they did happen it would be proved that I am deceived. I agree that many extraordinary things could happen, in the sense that there is no logical absurdity in the supposition. It could happen that when I next reach for this ink-bottle my hand should seem to pass *through* it and I should not feel the contact of any object. It could happen that in the next moment the ink-bottle will suddenly vanish from sight; or that I should find myself under a tree in the garden with no ink-bottle about; or that one or more persons should enter this room and declare with apparent sincerity that they see no ink-bottle on this desk; or that a photograph taken now of the top of the desk should clearly show all of the objects on it except the ink-bottle. Having admitted that these things *could happen*, am I compelled to admit that if they did happen then it would be proved that there is no ink-bottle here *now*? Not at all! I could say that when my hand seemed to pass through the ink-bottle I should *then* be suffering from hallucination; that if the ink-bottle suddenly vanished it would have miraculously ceased to exist; that the other persons were conspiring to drive me mad, or were themselves victims of remarkable concurrent hallucinations; that the camera possessed some strange flaw or that there was trickery in developing the negative. I admit that in the next moment I could find myself under a tree or in the bathtub. But this is not to admit that it could be revealed in the next moment that I am now dreaming. For what I admit is that I might be instantaneously transported to the garden, but not that in the next moment I might *wake up* in the garden. There is nothing that could happen to me in the next moment that I should call 'waking up'; and therefore nothing that could happen to me in the next moment would be accepted by me now as proof that I now dream.

Not only do I not *have* to admit that those extraordinary occurrences would be evidence that there is no ink-bottle here; the fact is that I *do not* admit it. There is nothing whatever that could happen in the next moment or the next year that would by me be called *evidence* that there is not an ink-bottle here now. No future experience or investigation could prove to me that I am mistaken. Therefore, if I were to say 'I know that there is an ink-bottle here', I should be using 'know' in the strong sense.

It may seem that Malcolm is claiming too much when he insists that nothing would count as evidence against his present knowledge that 'Here is an ink bottle' is true. Surely if he is prepared to concede that there is some evidence which would make him concede that perhaps he had no heart in his body it is unreasonable to insist that there is no evidence which would make him concede that there was no ink bottle in front of him? After all hallucinations are considerably more common than living men missing a vital organ! But Malcolm wants to bring out a difference in the two positions. In his *present* state he would concede that evidence about the heart (his heart) would make him withdraw his claim but in his *present* state *nothing* would make him withdraw his claim about the ink bottle. He has direct and immediate knowledge of it; it lies in front of him.

It will appear to some that I have adopted an *unreasonable* attitude towards that statement. There is, however, nothing unreasonable about it. It seems so because one thinks that the statement that here is an ink-bottle *must* have the same status as the statements that the sun is ninety million miles away and that I have a heart and that there will be water in the gorge this afternoon. But this is a *prejudice*.

In saying that I should regard nothing as evidence that there is no ink-bottle here now, I am not *predicting* what I should do if various astonishing things happened. If other members of my family entered this room and, while looking at the top of this desk, declared with apparent sincerity that they see no ink-bottle, I might fall into a swoon or become mad. I *might* even come to believe that there is not and has not been an ink-bottle here. I cannot foretell with certainty how I should react. But if it is *not* a prediction, what is the meaning of my assertion that I should regard nothing as evidence that there is no ink-bottle here?

That assertion describes my *present* attitude towards the statement that here is an ink-bottle. It does not prophesy what my attitude *would* be if various things happened. My present attitude towards that statement is radically different from my present attitude towards those other statements (e.g., that I have a heart). I do *now* admit that certain future occurrences would disprove the latter. Whereas no imaginable future occurrence would be considered by me *now* as proving that there is not an ink-bottle here.

He does not want his remarks to be taken as an autobiographical account of his own feelings as to what he, Malcolm, can claim to know. They apply to all claims of direct knowledge, the claims which we all make very often and every day. He points out that if we sometimes have to admit that something which we thought we knew is not so, we only do so because we accept some *other* claim as true. For example, if I say there is a dollar in a drawer, and then find that the drawer is empty, I must admit that my first statement was false, but I admit this because I accept the statement that the drawer is empty.

Malcolm says that there is an analogous situation in respect of mathematical and other *a priori* statements. If I am shown that 59 x 31 is not equal to 1839, but is equal to 1829, then I accept that my first calculation is incorrect only because I trust the reasoning which shows that the second calculation *is* correct.

By contrast if it is suggested that we should doubt that, say, there is an ink bottle before our eyes or that 5 x 5 = 25, then we are left with no certainty; we cannot affirm or deny anything. We are being invited to accept that there is no basis for any judgement whatever; for, if these statements (about the ink bottle and the simple calculation) are to be taken as uncertain and hypothetical, then we are in chaos. We must be able to claim to know some things, in the strong sense of 'know', if we are to be able to deny or to have doubts about other things.

These remarks are not meant to be autobiographical. They are meant to throw light on the common concepts of evidence, proof, and disproof. Every one of us upon innumerable occasions of daily life takes this same attitude towards various statements about physical things, e.g., that here is a torn page, that this dish is broken, that the thermometer reads 70, that no rug is on the floor. Furthermore, the concepts of proof, disproof, doubt, and conjecture *require* us to take this attitude. In order for it to be possible that any statements about physical things should *turn out to be false* it is necessary that some statements about physical things *cannot* turn out to be false.

This will be made clear if we ask ourselves the question,

When do we *say* that something turned out to be false? When do we use those words? Someone asks you for a dollar. You say 'There is one in this drawer'. You open the drawer and look, but it is perfectly empty. Your statement turned out to be false. This can be said because you *discovered* an empty drawer. It could not be said if it were only probable that the drawer is empty or were still open to question. Would it make sense to say 'I had better make sure that it is empty; perhaps there is a dollar in it after all?' Sometimes; but not always. Not if the drawer lies open before your eyes. That remark is the prelude to a search. What search can there be when the emptiness of the drawer confronts you? In certain circumstances there is nothing that you would call 'making sure' that the drawer is empty; and likewise nothing that you would call 'its turning out to be false' that the drawer is empty. You *made* sure that the drawer is empty. One statement about physical things *turned out to be false* only because you *made sure* of another statement about physical things. The two concepts cannot exist apart. Therefore it is impossible that *every* statement about physical things *could* turn out to be false.

In a certain important respect some a priori statements and some empirical statements possess the same logical character. The statements that $5 \times 5 = 25$ and that here is an ink-bottle, both lie beyond the reach of doubt. On both, my judgement and reasoning *rest*. If you could somehow undermine my confidence in either, you would not teach me *caution*. You would fill my mind with chaos! I could not even make *conjectures* if you took away those fixed points of certainty; just as a man cannot *try* to climb whose body has no support. A conjecture implies an understanding of what certainty would be. If it is not a certainty that $5 \times 5 = 25$ and that here is an ink-bottle, then I do not understand what it is. You cannot make me doubt either of these statements or treat them as hypotheses. You cannot persuade me that future experience could refute them. With both of them it is perfectly unintelligible to me to speak of a 'possibility' that they are false. This is to say that I know both of them to be true, in the strong sense of 'know'. And I am inclined to think that the strong sense of 'know' is what various philosophers have had in mind when they have spoken of 'perfect', 'metaphysical', or 'strict certainty'.

('Knowledge and Belief', *Mind*, 51 (1952) p. 178—89; also in Phillips Griffiths, *Knowledge and Belief*, p. 69 *et seq*)

Malcolm makes clear that any claim to know, even in the strong sense, may be disputed by *another* person. In other words just because he, Malcolm, will take nothing as evidence against his claim to know, say, that there is an ink bottle on the desk in front of him, it does not follow that he cannot be mistaken. *A fortiori* any claim to know in the weak sense, cannot be indubitable.

If I or Malcolm or anyone else knows that a statement is true, it must *be* true. This is a logical consequence of our definition of 'knowing that', and the criteria we adopted (see p. 231, criterion (2)). Therefore if the statement is shown to be false I, or Malcolm, or anyone who claimed knowledge, will have to admit that the claim was unjustified. We did not know after all. Thus, though all claims to knowledge have to be justified by an appeal to evidence and, if any individual makes a strong claim he or she will regard the evidence as irrefutable, it does not follow that it *is* irrefutable. Therefore it does not follow that what is held to be known (even in the strong sense) is itself logically and necessarily true.

Knowledge is true rational belief. A rational belief is a belief justified by evidence, and it is only if that evidence is thought adequate that knowledge can be claimed. But there are no undisputed criteria for judging evidence, be it evidence provided by reason[7] or by sense perception. So there will be cases where there is disagreement as to whether a claim to knowledge is justified.

The distinction between knowledge and belief is not that the objects of knowledge are different from the objects of belief even though, as we have seen, some statements are more likely to remain objects of possible belief (and not 'graduate' to being objects of knowledge) than are others. Nor does the distinction between knowledge and belief depend on the fact that there can be strong and weak beliefs, whereas knowledge is knowledge without degree. We have seen that it is reasonable to say that there are strong and weak claims to knowledge — what could be termed 'degrees of knowledge'.

The distinction is that belief is a psychological experience, and is a matter of subjective conviction. A belief ceases to be a belief when the *believer* is no longer convinced; he or she may cease to believe or may have doubts. Knowledge, on the other hand, is not *just* a matter of subjective conviction, it concerns an objective state of affairs. Belief that this state of affairs obtains is a necessary condition for knowledge but it is not sufficient. Knowledge ceases to be knowledge when the state of affairs no longer obtains (or it is shown never to have been knowledge if the state of affairs never did obtain); the subsequent fate of the belief is irrelevant.

FURTHER READING

R. J. Ackermann, *Belief and Knowledge* (Macmillan, 1972).
A. Phillips Griffiths (ed.), Essays IV, VI, IX, X, *Knowledge and Belief*.
N. Malcolm, Essay 8, *Thought and Knowledge*.

NOTES

1. Practical philosophy, as Aristotle appreciated, cannot be logically demonstrated and therefore cannot be an object of what he called 'scientific knowledge' (see chapter 3, p. 53). We are not dismissing it for that reason but rather because we are not concerned with rules and precepts.

2. Important objections have been raised to these criteria by Gettier (see discussion in Ackermann, *Belief and Knowledge*, p. 82) but we shall not consider them here.

3. Some mathematical statements are postulated as axioms; generally these are held to be self-evident and in no need of justification but, in any case, they are accepted without proof.

4. Plato and Aristotle believed that the attributes of Universals could be known; see also chapters 2, 3 and 11.

5. Many empirical generalisations are supported by established scientific theories but, since all such theories must be tested and corroborated by observation of particular objects and events, all generalisations are ultimately dependent on particular observations. See also chapter 3, and note 10.

6. Professor Malcolm also writes of this in his essay 'Moore and Wittgenstein or the Sense of "I Know"', in his book *Thought and Knowledge*.

7. In a complicated argument (logical or mathematical) there can be disagreement as to validity and therefore as to the truth of the conclusion.

11

Some Conclusions

We have considered various views as to the nature of objects of knowledge and the relation of knowledge to opinion or belief. Our subject has been epistemology.

It is a tautology that if a proposition is known to be true it must *be* true, for we cannot know that something is the case if it is not the case. This has led many philosophers to conclude that objects of knowledge must be necessary truths — that is that any proposition we know to be true cannot just be true as a matter of contingent fact, but must be a logical truth. Now this conclusion is incorrect, for it does not follow from the requirement that

'If we know, then what we know is necessarily true'

that

'What is known to be true must be a necessary truth.'

For example I may claim to know that it is raining, and, if I do indeed know, it follows logically and necessarily that it is indeed raining. The proposition 'It is raining' must (logically must) be true *in this context*. But it remains a contingent truth; it might not have been raining. Nevertheless we take the proposition as being one which we can claim to know, it is a proper object of knowledge.

We have seen that Plato held that it was only possible to know what was necessarily true, and so he would have denied that 'It is raining' was a proper object of knowledge — at best it could be but an object of true belief. We do not need to suppose that Plato would not have understood the argument of the preceding paragraph! Plato just had a different view of knowledge and of acceptable evidence to justify a claim to knowledge. For Plato knowledge had to be indubitable and he did not think that sense perception could provide evidence which would guarantee indubitability. The only evidence which he thought would guarantee truth was the evidence obtained by mental intuition or by reason.

Therefore for Plato, the only objects of knowledge were Universals: the higher order of Universals being Beauty, Justice, Goodness etc., the lower order being mathematical entities. Only Universals could be apprehended by the mind; they were apprehended either through recollection or by ratiocination. We can now appreciate that the dichotomy which Plato presented between objects of knowledge and objects of opinion or belief is analogous to that offered by Hume over 2000 years later.

Aristotle took a rather different view in that he did think that the objects of sense perception could be objects of knowledge. They were objects of knowledge only in so far as they were regarded as members of a species, and therefore possessed attributes of the species Universal. He took mathematical propositions as his paradigm of objects of knowledge: he regarded the axioms (e.g. 'Parallel lines never meet' or 'Things equal to the same thing are equal to each other') as self-evidently true, and he held that deductions from such axioms were also indubitable and therefore objects of knowledge. Because he thought that mathematical and geometrical axioms and theorems applied to objects perceived, e.g. actual lines drawn parallel would necessarily not meet, he was led to his view that there could be indubitable knowledge of things perceived. Non-mathematical objects, e.g. gold could also be objects of knowledge. For they had essential attributes which might be discovered by induction from observation; if a cause or reason for an observed association of attributes could be found (and it would be acknowledged to be a cause or reason by *nous*) then we had indubitable scientific knowledge — which could not be otherwise. But if no reason for the facts could be found, then the association, even though invariable was accidental and not an object of knowledge.

Though Aristotle preserved a dichotomy between accidental and essential properties, he ended the Platonic dichotomy between logical and empirical propositions, i.e. the dichotomy between relations of ideas and relations of matters of fact. For Aristotle both relations might be objects of knowledge. This was accepted by rationalists (epitomised by Descartes) and by empiricists (epitomised by Locke). And it is just because there *was* no strict dichotomy between the two relations *as objects of knowledge* that there is a latent empiricism in Descartes's account of knowledge and a latent rationalism in that of Locke.

We have seen that Berkeley was an empiricist in that he believed that knowledge came through sense perception, but for Berkeley 'things' were *ideas* – this is Berkeleyan immaterialism. Hence in his theory of knowledge *all* propositions about things stated relations between *ideas*. None of these relations were logically necessary relations; their truth depended on the consistency of God and it was not logically necessary that God should be consistent.

Now it might seem that this is a Cartesian view, for Descartes's whole philosophy of knowledge is grounded on his belief that God was no deceiver. But, for Descartes, this meant that we could trust *our* sense perceptions and *our* powers of reasoning – they were, so to speak, guaranteed by God. For Descartes the relations between matters of fact were relations between material substances and these were not *ideas* (ours or God's) for mental entities were an entirely different kind of substance. Material substances behaved according to laws of nature which had been ordained by God at the Creation and were necessarily obeyed. By contrast for Berkeley the laws of nature which we observed were simply the relations between God's *ideas*, and because God was consistent we were able to take one *idea* for a sign for another. The regularity we observed indicated that God was consistent in the signs He chose to give.

Hume, like Berkeley and Locke, thought that all knowledge was based on (impressions and) *ideas*, but he did reintroduce the Platonic dichotomy for he held that there could be a logical necessity between relations of *ideas* (it will be remembered that these were produced by reflection and hence were similar to what *we* mean by 'idea') and there could never be logical necessity in relations of matters of fact (that is knowledge from perception (*impressions* as Hume would have said)). Locke had admitted that there was a dichotomy in practice. Hume argued that there was a dichotomy in principle.

Hume's explanation of our notion of causal connection was that constant conjunction of events produced a psychological conviction of necessary connection — the prior event (or group of events) being cause(s) and the subsequent event (or group of events) being effect(s). Today we modify this account, for, though some events may be explained by causal laws based on direct observation 'If A then B', others are explained by causes derived from a theory, 'Theory T is true and therefore A will be followed by B'. For example:

A simple law based on observation is: 'If litmus is placed in acid it turns pink'.

An explanation of cause derived from a theory is 'Since there is a gravity pull the moon goes round the earth'.

But though our confidence in causal explanations need not be derived from direct experience of constant conjunction, it is still based on sense perception. For our explanatory theories are themselves supported by observation and therefore the explanations they offer are contingent. Hence all relations of matters of fact are contingent, be they explained by theories or no.

We should note that though Hume preserved the Platonic dichotomy between relations of ideas and relations of matters of fact, he did not deny that we could have no knowledge of relations of matters of fact. His point was that it was a different sort of knowledge; it was not logically necessary truth. Knowledge of events in the world must always be contingent.

It was in the eighteenth century that it began to be appreciated that mathematical knowledge was not *per se* knowledge about the world. The rationalist paradigm did not relate to the world after all. The French philosopher Buffon (1707—88) said:

There are several species of truths and usually mathematical truths have been put first; however they are only truths of definition: these definitions rest on suppositions that are simple but abstract, and all truths in this category are just abstract consequences of these definitions. We make suppositions, we combine them in all sorts of ways; this body of combinations is mathematical science: there is nothing therefore in this science that we haven't ourselves put there . . . . The final consequence is true only because it is identical with what precedes it, as this in turn is with what precedes it, and so on up to the initial supposition; and since definitions are the only principles on which everything is based, and since they are arbitrary and relative, all the consequences one can draw from them are equally arbitrary and relative. So what one calls mathematical truths are reduced to identities of ideas and have no reality. We suppose, we reason on our suppositions, we deduce consequences, we conclude; the conclusion or final consequence is a true proposition, relative to our supposition; but this truth is no more real than the supposition itself.

(Open University AMST 283 Unit 7 p. 56)

Buffon's views were not accepted at once, and indeed were regarded as dangerous by the Church. Apart from religious objections there were objections from empiricists, for example J. S. Mill (1806—67) held that mathematics was empirical in content.

But, though we may concede that we come to *understand* many elementary mathematical propositions by and through sense experience, this does not prove that mathematics describes a necessary aspect of the behaviour of objects perceived. Today we can and do construct systems of mathematics which are quite different from the classical system; but *all* the systems are equally abstract. They give logically necessary theorems as related to the definitions or axioms — which Buffon had called 'suppositions'.

However, it is because classical mathematical propositions do in fact give very good descriptions of the behaviour of perceived objects, and because it was known that mathematical propositions were logical consequences of axioms which seemed to be self-evidently true of physical objects, that the view that mathematics gave logically certain knowledge about certain aspects of the world was accepted for so long. Moreover, though we now admit that our classical mathematics is an abstract system of axioms and theorems which in no way depends on the behaviour of observable entities, we can surmise that did those entities behave in a different manner we would have constructed a very different mathematical system. For example, if it *happened to be the case* that physical objects did not keep a fixed position, but moved about in a given area,[1] if our space were much more 'curved' than it is, if lengths summed differently according to which end measurement started from, etc., we would almost certainly have a mathematics which reflected these contingent 'hypothetical facts'. That mathematics would be just as abstract as our classical mathematics but, in the new world it would be much more useful — it would be as useful there as classical mathematics is useful here. However, when we apply our mathematics to the world, when we use it for everyday calculations (the amount of fertiliser we need to buy for our rose beds for example) or when we use it in science (the stress which will produce metal fatigue in an aeroplane or a calculation as to the length of the DNA helix for example) it can not yield *logically* certain knowledge. As we have seen (p. 196) Einstein said:

'As far as the laws of mathematics refer to reality, they are not certain; and as far as they are certain, they do not refer to reality.'

(*Sidelights of Relativity*, p. 27)

In the later eighteenth century Kant made a noble attempt to bridge the division between ideas and facts by suggesting that there was an aspect of logical necessity in relations of matters of fact. He said that this was because facts were only known as facts, were only apprehended, because we ordered our sensations in accordance with *a priori* intuitions of space and time and then subsumed the subjective experiences produced under innate *a priori* concepts. Thus we constructed a world of phenomena which necessarily behaved in a manner determined by those intuitions and concepts. Therefore it was possible to have *a priori* synthetic judgements; judgements which were necessarily true. Although Kant's attempt failed he did show that any claim to knowledge must presuppose a framework of assumptions which cannot be justified by logical demonstration or by observation.

Nevertheless, even accepting that certain assumptions have to be made, we cannot claim logical certainty for the truth of any proposition relating to matters of fact. Yet it does not follow that we cannot claim *knowledge* of such types of relations. We can and do claim both common-sense and more specialised scientific[2] knowledge of many matters of fact. The evidence we need to support the claim is of a different kind from the evidence needed to support knowledge of relations of ideas but we do not regard it as inevitably less reliable.

Thus although we accept Hume's dichotomy[3] as regards two different types of statements we do not accept that there is a corresponding dichotomy between objects of knowledge and objects of belief. Also we take it that relations between ideas, i.e. mathematical and logical propositions are like relations between matters of fact in that their truth is not indubitable — it is always logically possible that we are mistaken in our reasoning as well as in our perceiving.

We may make the distinction suggested by Malcolm, between a strong claim to know (a claim which the claimant regards as irrefutable) and a weak claim (where he or she admits the *possibility* of refutation). But the strong claim is not necessarily strong for others apart from the claimant. It does not follow that if a person asserts that his or her claim is a strong claim that others will accept it as strong — they may not even accept it as a weak claim to knowledge; indeed they may even say that the proposition is false. All claims to knowledge, both strong and weak, must be supported by evidence. That evidence may be provided by sense perception or by reasoning and in both cases its value may be disputed.

At the last, all our claims to knowledge rest on our confidence that we are rational beings capable of intuitive appreciation of truth, of validity and of evidence provided by sense; capable also of understanding and assessing the testimony of others and of remembering events and arguments. Our philosophical analysis should enable us to appreciate that knowledge depends on judgement and that the claim 'I know what I know' is either an empty tautology or highly misleading. Philosophy teaches us not to be sceptical but to be critical of our own capacities and our beliefs. Our knowledge increases as we learn to appreciate what we can claim to know, and it also increases as we appreciate the circumstances in which we are not justified in claiming to know.

NOTES

1. This would be the case if Planck's constant were considerably larger.

2. There is no clear-cut distinction between common sense and scientific knowledge. Scientific inquiry is refined common-sense inquiry, and scientific knowledge is developed common-sense knowledge.

3. As mentioned earlier (chapter 8, note 3) the dichotomy has been questioned by Quine.

Glossary

Accident: not essential

Accidental attribute: non-essential attribute

Ampliative inference: an inference which leads to a conclusion which states more than is contained in the premises (see also 'Inductive inference')

Analytic judgement: one which can be shown to be true by analysing the subject of the judgement and which cannot be denied without contradiction

Analogues: things similar in attributes, circumstances and/or relations. Thus the analogues of philosophy, philosphers and philosophical problems in the natural sciences would be the content of the sciences, scientists and scientific problems

Apoditic judgement: one which is established incontrovertibly as an absolute truth. All analytic judgements are apoditic

Concept: an idea of a class of particular entities; grasp of a concept may be shown by the ability to recognise a particular of the class

Conceptualism: the view that Universals are mental concepts

Connote, Connotation: the *total* properties conveyed by a word *denoting* a class of entities. Increasing the connotation will limit the class, for example the connotation of 'spaniel' has greater connotation and therefore conveys more information that the connotation 'dog', but the class of spaniel is a smaller sub-class of the class of dog. [See also 'Denote, Denotation' below.]

Contingent: a non-necessary attribute, something that happens to be an attribute

Contingent fact: a fact that might have been otherwise

Contingent truth: a proposition that happens to be true but is not necessarily true

Cosmology: a theory of the structure of the universe

Demonstrate, demonstration (logical): to establish by logical deduction

Denote, denotation: to mark out or to signify. A word which *denotes* signifies an entity as a member of a class; it is to be compared with connote and connotation. The broader the denotation, e.g. 'dog', the less informative the connotation and vice versa. Thus 'dog' denotes a larger class than 'spaniel', but 'spaniel' connotes more than 'dog'.

Empirical: based on observation (perception)

Empirical inquiry: a method of inquiry based on observation

Empirical knowledge: knowledge based on observation

Empirical theory: a theory supported by evidence provided by observation

Empiricist: one who regards observation as the principal source of knowledge

Epistemology: the theory or science of the methods or grounds of knowledge

Essence, essential nature : those attributes which make an entity the kind of entity which it is, and without which it would not be that kind of entity

Euclidean triangle: a plane figure with three straight sides whose angles sum to 180°. A perfect Euclidean triangle is an ideal, or myth, first because no such figure can exist in our space (which does not strictly conform to the definitions laid down by Euclid) and second because even if this space did obtain the triangle could not be drawn so as to conform perfectly to the definition

Gene: a carrier of hereditary traits, a constituent of cell chromosomes

Hypothetico-deductive method: the method of scientific inquiry which seeks to establish knowledge by hypothesis (conjecture) followed by deduction of consequences and observational test, to see if they are fulfilled

Ideal gas: a gas which will behave so as to conform to the classical gas laws, such as those of Boyle. In fact there is no such gas

Immaterialism (Berkeley): the view that 'things' are nothing but *ideas* in the mind

Induction, inductive inference: inferring a general conclusion from particular instances. The conclusion applies to more than the particulars and therefore the inference may also be called an ampliative inference

Logical truth: a truth arrived at by valid deductive argument from true premises (see also 'necessary truth')

Manna: the miraculous food which God gave to the Children of Israel during their progress through the wilderness. Exodus XVI

Metaphysics: the study of what is beyond the scope of empirical science (physics), for example causality, space and time

Mode (Locke): a modification of an *idea*; a simple mode was a modification of a simple idea. For example we have a simple idea of space and distance, but each *idea* of different spaces and distances is a simple *mode* of the *idea*. See *Essay* II, XIII, 1—6

Molecular structure: the arrangement and bonding of atoms in a molecule

Molecule: the smallest part of an element or compound which can exist on its own — normally it will consist of more than one atom

Necessary connection: a relation between two events which *must* (logically) hold; thus before the time of Hume it was assumed that an established cause would necessarily be followed by its customary effect and that a substance, say water, which was recognised by one property would necessarily possess the other customary properties

Necessary truth: a logical truth which therefore must *necessarily* be true

Nominalism: the view which regards Universals as merely names for the group of particulars subsumed by the Universal

Numeral: see notes for ch. 1, p. 24

Objects of knowledge: what can be known; in respect of 'knowing that' objects of knowledge are statements or propositions *about* relations of ideas or matters of fact

Occasionalism (Malebranche): the theory that volition is followed by movement because God so wills it on each occasion. Thus mind and body interact on each occasion as a result of the miraculous powers of God

Particulars: single definite things

Peripatetic: walking, used in relation to the teaching of

Aristotle who is said to have lectured whilst walking. In Aristotle's school, the Lyceum, the covered portico, where he lectured, was called the *peripatos*

Phenomena (Kant): the objects which we construct in order to have objective knowledge from sensations

Phenomenalism: the view that all statements about physical objects are logically equivalent to statements about sense data

Physical object: entities which are accessible to the senses (usually more than one sense) and which continue to exist when not perceived

Plenum: space completely filled with matter

Primary qualities: those which inhere in objects, e.g. shape and extension; the term may also refer to the same properties of the corpuscles of which the material is composed

Proposition: an indicative sentence which can be true or false; to be distinguished from a question or a command (see also 'statement')

Rationalist: one who believes that knowledge is obtained by reasoning rather than from observation — therefore opposed to an empiricist

Realism (Plato)(Aristotle): one who believes that Universals have an existence analogous to that of particulars. In Plato's view, Universals existed *more* concretely than particulars

Realism (perception): the view that things *are* as they appear to sense perception

Secondary qualities: qualities which are not in the objects themselves but are powers which produce sensations (say taste or colour) in us

Sense data: direct sense experiences, Lockean *ideas*

Sense perception: what is conveyed by the senses: sight, sounds, tastes etc.

Solipsism: the view that the self and its experiences are the only objects of knowledge

Statement: see also proposition. Statements and propositions are what indicative sentences state. Thus 'John is older than Jim' and 'Jim is younger than John' are different sentences but the same statement or proposition

Synthetic judgement: a judgement which tells us something about the subject which is more than can be obtained by analysing the subject. It can be denied without contradiction

Tautology: a repetition, direct or indirect. All analytic statements are fundamentally tautologies

Teleological: relating to purpose; a teleological explanation is an explanation in terms of purpose

Third Man Argument (Universals): one proposed explanation of the relation of particulars to Universals is to say that each particular, say each particular man, is a man because he resembles the Universal Man. But, if we feel the need to explain the resemblance between particular men by saying that they resemble a Universal Man, then we also need to explain the resemblance of the particulars to that Universal Man. Therefore we need a third Man, a higher Universal, which the particular men and the original Universal Man resemble. But then we must explain *this* resemblance and postulate yet another higher Universal, and so on. We are in an infinite regress

Universal: the whole of a class, genus or species. Plato thought that they had an independent existence from the particulars of the class

Valid (of arguments): conforming to the rules of deductive inference such that valid arguments necessarily yield true conclusions from true premises

Bibliography

The place of publication is London unless otherwise stated.

R. J. ACKERMANN, *Belief and Knowledge* (Macmillan, 1972).

J. L. AUSTIN, *Sense and Sensibilia* (O.U.P., 1965).

ARISTOTLE, *Ethics*, trans. J. A. K. Thomson (Harmondsworth: Penguin, 1976). See also Ross below.

A. J. AYER, *The Central Questions of Philosophy* (Weidenfeld & Nicolson, 1973).

——, *The Concept of a Person and Other Essays* (Macmillan paperback, 1973).

——, *Hume* (O.U.P. paperback, 1980).

——, *Language, Truth and Logic* (Gollancz, 1970).

——, *The Problem of Knowledge* (Pelican, 1956).

G. BERKELEY, *A New Theory of Vision and Other Writings* (Everyman Dent, 1969).

R. DESCARTES, *Philosophical Writings*, trans. G. E. M. Anscombe and P. T. Geach (Nelson University Paperbacks, 1971).

W. DONEY (ed.), *Descartes* (Macmillan, 1970).

A. EINSTEIN, *Sidelights of Relativity* (New York: E. P. Dutton and Co. Inc., 1923).

A. FLEW, *An Introduction to Western Philosophy* (Thames and Hudson, 1971).

GALILEO, *Discoveries and Opinions of Galileo*, trans. Stillman Drake (New York: Doubleday Anchor Books, 1957).

A. PHILLIPS GRIFFITHS (ed.), *Knowledge and Belief* (O.U.P., 1973).

W. K. C. GUTHRIE, *The Greek Philosophers* (Methuen & Co. University Paperback, 1967).
D. HUME, *Enquiries concerning the Human Understanding and the Principles of Morals*, ed. L. A. Selby-Bigge (Oxford: O.U.P., 1970).
——, *A Treatise of Human Nature*, ed. L. A. Selby-Bigge (Oxford: O.U.P., 1973).
I. KANT, *Critique of Pure Reason*, ed. N. Kemp-Smith (Macmillan, 1929).
——, *Prolegomena*, trans. P. Lucas (Manchester University Press, 1971).
J. LOCKE, *An Essay Concerning Human Understanding*, ed. J. W. Yolton, vols I and II (Ithaca and London: Everyman Dent, 1968).
N. MALCOLM, *Thought and Knowledge* (Ithaca and London: Cornell University Press, 1977).
D. J. O'CONNOR, *John Locke* (New York: Dover Publications, 1967).
—— (ed.), *A Critical History of Western Philosophy* (Collier Macmillan, 1964).
OPEN UNIVERSITY, AMST 283 'Science and Belief from Copernicus to Darwin', Block 3 Units 6–8, 'Scientific Progress and Religious Dissent' (Milton Keynes: Open University Press, 1974).
PLATO, *The Complete Texts of Great Dialogues of Plato*, trans. W. H. D. Rouse (New York: Plume Books, 1961).
W. D. ROSS (ed. and trans.), *The Works of Aristotle translated into English*, vol. I (Oxford, 1953).
B. RUSSELL, *An Enquiry into Meaning and Truth* (USA: Humanities, 1946).
——, *History of Western Philosophy* (Allen & Unwin, 1969).
——, *The Problems of Philosophy* (New York and London: O.U.P. paperback, 1974).
J. S. SUTHERLAND (ed.), *The Oxford Book of Literary Anecdotes* (Oxford: Carendon Press, 1975).
A. E. TAYLOR, *Aristotle* (Nelson, 1943).
B. WILLIAMS, *Descartes* (Pelican, 1978).
R. P. WOLFE (ed.), *Kant* (Macmillan, 1968).
G. M. WYBURN, R. W. PICKFORD, R. J. HIRST, *Human Senses and Perception* (Edinburgh and London: Oliver and Boyd, 1964).

Index